The Hungry Voice:
THE POETRY OF THE IRISH FAMINE

The Hungry Voice

THE POETRY OF THE IRISH FAMINE

EDITED BY

CHRIS MORASH

WITH A FOREWORD BY

TERENCE BROWN

IRISH ACADEMIC PRESS

The typesetting of this book was produced by
Gilbert Gough Typesetting Dublin for
Irish Academic Press, Kill Lane, Blackrock, Co. Dublin.

BRITISH LIBRARY CATALOGUING IN PUBLICATION DATA
The hungry voice: the poetry of the Irish
famine.
1. Poetry in English. Special subjects.
Ireland. Famines. Anthologies
I. Morash, Christopher, 1963-
821'.008'0355

ISBN 0-7165-2437-6

The editor wishes to acknowledge the support of the
The Social Sciences and Humanities Research Council of Canada,
and The Trinity Trust.

Printed in England by
The Camelot Press Ltd, Southampton

Contents

PART II
'A Land Become a Monument'
AUBREY DE VERE & THE RELIGIOUS RESPONSE

PART VI
'Best Pillar of Thy Throne'
THE UNIONIST REACTION

Illustrations

All illustrations are reproduced courtesy of The Board of Trinity College Dublin.

Foreword

The demographer Brendan Walsh has suggested that had there been no emigration from Ireland in the last one hundred and fifty years the population of the island would now stand at about fourteen millions. What it might have been if we compute not only the emigrants but the famine dead in this ghostly calculation is the kind of tantalising historical speculation which can change one's perspective on the contemporary world. For a heavily populated Ireland would surely have played a different role in the life of the peoples on these islands than the one currently acted out by the small population of an island people whose historic destiny has been bound up with that of the inhabitants of the increasingly populous neighbouring island of Britain. But History's might-have-beens are useful only in directing the imagination to precise understandings of the implications of what did in fact happen. And what Professor Walsh's hypothesis does stimulate is an awareness of how profoundly anomalous Ireland is in late twentieth century northern Europe, in the quite unparalleled nature of the historic disaster which befell the nation in the nineteenth century. To find modern parallels one must look to the Armenian people, to the tragic experience of the famine-stricken nations of Africa. And in the light of such an understanding of our historic experience much that might seem difficult of comprehension in our national psychology becomes the more readily explicable. The black-humour of so much of our literature, our moods of desperation, our compulsive, fearful materialism, our pessimistic expectation of failure, our sense of national incompletion, of silence as our truest language, having lost the national tongue, of hunger as the defining appetite, stronger than the desire to procreate.

It is a measure of the significance of Christopher Morash's moving anthology of poems of the Great Hunger that much of this sense of a definitive and yet incomprehensible disaster comes from these ballads, verses and poetic attempts by men and women, most of whom had few pretensions to artistic competence of any special kind. What we have in these documents, which allow us access to the imagination of the disaster, are human documents, which as Morash rightly points out in his introduction, are testaments to the human need to comprehend what may in the end prove incomprehensible. As symbols of the human impulse to bear witness, to respond, to record, to speak of the worst that can be known, they constitute a kind of collective work of the imagination, a triumph of the spirit — which makes Morash's comparison of this body of writing with the literature of 'The Holocaust' an apt one, where it might have seemed somewhat factitious or even opportunistic. This is the book of a people, an effort to memorialize those vanished millions.

TERENCE BROWN
Trinity College,
Dublin

Introduction

It is not the literal past, the 'facts' of history' that shape us,
but images of the past embodied in language.'
Brian Friel, *Translations*

If you were to hike across Achill Island in County Mayo, you would find a
village of roofless cottages in the island's centre, the empty shells of an entire
community, piled stone upon stone. Their counterparts can be found singly
and in clusters throughout every county in Ireland. There, on that silent
hillside, it takes little effort of the imagination to see the peasant farmer of
the first half of the last century carrying each one of those stones from his
tiny, irregular field, lifting it and fitting it into place in the wall, stone upon
stone. The mind's eye sees his young wife, holding the first of many children,
tending to the pig, or digging at the small patch of ground that was to become
the potato garden. However, the imagination begins to strain when it tries to
imagine three million such farmers, each carefully piling stone upon stone.
And it balks entirely when asked to imagine all three million either dead or
packed into the holds of emigrant ships.

And yet, that is what happened. Early in the autumn of 1845, a fungus,
now known to have been *phythopthera infestans*, drifted invisibly across the
Irish Sea. The weather had been warm and damp — conditions which
favoured the blight — and by October the potatoes were in varying states of
rot throughout the entire country. That winter, stories of food shortages began
to filter in to the cities, and by the summer of 1846 streams of emaciated
refugees were beginning to flee from a countryside that had become a
nightmare to crowd the poorhouses, public works schemes, soup kitchens and
docksides. In the wake of this destitution, the diseases always endemic within
the population erupted, primarily typhus and dysentry; these in turn were
followed by the cholera epidemic which swept Europe in 1849. In April of
that year, a visitor to Limerick would report being shown 'one mass grave,
in a field on the outside of the city, near the poor house, into which nearly
two thousand bodies had been gathered in less than a month.'[1] The Census

1. Spencer T. Hall, *Life and Death in Ireland* (Manchester, J.T. Parkes, 1850), p. 38.

15

of 1851 shows an estimated 'excess mortality' for the period of over a million persons; a further two million are estimated to have fled the country. But those are only estimates; we will probably never know for sure how many anonymous thousands died alone in their remote stone cottages, or how many perished between the decks of the coffin ships.

This holocaust took place at a time of great turmoil throughout Europe. In Portugal and Poland there was civil war. In Italy, Guiseppe Mazzini was bringing together the disaffected and the ambitious under the banner of Young Europe. In England, the Chartist movement looked as if it might ignite a popular revolution. These stirrings of discontent came to a boil in 1848 when in February the poor of Paris took to the barricades; by May, Marx and Engels had published the Communist Manifesto, and by the year's end there had been serious uprisings in Berlin, Milan, Warsaw, Prague and Austria. 'In the past year thrones have been overturned, principalities shaken, and powers humbled', commented the *Dublin University Magazine* in January, 1849. 'From its centre to its extremities, Europe has been convulsed.'[2] One cartoon of the period in *Punch* shows a horse-drawn carriage, labelled 'The New Continental Coach', whipping along at breakneck speed, scattering monarchs in its path. In the background stands 'The British Lion Inn,' a bastion of stability; however, barely discernible in the dust behind the Inn the simianized figure of Paddy waves his shillelagh, cheering the coach on its way. Ireland in 1848 seemed ready to plunge into the European revolutionary maelstrom, possibly carrying England with her. And it could be argued that a revolution occurred, although it was not the one planned by those who were forging pikes and digging up their old muskets; that revolution fizzled out with a skirmish in a cabbage patch in County Tipperary. The real revolution lasted much longer, and had a much more profound influence on the future nation.

The social changes that took place in Ireland during the Famine were little different in kind from the types of change that had been in progress since at least the beginning of the nineteenth century. The fall in agricultural prices after the Napoleonic Wars, and the decreased profitability of tillage exports as compared to livestock exports all meant that, for a significant segment of the rural labouring population, hunger was common during that part of the year prior to the harvest, after the previous year's supplies had been exhausted. In 1800, 1817 and 1822 this hunger was so widespread as to have been designated as 'famine'. However, hardship was not the exclusive preserve of the small farmer; the large landowner, whose sole wealth was in his property, was finding it increasingly difficult to generate a profit from his impoverished tenantry. As the century progressed, the position of the landed

2. Kappa, 'France: A Retrospect of the Year 1848,' *Dublin University Magazine*, Vol. 33, No. 193 (January 1849), p. 134.

OLD CHAPEL-LANE, SKIBBEREEN.

gentry was further undermined by the granting of Catholic Emancipation in 1829 and the repeal of the Corn Laws in 1845; but it was the Famine of 1845-49 that gave the final push to the teetering edifice of many a country manor, just as it tumbled so many of the single-roomed cottages of the poor. As early as 1800, in Maria Edgeworth's novel, *Castle Rackrent*, we have an account of the old neo-feudal system of land-holding beginning to break down as more and more landlords became bankrupt and a predominantly Catholic middle class, made up of merchants, lawyers and larger farmers moved in to buy up portions of the old estates. As the self-made land speculator, Jason M'Quirk, asks in *Castle Rackrent*, 'When there's no cash, what can a gentleman do but go to the land?'[3] And it was from this chaos of evictions, bankruptcy, emigration and legislative change that we can trace the development of the middle class revolution that was to consolidate itself with the granting of the Land Acts in the latter half of the century. One novelist of the Famine, Elizabeth Hely Walshe, saw the situation like this:

> In 1850 the horizon was clearing. The lessening agricultural population had more elbow room . . . overgrown estates, encumbered with heavy charges, were broken into a variety of smaller properties, freed from

3. Maria Edgeworth, *Castle Rackrent*. Vol. I of *Tales and Miscellaneous Pieces* (London: Thomas Davison, 1825), p. 70.

burden, passing from the effete hands of the old possessors into the vigorous hands of men from the middle class.[4]

For the poet living in an age when social change is occurring on an epic scale, the nature of that change will influence the type of aesthetic decisions the poet must make. Famine, perhaps more than any other agent of change, forces the poet to make difficult choices; for while the sight of so many of his fellow creatures driven to the limits of existence cries out for some sort of response, famine does not sit comfortably in any of the established poetic idioms of the English tradition. Had the Great Famine taken place a half century earlier, it could have found expression in a native Gaelic tradition that embraced a long history of famine, exile and destitution. But by the 1840s, all of the great Irish language poets of the eighteenth century were gone, and the Gaelic revival that was to come at the end of the nineteenth century was still fifty years away. Although with some poets, notably Mangan, we see the first attempts to adapt Irish models to the English language, on the whole the only available poetic models came from a country in which famine was a foreign concept. Had the same number of people died in battle as died from hunger and disease, there would have been a tradition on which to draw going right back to 'The Battle of Maldon' (c. 1000) — the same tradition out of which Tennyson was able to create 'The Charge of the Light Brigade' (1854) only a few weeks after the event itself. Famine, however, left the poets of the 1840s abandoned by tradition. Many of the poets in this anthology turned to the all-embracing lyric, choosing to focus on an emotional expression of their own reactions to individual instances of suffering. Of those who tried to take a wider view, there was a contrary tendency to sidestep the physical realities of starvation by placing the Famine in a religious or mythological context.

In this respect, Sir Samuel Ferguson's two long satires of 1849, 'Inheritor and Economist', and 'Dublin', are virtually unique among the poems of the era in their attempts to comprehend the state of Famine Ireland in a verse form that takes account of the wider network of social and economic relationships in which any individual is necessarily enmeshed. When the potato blight first hit Ireland in the autumn of 1845, Ferguson, a successful lawyer and antiquarian, was on the Continent, researching manuscript sources of early Irish history. His verse translations of these ancient Gaelic epics in the years after the Famine were to earn him the respect of Yeats and to secure for him a place in the history of Irish literature. However, when he returned to Ireland in 1846 to find the country in a state of crisis, he not only laid aside

---

4. Elizabeth Hely Walshe, *Golden Hills* (London: The Religious Tract Society, 1865), p. 266.

the legendary material on which he had been working he also began to modify his political views. As a younger man, he had been a strong supporter of the union with England and had published anti-nationalist poetry, such as 'An Irish Garland', which appeared in *Blackwood's Magazine* in 1833. In the wake of the potato failure, Ferguson felt so perturbed at the sufferings of the peasantry, and the financial ruin of the gentry, that he felt himself uncharacteristically drawn to the politics of repeal. He even went so far as to address a meeting of the Protestant Repeal Association in May of 1848, at the height of the insurrectionary excitement, and later went on to make a successful defence of the poet Richard D'Alton Williams against a charge of treason felony.

However, the militant nationalism espoused by Williams and the Young Irelanders was not Ferguson's nationalism, and the difference registers itself in their respective verse forms. Williams favours short lines, strong rhymes, martial rhythms, and direct, imperative statements that aim to link the listener with the speaking voice of the poem:

> Come! hand in hand, at Heaven's command,
> Whose voice through the people rolls,
> Let us bravely stand, for our lives and land,
> And prove that men have souls!
>
> ('Hand in Hand', lines 9-12)

Although the internal rhymes might be taken to indicate an early Gaelic model, the exclamatory tone suggests that the strongest influence is probably an imitator of Shelley in an ecstatic moment. Ferguson, on the other hand, looks back beyond Romanticism; his two satires turn to the poets of Augustan England for their models, with their characteristic long lines, rhymed couplets, and cool, sardonic perspective. Indeed, 'Dublin,' which Ferguson tells us is 'In Imitation of the Third Satire of Juvenal,' owes more to Samuel Johnson's version of the Third Satire, his 'London' of 1738, than it does to Juvenal's original. This Augustan verse form, the urbane vehicle of oratorical wit, was the very antithesis of the overt emotionalism of Young Ireland, and, as such, was the perfect idiom for the nationalism to which Ferguson was attracted during the years of the Famine. The heroes of Ferguson's nationalist tradition, as he lists them in 'Dublin', are neither Wolfe Tone nor Robert Emmet; they are the august eighteenth century statesmen of the Parliament of 1782 — Grattan, Bushe and Plunket. And it is not on the historic fields of Tara and Clontarf, newly reconsecrated by O'Connell's 'monster meetings', that he finds the ruins of squandered nobility. For Ferguson, the monument to the Ireland that had been lost is the Parliament Building on College Green, forced into ignomious service as a bank:

> Here, where old Freedom used to wait
> Her darling Grattan at the gate,
> Now little clerks in hall and colonnade
> Tot the poor items of provincial trade;
> So changed, alas! — since, sped by cruel fates,
> Our three-per-cents expelled our three estates.
>
> ('Inheritor and Economist,' lines 23-26; 33-34)

As Ferguson was writing his satires in the spring of 1849, the dust was still settling from the previous year — a year which not only had seen the dramatic spectacle of widespread revolution but also had witnessed a much more low key event in the publication of J.S. Mill's *Principles of Political Economy*. While most of his contemporaries were luridly imagining — either in fear or in anticipation — an Ireland overrun by bands of rebels, Ferguson was able to perceive that the slow, unheroic implementation of the theory of free market 'political economy' was the agent of change that formed the more potent threat to the Ireland to which he wanted to belong. And just as the 'little clerks', whom Yeats was later to describe 'fumbling in a greasy till,'[5] oust the noble Grattan from the Parliament Buildings in 'Dublin,' so too does the 'Economist' in 'Inheritor and Economist' drive the landed 'Inheritor' and his family from their ancestral acres. In both poems, Ferguson is turning back to the eighteenth century, to the age from which he had taken his verse forms, to find the two figures who represented the last hope of a real possibility of leadership for the Protestant Ascendancy — the parliamentary nationalist, and the eighteenth century landed nobleman — both of whom had been made anachronistic not by any pike-wielding revolutionary, but by the utilitarian determination of a mercantile class to create a cash-based economy:

> So shall we speedily the land behold
> Once more exchangeable for British gold;
> And in its Castle-Rack-Rent mansions see
> A bran-new Cheesemonger propriet'ry,
> Able in all things, save alone thy grace,
> Gentility, to fill a gentry's place.
>
> ('Inheritor and Economist', lines 505-510)

Ferguson was not to go as far as Yeats in embracing the revolutionary tradition as a means of ennobling the 'bran-new Cheesemonger propriet'ry', (although his 'Lament for Thomas Davis' takes him several steps in that direction); nonetheless, in 'Inheritor and Economist', he is battling,

---

5.   W.B. Yeats, 'September, 1913,' in *Collected Poems* (London: Macmillan, 1985), p. 120.

Cuchulain-like, the first waves of Yeats' 'filthy modern tide'.[6] The ultimate futility of any challenge to such a complex and widely-based social change registers in the internal stresses and strains in Ferguson's verse. Both 'Dublin' and 'Inheritor and Economist' use the freedom of the couplet to allow the ramifications of political and economic theories to develop from a perspective which, if somewhat jaundiced, is nonetheless emotionally detached. However, towards the end of 'Dublin', the speaking voice of the poem changes as Ferguson introduces a section that is stylistically inconsistent in its emotional immediacy and yet is justified by the latent bitterness of the rest of the poem:

> Here men of feeling, ere they grow old,
> Die of the very horrors they behold.
> 'Tis hard to sleep when one has just stood by
> And seen a strong man of sheer hunger die;
> 'Tis hard to draw an easy, healthful breath,
> In fields that sicken with the air of death.
>
> ('Dublin', lines 177-182)

A similar breakdown in the satiric distance maintained throughout the poem takes places at the end of 'Inheritor and Economist.' Even more than 'Dublin', this poem constitutes a sustained analysis of the economic factors at work in Ireland during the Famine years, doggedly outlining the day-to-day realities of managing an estate. However, in its final lines, the poem transforms itself into an apostrophe to the poet's 'poor native land':

> Thy day prefixed in God's eternal doom,
> May long be longed for; but the day will come
> When heaven shall also give its sign to thee,
> Thy Diocletians fallen, thy people free.
>
> ('Inheritor & Economist', lines 549-552)

Faced with an unrecoverable past, and the unpalatable present that the harsh light of satire has shown him, Ferguson takes a third option; he chooses to place the fate of Ireland in the context of a divinely ordered history. Ireland must wait for the 'sign' before coming into her kingdom.

Ferguson was too deeply rooted in Enlightenment ideals of rationality to promote such doctrines at any length. His slip into the language of prophecy is no more than an illuminating aberration. For many of his contemporaries, however, the images of the prophetic books of the Bible provided a central means of comprehending the accelerated change brought on by the Famine.

6.   Y.B, Yeats, 'The Statues,' in *Collected Poems*, p. 376.

In the light of the research that has been done on millenarianism since the publication of Norman Cohn's *Pursuit of the Millennium* in 1957, this should hardly seem surprising. In his pioneering study, Cohn found that poverty, even the direst poverty, is not in itself sufficient to trigger millenarian hopes, for the impoverished society very often generates a passive stability of the sort J.M. Synge was to idealize in his portrayal of the remnant of the pre-Famine peasantry on the Aran Islands. Millenarianism is much more likely to arise when the impoverished society comes into close contact with a more affluent society, creating a disparity between expectations and their possibilities for fulfilment. 'The torture of Tantalus' is how William Drennan Jr describes the aggravated colonial situation of Famine Ireland in his poem '1848'. When the political apparatus for change seems to be out of control, one of the few historical paradigms to offer the possibility of a return to an ordered society is that which promises complete this-worldly salvation brought about by an other-worldly agency — the millenarian paradigm.

If Famine Ireland was ripe for a millenarian prophet, no one was better suited to fill that role than James Clarence Mangan. More than any other single poet, Mangan established the millenarian idiom of Famine poetry with 'The Warning Voice', 'The Peal of Another Trumpet' and 'A Vision: 1848'. Born in penury, and struggling all of his life with drug addiction, Mangan was to carry the mantle of poet-prophet from his verse into his public persona, transforming himself into an urban version of the prophecy man desribed by Carleton in *The Black Prophet*. One contemporary describes Mangan thus:

> When he emerged into daylight, he was dressed in a blue cloak, mid-summer or midwinter, and a hat of fantastic shape, under which golden hair, as fine and silky as a woman's, hung in unkempt tangles, and deep blue eyes lighted a face as colourless as parchment. He looked like the spectre of some German romance rather than a living creature.[7]

Whether he believed, or believed intermittently, in the power of Mangan the prophet, it was a posture that provided Mangan the poet with the metaphor for which he had been searching throughout his career in his exploration of sublime terror in the face of death, and what might lie beyond death. Although his early work is an idiosyncratic mixture of giddy parodies, acrostics, Wertherian melancholia, 'translations' from imaginary Persian poets, as well as successful translations from the Irish, the backbone of this eclectic collection is comprised of a group of deeply personal poems of spiritual desolation. As early as 1833, the imagery of his Famine poetry is presaged

7. Sir Charles Gavan Duffy, 'Personal Memories of James C. Mangan,' *Dublin Review*, Vol. 142, No. 285 (April, 1908), p. 278.

in such pieces as 'Life is the Desert and the Solitude', 'Disaster', and 'A Broken- Hearted Lay':

> Weep for one blank, one desert epoch in
> The history of the heart; it is the time
> When all which dazzled us no more can win.[8]

In the years leading up to the Famine, Mangan began to explore the potential of the role of prophet in the desert; in 'The Coming Event', written on the very eve of the Famine in 1844, he makes the link between the imminence of his own approaching death and the imminence of the Last Judgement:

> Shadows of changes are seen in advance,
>   Whose epochs are nearing;
> And days are at hand when the Best will require
>   All means of salvation,
> And the souls of men shall be tried in the fire
>   Of the Final Probation.

By the end of the poem, however, the world historical nature of the 'Coming Event' has shrunken to the dimensions of a skull, as a single man confronts his end alone:

> Spend all, sinew, soul, in your zeal to atone
>   For the past and its errors;
> So best shall ye bear to encounter alone
>   THE EVENT and its terrors.[9]

As the world around Mangan came increasingly to resemble the desert of his nightmares in the final years of his life, the themes which had long haunted his work, themes of isolation, spiritual exile, and metaphysical terror, found their objective correlatives in the state of Famine Ireland. It was as if the spiritual malaise of one man had been realized in the landscape of a nation. As he saw the horsemen of war, famine and pestilence ride roughshod over Ireland, the millenarian dimension of Mangan's confrontation with death became inflamed and its images more sharply defined. He found omens and portents in public events, and these in turn, by their life-threatening nature,

8. James Clarence Mangan, 'A Broken Hearted Lay,' *Poems of James Clarence Mangan*, ed. D.J. O'Donoghue (Dublin: M.H. Gill, 1922), p. 124.
9. James Clarence Mangan, 'The Coming Event,' *Poems*, p. 143.

both intensified his spiritual anxiety and expanded the metaphorical possibilities for its expression. By the time he came to write 'A Vision' in 1848, Mangan was finding places for specific political developments of the recent past in the jigsaw puzzle of Biblical prophecy, identifying the young men of the nationalist movement with the divinely chosen elite to whom he increasingly addressed himself:

> Youths! Compatriots! Friends! Men for the time that is nearing!
> Spirits appointed by Heaven to front the storm and the trouble!
> ('A Voice of Encouragement', lines 1-2)

However, as in most millenarian visions of salvation drawn from the Judeo-Christian tradition, Mangan's young heroes are not to come into their kingdom unscathed. If one is to usher in an apocalypse, the reasons for doing so can not be more or less correct; they must be absolutely correct. The enemy must be absolutely evil, and the chosen absolutely good. In the Old Testament and Book of Revelations, the chosen remnant achieve this purity by suffering conquest, exile, famine and pestilence. As those very tribulations were visited upon Ireland in the 1840s, it became possible for a poet like Mangan to interpret the suffering they caused as being directed toward a similar purpose:

> The ANOINTED must fall —
> The Weak Ones must yield
> Up in silence their breath
> Ere the Last Scene of all,
> For that scene must behold
> But stern spirits and bold,
> When the Lord takes the field.
> Therefore Famine first came
> And then Pestilence came.
> ('A Vision,' lines 64-72)

Later, we will see how Aubrey De Vere developed the theme of the sanctity of suffering in a more orthodox religious context. Mangan, however, lacked the stabilizing influence of orthodoxy, and as a consequence his prophecy poems of the Famine veer wildly between poles of wild elation and profound despair. The years of crisis and sorrow constitute a test; to succeed is to win the favour of God; to fail is damnation. Hence, he is able to exult in 'When Hearts Were Trumps':

> Love will yet abolish Pain,
> As by necromancy;

And, friends, trust me; your — (not *my*) —
　　Offspring will have wondered
Much at myriad changes — by
　　ANNO NINETEEN-HUNDRED!

('When Hearts were Trumps', lines 41-48)

Yet, in another poem, 'The Groans of Despair', he writes:

The wrath of God, the avenging sword
　　Of Heav'n burns in my breast alway
With ever freshly torturing flame!
　　And desolateness and terror
　　　Have made me their dark mate —
The ghastly brood of sin and error
　　Repented all — TOO LATE![10]

MULLINS'S HUT, AT SCULL.

What began as a structure to impart meaning to physical suffering becomes itself the source of a deeper spiritual suffering under the burdensome sense of sin and isolation which permeates Mangan's world. His best work is to be

10. James Clarence Mangan, 'The Groans of Despair,' *Poems*, p. 125.

found in the handful of poems written during the Famine years in which he is able to go beyond the sources of his almost unbearable anxiety to a direct apprehension of that anxiety itself. In the realm of 'pain acute, yet dead' of 'Siberia', for instance, Mangan is able to unite the existential horror he had long felt at the knowledge of his own impending death with the bleak, death-strewn landscape of Famine Ireland in a single, forceful image of desolation in which neither the public nor the private is foregrounded. He was to write increasingly in this mode right up until the end. Although not up to the standard of 'Siberia', the same painful awareness of death haunts the final poem he was to publish, 'The Famine', which appeared eleven days before cholera and malnutrition finally brought about his death on June 20, 1849:

> Despair? Yes! For a blight fell on the land —
> The soil, heaven-blasted, yielded food no more —
> The Irish serf became a Being banned —
> Life-exiled as none ever was before.
> The old man died beside his hovel's hearth,
> The young man stretched himself along the earth,
> And perished, stricken to the core!

('The Famine,' lines 22-28)

   While Mangan presents us with the unique case of a poet whose private obsessions found a form in millenarian interpretations of the world around him, he was not alone in his use of the images and paradigms of prophecy during the Famine years. Thomas D'Arcy McGee, Richard D'Alton Williams, Speranza, John De Jean Frazer, and other less prolific nationalist poets, as well as the Orange poet Robert Young, were all to attempt the role of prophet in the years leading up to 1848. But can this flood of chiliastic verse, particularly among nationalists, be taken as evidence of a full-fledged millenarian movement in Ireland during the 1840s? Comparative studies have shown that 'millenarianism is born out of great distress coupled with political helplessness.'[11] In order to begin to determine the millenarian status of Famine Ireland, it is necessary to ask who was in great distress, and who was feeling the burden of political helplessness. With a few notable exceptions, the main poetic activity of those years took place in the periodicals, the most important of which was *The Nation*, and its successors, the *United Irishman*, and *The Irishman*. A closer look at these newspapers reveals that their contributors were by and large professionals from the middle class: Thomas Davis, John Mitchel, and John O'Hagan were lawyers. Kevin Izod

---

11. Yonina Talmon, 'Millenarian Movements,' *Archives euroéennes de sociologie*, Vol. 7, No. 2 (1966), p. 185.

O'Doherty, and Richard D'Alton Williams were doctors. Indeed, it was said at the time that if you were ill you had a better chance of finding a doctor in D'Olier street (where *The Nation* had its offices) than you did in Jervis street (site of one of the main Dublin hospitals). There were, of course, exceptions. Mangan was never far from abject poverty. John Keegan, educated at a hedge school, was buried in a pauper's plot when he died in 1849. But, on the whole, the men and women who were writing prophecies of the coming millennium were members of a class who, were it not for Ireland's colonial status, would have been in positions of political power. While this urban, Dublin-based middle class were agitating for reform, the real impact of the Famine was

being felt by an entirely different class of rural peasantry, who were, for the most part, politically passive during the Famine years. It is difficult to measure political involvement in what was a limited democracy; however, one indicator suggests the political apathy that covered the countryside. Daniel O'Connell had funded both the earlier Catholic Emancipation movement and his later Repeal Association by means of a weekly 'rent,' donated primarily by small farmers throughout the countryside. For years this 'rent' had brought the Association a substantial weekly sum. But as the Famine progressed, the amounts dwindled, until, on the week of June 6, 1848 — at the very height of the insurrectionary fever, if one reads *The Irishman* or the

Irish Felon — the 'rent' collected from the entire country amounted to a mere £12. The following week the Repeal Association was disbanded.

It is because of this disjunction between the class who were suffering the greatest oppression, and the class who were using the imagery of Biblical salvation to articulate their struggle to free themselves from a situation of political helplessness that Irish millenarianism takes its peculiar form. There is an air of unreality about the whole enterprise, beginning with the notion of using English language newspapers to preach rebellion to a largely Irish speaking peasantry, most of whom would have had no money to buy newspapers and considered themselves lucky if they had enough to buy their food and pay their rent. The western peasantry, desperately trying to survive, were oblivious to the affluent young Dublin poets like Richard D'Alton Williams who were fascinated by the idea of an apocalypse that would right every wrong:

> Ere we burst the chains that gore us,
> Ere the tide of battle rolls,
> May thine angels camp around us,
> Nerve our hearts and cleanse our souls!
>
> ('Lord of Hosts', lines 21-24)

The same newspaper that carried Williams' strident cries for the tide of battle to roll forth and rejuvenate the soil with the blood of young heroes was also publishing a series of lengthy pieces of undergraduate humour that Williams was writing, entitled 'The Adventures of a Medical Student'. While it may not seem remarkable that Williams should have exhibited this form of cultural schizophrenia, it does seem striking in retrospect that neither he nor his editors should have found it disturbing or even incongruous that a university prankster should have been praying for Armageddon. Like many of his contemporaries in the nationalist press, Williams was promoting a millenarian fantasy that had little correspondence to the reality of the world around him. Nonetheless, *The Nation* poets repeatedly used the chiaroscuro opposition of absolute good and absolute evil to rehearse the tale of the perfidious Saxon and the sorrowing Gael; and they dropped delicious hints as to the nature of the golden age that was to follow the cleansing blood bath. For Thomas D'Arcy McGee in particular, the New Jerusalem was to be a world peopled by refugees from the poems of Thomas Moore — harp-plucking bards, stout-hearted warriors, and holy monks living in round towers. This dream perspective permeates even to the level of details such as the weapons that the peasantry are urged to take up: spears, swords and staffs predominate — hardly very effective tactical weaponry in 1848. Indeed, the unreality of the whole neo-mediaeval vision of bardic Ireland became glaringly apparent in August of 1848 when William Smith O'Brien attempted to conduct a rebellion with due respect for the laws of property and chivalry, and promptly earned himself a passage to Australia at Her Majesty's expense, after a farcical, but gentlemanly, skirmish.

The difficulty of the nationalist position registers itself in this tension between the rhetorical ideal and the reality of conditions in Famine Ireland. A comparison between the newspapers that supported the Union with Britain, and those which were in favour of Repeal, shows a marked tendency among the latter to emphasize the more graphic physical details of death by starvation. John Mitchel's *United Irishman*, for instance, was filled week after week with headlines such as 'Horse Eaten By Human Beings', and 'The Shroudless and Coffinless Dead', which shared the page with Mitchel's own  militant harangues.[12] Some of the most successful poems of the period are the sentimental pieces from occasional contributors that focus on a single graphic image of suffering. James Tighe's 'The Boreen Side', for instance, appeared in the radical *Irishman*:

> A stripling, the last of his race, lies dead
>   In a nook by the Boreen side;
> The rivulet runs by his board and bed,
>   Where he ate the green cresses and died.
>
> ('The Boreen Side', lines 1-4)

Yet, the very degradation that was generating so much sympathy for the nationalist cause, even among such unlikely people as Samuel Ferguson, was the very thing that was withering the strong arms of the Celtic warriors, belying the shining utopia of the nationalist rhetoric. As reports of the numbers who had died began to reveal the horrific extent of the disaster, it became increasingly difficult to reconcile rhetoric and reality — a difficulty which takes an explicit form in the rejection of statistical truth in Speranza's 'The Exodus':

12. *The United Irishman*, Vol. 1, No. 2 (Feb. 19, 1848), p. 23.

> 'A million a decade!' calmly and cold
>   The units are read by our statesmen sage;
> Little they think of a Nation old,
>   Fading away from History's page.

('The Exodus', lines 1-4)

Because the nationalist use of millenarianism entailed this uneasy rejection of the world of statesmen and statistics, and yet tried to operate at the same time as political allegory, it occupies a poetic space supported by neither public nor personal truth. Whereas Mangan believed that if the 'Coming Event' did not take a collective, earthly form, it was sure to take a personal, spiritual form, there is no evidence of this personal conviction in a poet like Williams. Consequently, whereas millenarian imagery provided Mangan with an accurate metaphor for the awesome reality of personal judgement, for many of his co-contributors to the nationalist press such imagery was an evasion of the reality of political impotence.

And yet, in spite of their weaknesses and blind spots — or perhaps because of them — the verses published by these young nationalists have been among the most popular and influential works of Famine poetry. If anything, this body of poetry gained in effectiveness as the ever increasing assimilation of the peasantry into the rural middle classes eased the disjunction between image and audience that had existed when the poems were first published. As the descendants of the Famine generation were becoming a part of the struggle for land and power, they were also becoming a part of the book-buying public. Between the founding of the Tenant League in 1850, and the final Land Act of 1923, the poetry of *The Nation* was republished in an avalanche of anthologies and garlands; indeed, it was often claimed that the best selling Irish book of the entire nineteenth century was *The Spirit of the Nation* anthology. The influence of individual pieces extended even further. Williams' 'Lord of Hosts' can be found sharing the page with popular music hall numbers and 'minstrel' songs in the weekly *Harding's Dublin Songster* in the first decades of this century. Speranza's 'Famine Year' made its way into the school textbooks in 1929, when it was included in *Ballads of Irish History for Schools*, where it would have left several generations of Irish school children with a millenarian interpretation of the Famine:

> We are wretches, famished, scorned, human tools to build your
>   pride,
> But God will yet take vengeance for the souls for whom Christ
>   died.
> Now is your hour of pleasure — bask ye in the world's caress;
> But our whitening bones against ye will rise as witnesses,

From the cabins and ditches, in their charred uncoffin'd masses,
For the Angel of the Trumpet will know them as he passes.
A ghastly spectral army, before the great God we'll stand,
And arraign ye as our murderers, the spoilers of our land.

('The Famine Year', lines 41-8)

The very exuberance of the vision of the brave new Ireland that was the key to the popularity of this body of verse held within itself the seeds of a corresponding despondency. As might have been expected, the inability of a nation devastated by famine to become the New Jerusalem led many of those who had preached that dream most fervently — including McGee and Williams — to emigrate after the collapse of the rising in 1848. Others, like Speranza and John O'Hagan, settled back into that world of statisticians and statesmen which their poetry had previously rejected. It was not only the social structure of Ireland that was undergoing a massive change during the Famine years. These young men and women themselves — most of whom were in their early twenties — underwent personal change at the same accelerated pace as the world around them, as they were forced to abandon the adolescent idealism of romantic nationalism and accept the disillusioning realities of their situation in a famished colony. At the age of twenty-four, Martin MacDermott wrote:

I have seen death strike so fast
    That the churchyards could not hold —
Though torn into one yawning grave—
The remnants of the young, the brave,
    The bright-eyed and the bold.
I must be very, very old —
    A very Old, Old Man.

('A Very Old, Old Man', lines 54-60)

This tone of exhaustion is echoed throughout much of the later Famine poetry from *The Nation*. John De Jean Frazer, for instance, was a young carpenter who in 1848 was writing some of the most overtly militant verse of the period. His 'Harvest Pledge' appeared in *The Nation* in July, embellished with all of the neo-mediaevalisms of the genre:

So the serfs, in the face of the Lord of the Manor,
Set a spear for a shaft and sheaf for a banner;
And said: 'If *we* choose, from the sward to the sky,
From centre to shore, thou shouldst yield — or die!'

('The Harvest Pledge', lines 31-34)

31

However, by the following year his ringing confidence had fled. Although he still reiterated his constant theme of a workman's right to a decent living, it had become a plea rather than a demand in 'The Artisan's Apology for Emigrating' of 1849:

> Day and night we are wrapped in a desperate strife,
> Not for national glory, but personal life;
> And our hair raineth sweat, like the clouds on the soil;
> Yet the ass, with his thistle, has more for his toil!
> Or, lacking employment, our energies rust;
> Our ambitions decay into ashes and dust.
>
> ('The Artisan's Apology For Emigrating', lines 39-44)

Like the English Romantic poets of a generation before him, faced with the degeneration of the ideals of the French Revolution, or like many of the poets to have emerged out of Northern Ireland after the collapse of the Civil Rights movement, Frazer seems to have been attempting to find a more personal poetry, a poetry 'not for national glory, but personal life'. However, unlike most of his co-contributors to the nationalist press, Frazer was a working man whose 'desperate strife' to support himself and his family in the shattered economy of Famine Ireland made it impossible for him to disentangle the personal from the political. He stopped writing poetry after the death of his son during the cholera epidemic of 1849. In 1851, some of his more affluent associates from *The Nation* attempted to help him out financially by publishing a collected edition of his poems; it did little good. The following year he died in poverty.

Where Frazer's precarious social position made the personal political, Aubrey De Vere, ensconced in his Curragh Chase estate, was able to confine his public work during the Famine to his efforts on behalf of his tenantry, and to his prose writings, chief among which is his *English Misrule and Irish Misdeeds* of 1848. His Famine poetry, however, is delimited to a personal exploration of spirituality. Indeed, the Famine seems to have generated much of its compelling literary interest for De Vere precisely because the suffering he saw about him brought him into an active dialogue with his faith, heightening an already intense religious awareness that owed much to his friendship with Newman and his interest in the Oxford Movement. In his 'Ode: After One of the Famine Years', he writes:

> A cry from famished vales I hear,
>   That cry which others hear not.
> Sad eyes, as of a moontide ghost,
>   Whose grief, not grace, first won me,

32

'Mid regal pomps ye haunt me most: —
There most your power is on me.
('Ode: After One of the Famine Years', lines 27-32)

There is a stately, almost languid elegance to the world of 'moontide ghosts'
of De Vere's Famine poetry. His is an empty landscape of:

Far-circling wastes. Far-bending skies,
Clouds as at Nature's obsequies
    Slow trailing scarf and pall.
('The Desolation of the West', lines 7-9)

The peace that De Vere finds in this 'realm untenanted' ('The Desolation of
the West', line 6) begs comparison with the Famine landscape of Mangan.
Whereas Mangan's world is one where 'Nought is felt but dullest pain/Pain
acute, yet dead' ('Siberia', lines 14-15), De Vere is able to move beyond the
pain to a beatific vision. The chief difference between the two lies in their
respective temporal perspectives. Mangan's best Famine poetry, such as
'Siberia', speaks with a Beckettian voice from the interminable, tormented
'now' of the last seconds of doubt before death. De Vere, on the other hand,
is usually writing in the past tense:

And in my spirit grew and gathered
Knowledge that Ireland's worst was weathered,
    Her last dread penance paid;
Conviction that for earthly scath
In world-wide victories of her Faith
    Atonement should be made.
('The Desolation of the West', lines 49-54)

De Vere's Famine poetry takes an essentially preterist stance; the apocalypse has taken place, and it is now time to look to the New Jerusalem. He is
able to work from this position because unlike Mangan he never shows any
doubt of his own salvation, and unlike the young political millenarians of *The
Nation*, he does not think of the golden age to be ushered in by the suffering
of the Famine in political terms. De Vere's interpretation of the Famine was
rather 'Conviction that for earthly scath/In worldwide victories of her Faith/
Atonement should be made.' Consequently, he is able to proclaim at the end
of 'The Desolation of the West':

A Land become a Monument!
Man works: but God's concealed intent

33

> Converts his worst to best.
> The first of altars was a tomb —
> Ireland! thy grave-stones shall become
>   God's altar in the west!
>   ('The Desolation of the West', lines 73-78)

When a poet uses such a vast frame of reference, there is always the danger that the central problem of suffering will be dwarfed, and ultimately dehumanized. Although De Vere occasionally does allow the interpretation to overwhelm the event, his poetry is never less than a serious attempt to assail the problem of suffering. In his 'Ode', for instance, he voices a doubt as to the very legitimacy of writing poetry about the Famine:

> I come, and bring not song; for why
>   Should grief from fancy borrow?
> Why should a lute prolong a sigh,
>   Sophisticating sorrow?
>   ('Ode: After One of the Famine Years', lines 73-76)

De Vere's question foreshadows T.W. Adorno's assertion that to write poetry after Auschwitz would be barbaric. There is a fundamental ethical question at stake here: is it morally correct to allow art to impose its order on an experience whose essentially horrific nature lies in its very chaos? Is it right to 'sophisticate sorrow?' Writing from a Christian perspective, De Vere's position seems to be that not only is it right, but it is necessary to understand the Famine as a part of the unfolding of God's design for humanity extending back through centuries of suffering:

> Sleep well, unsung by idle rhymes,
>   Ye sufferers late and lowly;
> Ye saints and seers of earlier times,
>   Sleep well in cloisters holy!
>   ('Ode: After One of the Famine Years', lines 105-108)

When De Vere equates the Famine dead with the 'saints and seers of earlier times', he is creating a context in which the deaths of the anonymous thousands who died of starvation and disease have a meaning. His Christian strategy parallels that of the nationalist writers who attempted to include the Famine dead among the pantheon of martyrs who had died for Irish freedom. However, what struck so many observers of the period was the banality conferred on suffering by the sheer scale of the Famine. A manufacturer from Manchester, Spencer T. Hall, arriving in Limerick in 1847, shared the surprise

34

of many who were shocked at the almost complete absence of burial rites in a society so famous for its wakes. 'It happened', he records in his journal, 'that a man died of hunger and lay for the greater part of a week in a cow cabin, without any one making the slightest preparation for burying him!'[13] As we find in so many accounts of the Famine, it is not the fact of death itself which so affronts the observer, but the ignoble means of death, and the facelessness of the victims after death. Although it would be unwise to equate the Irish Famine and the Holocaust too rigorously (for there are major causal and motivational differences), it is worth remembering that the bureaucratic nature of evil during the Third Reich remains one of the most problematic features of the Nazi era. Similarly, when writing of the Famine, contemporary authors repeatedly refer to the Kafkaesque nature of the world around them. In 'Inheritor and Economist', for instance, Ferguson describes the proliferation of bureaucrats in an Irish Poor Law Union thus:

> Make haste, appoint one Chief Commissioner
> To supervise all Beggarland's concerns,
> Fifty inspectors, chiefs, and subalterns;
> Fifty collectors, with good sureties,
> To gather in the dues: then add to these
> Five hundred guardians, vice and volunteer —
> Five hundred clerks at fifty pounds a-year;
> Five hundred masters, and five hundred dames,
> Five hundred Health-Board doctors of all names;
> Five hundred builders from the Board of Works,
> Five hundred Chaplains, and five hundred clerks.
> ('Inheritor and Economist', lines 220-230)

At the opposite end of the political spectrum, John Mitchel can be found grappling with the same invasion of civil servants in his *Last Conquest of Ireland (Perhaps)*:

> If one should narrate how the cause of his country was stricken down in open battle, and blasted to pieces with shot and shell, there might be a certain mournful pride in dwelling upon the gallant resistance . . . but to describe how the spirit of a country has been broken and subdued by beggarly famine; — how her national aspirations have been not choked in her own blood, nobly shed on the field, but strangled by red tape; — how her life and soul have been ameliorated and civilized out of her; —

---

13. Hall, *Life and Death in Ireland*, p. 20.

how she died of political economy, and was buried under tons of official stationary; — this is a dreary task, which I wish some one else had undertaken.[14]

Such honesty about the problem of finding a response is rare; the Famine cried out to be falsified, for the random and widespread devastation caused by the intangible agents of fungus and bureaucracy did not lend itself to models of heroic martyrdom, either religious or political, that were capable of giving a meaning to death in other circumstances.

WOMAN BEGGING AT CLONAKILTY.

The questions this posed for the poet of the 1840s go straight to the heart of pre-modernist aesthetics. Victorian poetry and the various traditions to which it was heir had meaning; it had form, and was about the imposition of form and meaning on those aspects of experience, whether love or nature, that threatened to escape the snares of meaning. A poet such as Aubrey De Vere simply did not have at his disposal forms that allowed for formlessness, nor structures that admitted the existence of meaninglessness. In such a context, Mangan's verse appears more modern (and hence is attracting more recent critical attention than De Vere's), because his personal idiosyncrasies led him to break forms and admit the possibility of meaninglessness in the interstices of his own radical metaphysical doubt; De Vere, by comparison, with his formal and theological confidence, today sounds distinctly dated. Much of the poetry in this anthology shows the strain of having been created within a conventional framework that did not pertain to the situation to which it strove to respond. The millenarian imagery examined at length above is but one example of the latent apprehension of meaninglessness generating a search for alternative conventions. Instead of turning to the obvious Biblical text with which to encompass the problem of suffering, the Book of Job, or even instead of turning to the passages dealing with suffering in the Gospels, the majority of the Famine poets who attempted to work within a Biblical framework drew on what is probably the most imagerially chaotic book in the Bible, the Book

14. John Mitchel, *The Last Conquest of Ireland (Perhaps)* (London: Burns, Oates & Washbourne, 1861), pp. 138-9.

of Revelations, as the only Biblical text capable of providing images as extreme and as disorienting as the world around them had suddenly become:

> The wondrous things foretold by JOHN were realized at last,
> And APOLLYON came on earth, to blacken and to blast.
>
> ('Thanatos, 1849', lines 9-10)

But let us return to Adorno's challenge, adapted to to the present circumstances.

No poetry after the Famine?

The answer of the combined voices of the poets in this anthology would seem to say that poetry is not only a possibility in such conditions, it is a necessity; for it is that which cannot be articulated which must be articulated. History provides us with facts, and continues to do so with increasing sophistication; but literature provides us with the response to those facts — or, if not the response, at least the possibility of a response. It still remains impossible to fully comprehend what it meant for those three million small farmers to stand outside their stone cottages and watch their sole source of food decay into black putrification. In *Language and Silence*, George Steiner writes: 'The world of Auschwitz lies outside speech as it lies outside reason.'[15] The same could be said of the world of the Famine. But the attempt to contain that world within language, even if doomed to failure, had to be attempted, just as we must try to understand the images that those attempts have bequeathed to us. So while we can recognize the basic inadequacy of all paradigms of comprehension — whether rational, romantic, political, religious, or millenarian — and the continued inadequacy of all subsequent paradigms, including this one, we must also recognize that their failure does not entail their dismissal. Even if each individual paradigm can be said to have failed, the plurality of views presented in this anthology constitutes a multifaceted text with more extensive claims to adequacy than any single one of its constituent parts; indeed, it could even be said to have greater claims to adequacy than a single long unified text, such as a novel. However, this does not mean that we should ignore the uniqueness of each one of the poems that follows: they are not merely a variety of strategies of evasion. Each of the poems in this anthology is an attempt at understanding that in itself constitutes a simple, Sisyphusian form of heroism that is at the basis any movement towards an adequate response to atrocity.

15. George Steiner, *Language and Silence* (London: Faber & Faber, 1985), p. 146.

PART I

'Whence Came You, Pallid Wanderer?'

LAYS AND LAMENTS

A Lay of the Famine

ANONYMOUS

Hush! hear you how the night wind keens around the craggy reek?
Its voice peals high above the waves that thunder in the creek.

'Aroon! aroon! arouse thee, and hie thee o'er the moor!
Ten miles away there's bread, they say, to feed the starving poor.

5   'God save thee, Eileen *bawn astor*, and guide thy naked feet,
And keep the fainting life in us till thou come back with meat.

'God send the moon to show thee light upon the way so drear,
And mind thou well the rocky dell, and heed the rushy mere.'

She kissed her father's palsied hand, her mother's pallid cheek,
10   And whirled out on the driving storm beyond the craggy reek.

All night she tracks, with bleeding feet, the rugged mountain way,
And townsfolk meet her in the street at flushing of the day.

But God is kinder on the moor than man is in the town,
And Eileen quails before the stranger's harsh rebuke and frown.

15   Night's gloom enwraps the hills once more and hides a slender form
That shudders o'er the moor again before the driving storm.

No bread is in her wallet stored, but on the lonesome heath
She lifts her empty hands to God, and prays for speedy death;

Yet struggles onward, faint and blind, and numb to hope or fear,
20   Unmindful of the rocky dell or of the rushy mere.

But, ululu! what sight is this? — what forms come by the reek:
As white and thin as evening mist upon the mountain's peak.

Mist-like they: glide across the heath — a weird and ghostly band;
The foremost crosses Eileen's path, and grasps her by the hand.

25   'Dear daughter, thou hast suffered sore, but we are well and free;
For God has ta'en our life from us, nor wills it long to thee.

'So hie thee to our cabin lone, and dig a grave so deep,
And underneath the golden gorse our corpses lay to sleep —

'Else they will come and smash the walls upon our mould'ring
    bones,
30   And screaming mountain birds will tear our flesh from out the
    stones,

'And, daughter, haste to do thy work, so thou mayst quickly come,
And take with us our grateful rest, and share our peaceful home.'

The sun behind the distant hills far-sinking down to sleep;
A maiden on the lonesone moor, digging a grave so deep;

35   The moon above the craggy reek, silvering moor and wave,
And the pale corse of a maiden young stretched on a new-made
    grave.

The Song of the Famine
ANONYMOUS

Want! want! want!
    Under the harvest moon;
Want! want! want!
    Thro' dark December's gloom;
5   To face the fasting day
    Upon the frozen flags!
And fasting turn away
    To cower beneath a rag.

Food! food! food!
10   Beware before you spurn,
Ere the cravings of the famishing
    To loathing madness turn;
For hunger is a fearful spell,
    And fearful work is done,
15   Where the key to many a reeking crime
    Is the curse of living on!

For horrid instincts cleave
    Unto the starving life,
And the crumbs they grudge from plenty's feast
20   But lengthen out the strife —
But lengthen out the pest
    Upon the foetid air,
Alike within the country hut
    And the city's crowded lair.

25   Home! home! home!
    A dreary, fireless hole —
A miry floor and a dripping roof,
    And a little straw — its whole.
Only the ashes that smoulder not,
30   Their blaze was long ago,
And the empty space for kettle and pot
    Where once they stood in a row!

Only the naked coffin of deal,
    And the little body within,
35   I cannot shut it out from my sight,
    So hunger-bitten and thin; —
I hear the small weak moan —
    The stare of the hungry eye,
Though my heart was full of a strange, strange joy
40   The moment I saw it die.

I had food for it e'er yesterday,
    But the hard crust came too late —
It lay dry between the dying lips,
    And I loathed it — yet I eat.
45   Three children lie by a cold stark corpse
    In a room that's over head —
They have not strength to earn a meal,
    Or sense to bury the dead!

And oh! but hunger's a cruel heart
50   I shudder at my own,
As I wake my child at a tearless wake,
    All lightless and alone!
I think of the grave that waits
    And waits but the dawn of day,

55 And a wish is rife in my weary heart —
  I strive and strive, but it won't depart —
   I cannot put it away.

 Food! food! food!
  For the hopeless day's begun;
60 Thank God there's one the less to feed!
  I thank God it is my son!
 And oh! the dirty winding sheet,
  And oh! the shallow grave!
 Yet your mother envies you the same
65 Of all the alms they gave!

 Death! death! death!
  In lane, and alley, and street,
 Each hand is skinny that holds the bier,
  And totters each bearer's feet;
70 The livid faces mock their woe,
  And the eyes refuse a tear;
 For Famine's gnawing every heart,
  And tramples on love and fear!

 Cold! cold! cold!
75 In the snow, and frost, and sleet,
 Cowering over a fireless hearth,
  Or perishing in the street,
 Under the country's hedge,
  On the cabin's miry floor,
80 In hunger, sickness, and nakedness,
  It's oh! God help the poor.

 It's oh! if the wealthy knew
  A tithe of the bitter dole
 That coils and coils round the bursting heart
85 Like a fiend, to tempt the soul!
 Hunger, and thirst, and nakedness,
  Sorrow, and sickness, and cold,
 It's hard to bear when the blood is young,
  And hard when the blood is old.

90 Death! death! death!
  Inside of the work-house board,

Where maybe a bed to die upon,
    And a winding sheet is found.
For many a corpse lies stiff and stark —
95   The living not far away —
Without the strength to scare the hateful things
    That batten upon their prey.

Sick! sick! sick!
    With an aching, swimming brain,
100 And the fierceness of the fever-thirst,
    And the maddening famine pain.
On many a happy face
    To gaze as it passes by —
To turn from hard and pitiless hearts,
105   And look up for leave to die.

Food! food! food!
    Through splendid street and square,
Food! food! food!
    Where is enough and to spare;
110 And ever so meagre the dole that falls,
    What trembling fingers start,
The strongest snatch it from the weak,
For hunger through walls of stone would break —
    It's a devil in the heart!

115 Like an evil spirit, it haunts my dreams,
    Through silent, fearful night,
Till I start awake from the hideous scenes,
    I cannot shut from my sight;
They glare on my burning lids,
120   And thought, like a sleepless goul,
Rides wild upon my famine-fevered brain —
Food! ere at last it come in vain
    For the body and the soul!

The Wanderer

ANONYMOUS

'Whence came you, pallid wanderer, so destitute and lorn,
With step so weak and faltering, and face so wan and worn?
Our eyes are used to misery, that day by day endures,
Yet never have they looked upon so sad a form as yours,'
5   'In a glen of distant Munster, my infant breath I drew,
Where the summer sun falls brightly on the lovely Avondhu —
Oh! oftentimes beneath his beams I've watched the river shine,
And never thought such bitter woe and hardship would be mine.
I was born to strive with poverty, as all my people were,
10   But I never thought of better, and my heart was free from care;
We knew that ours must be a life of penury and toil,
For what were we but Irish — the children of the soil?
But the famine and the pestilence swept o'er us with their breath,
And gather'd many a one I lov'd into the arms of death;
15   While, crueller than famine — than pestilence more sure,
Came the landlord's hireling drivers — the wreckers of the poor.
Then woe unto the cabin homes within that little glen,
We never felt dependence in its bitterness till then;
The living and the dying lay unsheltered on the sod;
20   No earthly succour near them — no refuge save in God.
When our friends and our defenders rais'd the emerald flag on
        high;
And hope had whisper'd a return of long lost liberty,
Thus did our masters counsel those who to this standard pour'd,
'Be tranquil, and be loyal, or ye perish by the sword.'
25   But better had it been for them to lie among the slain
Than to end a life of sorrow by a lingering death of pain;
And hardly would the sword have stuck all that famine slew,
In the glen of rushing waters — my lovely Avoudhu!
Now I, a lonely wanderer, come in my sorrow forth,
30   To seek for help and pity in the bosoms of the North.
An orphan and a stranger — in sickness and in woe,
May Heaven return the merciful the mercy they bestow!'

The Poor Little Maiden

WILLIAM ALLINGHAM

A gentle face and clear blue eyes
The little maiden hath, who plies
Her needle at the cottage door,
Or, with a comrade girl or more,
5   Group'd on the shady hedgerow-grass, —
I love to find her as I pass, —
Humbly contented, simply gay,
And singing sweetly; many a day
I've carried far along my way
10   From that fair infant's look and voice
A strength that made my soul rejoice.

O sad! her father died last week;
Her mother knows not where to seek
Five children's food; the little maid
15   Is far too young for others' aid.
Willingly would she do her best
To slave at strangers' rude behest;
But she is young and weak. Her thread,
From dawn till blinding rushlight sped,
20   Could never win her single bread,

And must the Poorhouse save alive
This Mother and her helpless five,
Where Guardians, no Angelic band,
With callous eye and pinching hand,
25   Receive the wretched of their kin,
Cursing the law that lets them in?
I see her growing pale and thin,
Poor Child; (the little needle-song
Is ended) — and perhaps ere long
30   Her coffin jolting in their cart
To where the paupers lie apart.

Just from that cottage-step one sees
A Mansion with its lawn and trees,
Where man and wife are wearing old
35   Within a wilderness of gold,
Amidst all luxuries and graces,

Except the light of children's faces.
Ah, had the little Maid forlorn
In that fine house been only born,
40   How long she were tended, night and morn!
A long-tail'd pony then were hers,
And winter mantles edged with furs,
And servants at her least command,
And wealthy suitors for her hand.

The Young Street Singer
WILLIAM ALLINGHAM

How sad! — to hear a song of mirth
   Sung in the homeless street,
By one in melancholy dearth
   Of clothes, and food to eat,
5   Or place beside the poorest hearth
   For bare and blistered feet.

Some tones of softness still retains
   This worn and feeble voice,
That once, perhaps, in hawthorn lanes
10   Helped spring-time to rejoice;
Not then impelled by hunger-pains,
   But childhood's merry choice.

Mayhap the mother little thought
   Her darling and her pride,
15   Portioned with but songs she taught,
   Must face the world so wide,
And give the starving outcast's lot
   A speech so unallied.

How weary are the unknown ways,
20   How sharp the pitiless stones,
What haughty heads the houses raise
   From one whom no one owns,
Whose mouth is singing lively lays,
   Whose heart is utt'ring groans!

47

25 The careless window's happy glow
        Displays the lighted room,
    The very pools of rain below
        The ruddy tint assume;
    But not a ray doth it bestow
30   To cheer the wanderer's gloom.

    Save that a petty hope has strayed
        Into the aching breast:
    Nor be the slender fee delayed,
        But may thy weary quest
35 Alight on more effectual aid;
        Or may'st thou soon find *rest!*

Lay of the Famine:
The Irish Husband to his Wife
W.C.B.

    Bright was your blue eye, Kathleen,
        Smooth was your sunny brow,
    On that fair morn, my Kathleen,
        When you breath'd your bridal vow.
5   Joy wove his choicest treasures round us,
                Peace came with all her smiling train;
            Mirth in his magic circle bound us,
                Whence fled the phantoms Grief and Pain.

    Few years have pass'd, my Kathleen,
10   Since you breath'd your bridal vow,
    Hope smiling o'er us, Kathleen, —
        O God, to see you now!
            To see your blue eye waning, waning,
                To see your brow so seam'd with pain,
15   To see gaunt Hunger's red tooth draining,
                The lifeblood from each throbbing vein!

    Fair was our first-born, Kathleen,
        As it hung upon your breast:
    Oh! weep not, weep not, Kathleen,

48

20   Why mourn its speedy rest?
            And tell me not its smiles would lighten
                The pangs that revel through this heart,
            Say how could smiles its young cheek brighten,
                While Famine struck with venom'd dart!

25   Our last, our youngest, Kathleen, —
            Forgive this struggling tear, —
       Its sinking cries, my Kathleen,
            Ring ever on my ear.
               O God, to hear its plaintive wailing,
30   To see your look of dark despair,
            When the mother's fountain failing,
                Its lips convulsive drank but air!

       Rest on this bosom, Kathleen,
            All, save your love, is fled,
35   Ha, what, — my wife! my Kathleen!
            Fiend, Tempter, she's NOT dead!
               Stare not with those eyes so blindly,
                Fan me with thy gentle breath,
               Speak! even coldly or unkindly, —
40   Kathleen, Kathleen, IS this Death?

The Last Appeal
T.C.D.

I.

And must I die — oh! gracious God —
            And perish in my prime?
       My arm is nervous still; my brow
            Unfurrowed yet by time;
5   By this bleak ditch-side must I fall unknown,
And none to raise my fever'd head, weak, famine-struck, alone?

Jesu Maria! Son of Man!
            In mercy hear my prayer:
            Thou, too, hast felt what hunger is —
10   A crown of thorns didst wear.

rt God, and in thy dying hour
'st defy both madd'ning want and gnawing famine's
r.

thou, at Creation's birth,
      Ere time was a full week old,
forming Earth's nobility,
      Employ a different mould?
lidst thou fashion, of mere common clay,
The baser sort, for Pestilence and Plague to waste away?

    Is not this bright and fruitful earth
20   Sufficient to sustain
    The creatures of thy framing, Lord!
          With root and bursting grain?
Are *we* mere step-sons of this teeming soil —
Contaminated, worthless serfs — plague-smitten slaves of toil?

And the Famine Was Sore in the Land: 1847

JOHN SWANWICK DRENNAN

    Where hoarse th' Atlantic billow raves
        On southmost Cork's dejected stand,
    What cry outsounds the troubled waves?
        The wailing of a famish'd land.
5   Whilst borne from every bleak abode,
        As Winter rears his icy wall,
    The same funeral accents load
        The mountains of Donegal.

    The songs that made our hearths rejoice,
10   Pale Woman's lips no longer pours,
    Whilst Manhood's hesitating voice
        For bread — bread only — now implores.
    For bread life's sinking powers to nurse —
        Bread which the *hand* would earn in vain,
15   Till the earth with mitigated curse
        Bid baffled Labour *strive* again.

On his lone threshold see him stand,
    That pining peasant spectre-thin;
Without, his rood of traitor land;
20   Starvation and despair within.
His wife — his babes — his festered food,
    Her urgent plaint — *their* failing breath —
Ah, shield that wretch from thoughts of blood!
    That hut reprieve from sin and death!

25 Much, much the meanest boon avails
    When 'famine clings' in dubious strife;
A crust of bread may fix the scales,
Where tremble innocence and life.
One ray of sympathy supplied,
30   Correct a brain that darksome erred;
Revive a heart that, longer tried,
    Had frozen been from warmth deferred.

By gentle stress — with patient skill,
    Each link of human wrong is loosed;
35 The mountain mass of human ill
    By pity's slend'rest stream reduced.
And, lightened thus, misfortune shows
    The purpose of her earthly woes
Pointing a meaning for our woes
40   In every virtue they evoke.

If, Erin, thine abortive toil
    Have yielded yet a warning wise;
If from the ruins of thy soil
    A *moral* harvest shall arise;
45 If prudence, vigour, justice lost,
    Thence renovate thy growth of *men*,
Though dear the rigid culture cost
    The fruit will recompense thee then.

A Wail: 1847

JOHN SWANWICK DRENNAN

Lament for the land where the sun beams wander,
    And shadows deeper than elsewhere fall,
And the listless winds seem to wail and ponder
    Over glories past which they can't recall.
5   Fair are its cities, but despair frequents them
    From its fertile valleys must the famished flee;
And coasts safe smiling where the wave indents them,
    Invite, Isle of Ruin, no hope to thee!
        Ochone for thee, Erin, ochone a ree!

Round thy mystic towers and cromlechs lonely
10   Flit shadows majestic, of chief and sage,
But the light on each clarsech and torque is only
    Dimly reflected to this darkened age.
Fell are thy tall trees that erst branched so boldly,
    Hushed thy sweet singers that once warbled free;
15   O the bleak fortune that now clasps thee coldly,
    When, Isle of Ruin, shall it pass from thee?
        Ochone for thee, Erin, ochone a ree!

It has reached the Dead in thy green raths lying,
    'Tis troubling the calm of stone-girt rest,
Till a dreary sound of sepulchral sighing
20   Echoes the groans of the living breast.
From the Cairns of Meath to grey Cashel's Station
    Dim hands are shudd'ring from sea to sea,
Through Cein-an-each's Pass floats thy knell, lost nation,
    And o'er Glendalloch spirits 'keen' for thee;
25   Ochone for thee, Erin, ochone a ree!

1848

WILLIAM DRENNAN, JR

The birth of another year, ghastly with graves,
For famine stalks on through the hovels of slaves;
A funeral wail! But my heart feels so blank!
Slaves, fill me out wine, such as Thrasea drank.

5   When he and Helvidius, monarchs in worth,
Sate crown'd on the day that gave Brutus to earth.
Oh, those Romans of old, and this chain's weary clank!
Slaves, pour me out wine, such as Thrasea drank!

The torture of Tantalus, ever to read
10   Of Greece and Rome; of the word and the deed;
High heaven! have *we* souls, among men do *we* rank?
Slaves, lavish such liquor as Thrasea drank.

In a bowl of beechwood, or my lord's kindly clay,
Men are starving, hence, goblet of silver, away.
15   There were blood on your brim, there were tears in the draught,
Slaves, crown it with wine, such as Thrasea quaff'd.

Bead the bowl, fill it high, higher, up with it yet!
He drank to remember, I drink to forget;
We have couch'd to be famish'd; at insult have laugh'd.
20   Slaves! this is not wine such as Thrasea quaff'd.

The wine, ah, what was it; the thoughts it inspired,
Proud memories it woke, and high hopes which it fired,
Freedom's smile over all; in each heart how it sank!
Slaves! ye have no wine such as Thrasea drank!

Lament of the Irish Emigrant

LADY DUFFERIN

I'm sittin' on the stile, Mary,
    Where we sat side by side,
On a bright May mornin' long ago,
    When first you were my bride:

5 The corn was springin' fresh and green,
   And the lark sang loud and high —
 And the red was on your lip, Mary,
   And the lovelight in your eye.

 The *place* is little changed, Mary;
10   The day is bright as then;
 The lark's loud song is in my ear,
   And the corn is green again;
 But I miss the soft clasp of your hand,
   And your breath, warm on my cheek,
15 And I still keep list'nin' for the words
   You never more will speak.

 'Tis but a step down yonder lane,
   And the little church stands near —
 The church where we were wed, Mary;
20   I see the spire from here.
 But the graveyard lies between them, Mary,
   And my step might break your rest —
 For I've laid you, darling! down to sleep
   With your baby on your breast.

25 I'm very lonely now, Mary,
   For the poor make no new friends:
 But, oh! they love the better still,
   The few our Father sends!
 And you were all I had, Mary —
30   My blessin' and my pride!
 There's nothin' left to care for now,
   Since my poor Mary died.

 Yours was the good, brave heart, Mary,
   That still kept hoping on
35 When the trust in God had left my soul,
   And my arm's young strength was gone;
 There was comfort even on your lip,
   And the kind look on your brow —
 I bless you, Mary, for that same,
40   Though you cannot hear me now.

 I thank you for the patient smile

When your heart was fit to break,
    When the hunger-pain was gnawin' there,
        And you hid it for *my* sake;
45   I bless you for the pleasant word
        When your heart was sad and sore —
Oh! I'm thankful you are gone, Mary,
        Where grief can't reach you more!

I'm biddin' you a long farewell,
50   My Mary — kind and true!
But I'll not forget *you*, darling,
        In the land I'm goin' to:
They say there's bread and work for all,
        And the sun shines always there —
55   But I'll not forget Old Ireland,
        Were it fifty times as fair!

And often in those grand old woods
        I'll sit and shut my eyes,
And my heart will travel back again
60   To the place where Mary lies;
And I'll think I see the little stile
        Where we sat side by side,
And the springin' corn, and the bright May morn,
        When first you were my bride.

A Christmas Chime for 1849

K.

'Tis the day of the dawn of the long-hoping soul,
When despondence was crush'd with the serpent's control!
'Tis the Feast of the Christian — the day of *His* birth
Whose life first ennobled the suff'rings of earth:
5   When the Virginal Mother, rejected by all,
Plac'd her Maker and Babe in the Bethlehem stall!
        Then help, young and old,
        And cover the cold,
        And feed all the fasting,
10   For life everlasting!

'Tis the season of gladness, thanksgiving, and love,
When the Son came to open the portals above;
'Tis the happiest hour that creation has known
Since the credulous Eve caus'd our fall and her own!
15   But, while we rejoice, let us wisely remember
That now blow the blasts of bleak, blytheless December
    Let's succour the old,
    And cover the cold,
    And feed all the fasting,
20   For love everlasting!

All the proud hearths are blazing, gay groups gather round,
With the warmest attire, and the gleesomest sound;
Brilliant boards are beladen with costliest fare,
And no signals of sorrow and suff'ring are there.
25   May their pleasures be true, as thus bright they appear;
But, to make them *more real*, I'd breathe in each ear —
    'Oh! cherish the old,
    And cover the cold,
    And give food to the fasting,
30   You'll reap life everlasting!'

There are hoary heads bow'd beneath patience and pain —
Ay, and youthful limbs tott'ring in tempest and rain;
There are young mothers yet, without shelter or aid,
With their shiv'ring babes still in some lone hovel laid;
35   There's no feasting for these, save the *hope the day brings,*
And the wish that their souls would spread upwards their
    wings—
    Where nothing is old,
    And there's no more cold,
    And no one is fasting,
40   In life everlasting!

To the Cholera

JOHN KEEGAN

Oh! thou, who comest, like a midnight thief,
    Uncounted, seeking whom thou may'st destroy;
Rupturing anew the half-closed wounds of grief,
    And sealing up each new-born spring of joy.

5   Sprite, goblin, demon, whatsoe'er thou art,
    Fain in thy ears my terrors would I whine;
Fain would I seek the portal to thy heart,
    To pray thy pity upon me and mine.

I will not bid thee welcome, for to that
10   Uncalled-for show of canting courtesy
My blanching cheek would give denial flat,
    And shame the poet's boasted chivalry.

We've seen, or heard, or read of human bones,
    Oh! History tells of many a dire mishap —
15   Securely propping up the blood-stained thrones
    Of Tamerlaine, Attila, or old Nap.

And we can boast full many a tyrant still,
    Far worse than these destroyers of their kind;
But thou, grim terrorist, with matchless skill,
20   Dost beat such clumsy devastation blind!

Through duchies, kingdoms, empires great and small,
    Thou'st long been wandering with gigantic stride,
Casting thy shadows like a funeral pall,
    Upon the nations trembling far and wide.

25   With well-nerved arm you poised the fatal shaft,
    Kings, peasants, bards are equal in thy view;
Though sadly favouring all unholy craft,
    If we may credit the Romaunt of Sue.

No gibbets, racks nor molten lead attend
30   Thy works of ruin, nor the savage roar
Of hideous monsters, in the circus penned;
    One grasp, one spasm, and thy job is o'er.

Nor can all sublunary power avail,
    A Leo's rhetoric, or a Wellesley's sword —
35   To stay thy arm uplifted to assail
    The steel-girt city or the wandering horde.

But if you're strong, be merciful, and spare
    The trembling poet to his country's cause;
Oh! let his sons inspire thee to forbear
40   And in thy march of crimson havoc pause.

Albeit, regardless of my prayers and tears,
    Thy heart, though hard as adamant or stone,
If not yet blasted by the crime of years,
    Perchance a spice of gallantry may own.

45   You must have heard, with rapture and surprise,
    In other lands where thou hast chanced to be,
The dulcet warbler of the northern skies,
    Pour her full tide of matchless melody.

Even now she's picking up a few crumbs here,
50   And whilst the *gods* proclaim her heavenly sway,
And jewelled damsels pet the little dear,
    Ah! canst thou come to scare the bird away.

The Dying Mother's Lament
JOHN KEEGAN

'Oh God, it is a dreadful night — how fierce the dark winds blow!
It howls like a mourning *Banshee*! Its breathing speaks of woe;
'Twill rouse my slumbering orphans — blow gently, oh wild blast,
My wearied hungry darlings are hushed in peace at last.'

5   'And how the cold rain tumbles down in torrents from the skies,
Down, down, upon our stiffened limbs, into my children's eyes:
Oh God of Heaven, stop your hand until the dawn of day,
And out upon the weary world again we'll take our way'.

'But, oh! my prayers are worthless — oh! louder roars the blast

10 And darker from the pitchy clouds the rain falls s\
Oh God, if you be merciful, have mercy *now*, I pra\
Oh God, forgive my wicked words, — I know not \

'To see my ghastly babies — my babes so meek and\
To see them huddled in that ditch like wild beasts in t\
15 Like wild beasts! No! the vixen cubs that sport on yon\
Lie warm this hour, and, I'll engage, of food they've ha   .. iill'.

'Oh blessed Queen of Mercy, look down from that black sky —
You've felt a mother's misery, then hear a mother's cry;
I mourn not my own wretchedness, but let my children rest;
20 Oh watch and guard them this wild night, and then I will be blest'!

Thus prayed the wanderer, but in vain! — in vain her mournful cry;
God did not hush that piercing wind, nor brighten that dark sky;
But when that ghastly winter's dawn its sickly radiance shed,
The mother and her wretched babes lay stiffened, grim, and dead!

Home Again

MARY KELLY

Aye! twenty years and more it was, and home across the sea
A grey-haired man came sailing, and all alone was he;
But the well-lov'd smiles of kindred, the friends he left behind,
Sure the stranger won't be lonely, if these he still can find.

5 They're all before him, warm and bright, as in the days of yore;
And he paints the dear old faces with the look that once they wore;
And he thinks of that low cottage among the distant hills,
And the orchard and the meadow, water'd by the silver rills.

Yes! yes! they must be very old, the mother and the sire,
10 If they are still together beside the winter fire.
They must have mourned him deeply, the boy they lov'd so true;
But, oh! for that sweet welcome they'll give him as his due.

It is a dreary length of years that o'er his head has roll'd;
'Tis over now for ever, and he brings them hard-won gold.

59

The strong man's honest earning; and want shall come no more,
With care and sorrow hand in hand, around that cottage door.

The good ship flies across the wave; the distant cliffs arise —
The grey, old, misty Skelligs faintly pictur'd on the skies;
The breeze is freshly blowing, all impatient on its way,
20   And the sea-gulls hurry onward, glistening thro' the sunny ray.

But faster than the wild wind blows, and faster than the bird,
His heart is speeding onward — to its deepest pulses stirr'd —
'Till once again he treadeth on the well-remembered shore,
Where he parted friends and kindred more than twenty years
        before.

25   'Come, tell me, neighbours good and true, what news have you
        to tell?
What changes have been since I went? — my people, are they
        well?
Oh! little good is there to hear: your pitying eyes I see;
And after all the toil of years, but sorrow waits for me!'

'Aye! bear it bravely, Fergus, and say "God's will be done":
30   The poor old pair are lying low — they blest their absent son.
They died; be thankful for it: they were spared that bitter woe —
The crowbar, and the poorhouse — that some amongst us know.'

'And Maurice — brother of my heart! — and Mary, where is she?
And little Eileen? — dark the days they one and all did see.'
35   'Poor Maurice followed in your track across the stormy wave,
And in the wild Atlantic deep is now his lonely grave.'

'And Mary married far away — bad news of her is come —
The famine and the fever have been both within her home.
And little Eileen — none can tell where she may now be found:
40   Ah! there are changes, sad indeed, since you left Irish ground!'

Oh! weary, weary Pilgrim of all the mournful years,
Now run to earth, his heart pours out its flood of bitter tears.
Oh! darker than the exile far distant he has known
Is the consolation round him in the land he calls his own!

A Scene for Ireland

MARY KELLY

It was a wild and rainy day,
    The last of dark December's —
A ragged 'pauper', drooping, lay
    Above the dying embers.
The drops fell from the rotting roof,
    Marking the hours so dreary,
The hungry children stood aloof,
    Pallid, and cold, and weary.

Sad was the wretched mother's brow,
    Her baby's wailings hushing:
She has no food to give it now
    Save those hot tears outgushing.
Colder and colder blew the wind,
    Louder the dark rain splashes;
And dimmer grows the fire behind
    The heavy pile of ashes.

Far, far away, with pearls and gold
    My lady's hair is gleaming;
For every gem our eyes behold
    A crimson drop is streaming! —
For all the grace of silks and lace
    Some wretches naked shiver;
For every smile upon her face
    Some death-blue lips will quiver!

There's not a scene of lordly pride
    (Did heaven's good light illumine)
But we should know had, far and wide,
    Its meed of victims human.
We drain, perchance, some life away
    From out the sparkling chalice —
Some humble home in ruins lay
    Decking the gilded palace!

Black thoughts came from the Famine Fiend —
    He whispers low and stealthy —
'The poor man has no law or friend;

'Tis not so with the wealthy!
'Tis hard to see God's lights above,
    While clouds and darkness bound us;
'Tis hard to hear God's words of love
40   With storms like those around us.'

'Pray, pray!' so says the devotee,
    'Thus is temptation warded:'
Ah, little prayer had guided *thee*,
    Perchance, not gold-enguarded.
45   It is an easy thing to pray,
    No want or sorrow knowing —
It is an easy thing to say,
    'I praise God for bestowing.'

Within your hand the gilded book,
50   Upon the cushion kneeling;
And in your home no word nor look,
    One geyser spring unveiling.
But try to pray and try to love,
    Pain-wrung and soul-degraded —
55   The Lord God judges 'crime' above,
    But not as man has weighed it.

One of Many

MATTHEW MAGRATH

'Saw you a woman of yester-e'en
Pass slowly here — who once, I ween,
Had a heart as light, and a face as fair
As ever yet breathed the fresh mountain air?'

5   'I saw her, yes, and will never forget
That face, on which sorrow's seal was set;
'Twas a pale-white hue, and her light blue eyes
Were glazed like a dead-man's ere he dies.

'A sleeping child to her bosom she prest,
10   'Twas covered o'er with a tattered vest;

She looked at its face, heaved a long, long sigh,
Then turned up to Heaven with a prayerful eye.

'With a tottering step she passed slowly by,
And anon to the rich man's house grew nigh;
15   She stood at the door like a statue tall.
And the wind whistled through her garments all.

'I saw the rooks in the old ash tree,
They were building their nests right joyously:
The lowing herds grazed in the fields so green,
20   'Twas a peaceful, happy, contented scene.

' 'Twas so wherever I cast my eye,
On the hill, on the plain, on the vaulted sky;
The earth seemed of Nature's gifts a store,
I rapturously gazed on it o'er and o'er —

25   'Till I turned my eyes to where she stood,
Motionless; waiting, not asking for food;
On the fields, on the plains, did she gaze on them? Never;
They seemed but to mock her, for aye, and for ever!

'And the rich man came out with his face so red —
30   ''I can give you nothing'', he harshly said;
Not the heart of the fatally wounded bird
Could throb like hers when she heard that word!

'One hapless glance on her babe she cast,
Her glazed eyes were filled with tears at last;
35   And she hurried away by the hedge that shields
The northern blast from your verdant fields.'

'Say, where did she go to seek for bread?
Say, where did she rest her weary head?
Say, why does she ever thus wander away?
40   In her home, with her kindred, why did she not stay?'

'Alas, since you saw her she asked not for bread,
And the raven knows well where she rests her head,
From her once happy home she was forced to go,
For the ruthless landlord had laid it low!

45   'With her friends or her kindred she'll never abide,
On yonder pathway last night she died!
Her infant lay close to her clay-cold breast;
In the world to come they are both at rest.'

A Lament

WILLIAM PEMBROKE MULCHINOCK

'The potato is gone! We are now on the brink of another famine, more fearful than that of 1846. What are the ministers doing?' *Evening Freeman,* August 9, 1848.

With wailing and weeping
Our vigils we're keeping,
    Both daily and nightly;
Death garlands we're twining;
5   The hopes that shone brightest
Are darkly declining —
The hearts that beat lightest
    No longer beat lightly.

Than worker or toiler,
10   The hand of the spoiler,
    Dread famine is stronger;
In lowland and highland
The green stalks are faded —
In far-land and nigh-land
15   The toilers unaided,
    Can struggle no longer.

No hope for the weeper,
But darker, and deeper,
    And deadlier sorrow;
20   To us has high Heaven
    Sent ills without number —
Our hearts crush'd and riven,
    Can rest not as slumber,
    With dread of the morrow.

25   And cometh, remember,
The bitter December —
      On wings it speeds hither,
To find hearts wrung sorest,
     Without a roof's cover,
30   Like leaves of the forest,
     When summer is over,
      Foredoomed but to wither.

That sharp winter weather
Will pierce us together —
35   Like aspens we'll shiver;
Our dark fate pursuing,
     With light'ning quick motion
We glide on to ruin,
     As rushes to ocean,
40   A rain-swollen river.

A glad hour we know not,
The future can show not,
      Our barque lacks a haven;
Our iron soul'd master,
45   Deaf, deaf to our plaining,
But plies the scourge faster,
     Our limbs again chaining,
      As food for the raven.

The rats shall ply over
50   The loved and the lover
      Their loathsome vocation,
No hand rais'd in anger
     To threaten or smite them —
No voice, save of languor,
55   To scare, or affright them,
      Gnawing on to repletion.

Like unto Gomorrah,
Or Sodom of sorrow,
      Our land shall a waste lie,
60   While famine and fever,
     Those toilers unresting —
By day or night ever,

His food go out questing
    For Death pale and ghastly.

65   Our dead from their prison
Of cold clay, arisen,
    In spectral bands gather;
Our hearts hear their moving,
    Low calls in the even —
70   In tones soft and loving,
    They whisper of Heaven
        And God the All-Father.

Haste, haste, then ye grieving,
Your white shrouds be weaving,
75   Though little you need 'em;
Kind Death, whom, in madness,
    We call 'Desolator,'
Will place you in gladness
    Beside your Creator,
80   Where only is Freedom.

The Old Story

WILLIAM PEMBROKE MULCHINOCK

When first upon my country's lyre
    My trembling finger lighted,
I thought its first faint note of fire
    Should be with Fame requited;
5   The blood within my youthful frame
    So boiled with exultation,
When brightly o'er my dark mind came
    The dawn of Inspiration.

The meanest shapes of earth and air
10   For me had queenly beauty;
Religion, Freedom, Nature fair,
    Claim'd each and all my duty;
The woes and wrongs of human kind,
    In weak and humblest station,

15   Flashed lightning-like upon my mind
       The fire of Inspiration.

    I've seen the manly peasant's eye
       By tears of sorrow shaded —
    I've seen the maiden's beauty fly
20   By want and hunger faded —
    I've seen around me scatter'd wide
       Decay and desolation —
    I've seen it, and I sadly sighed,
       To draw thence Inspiration.

25   My burning thoughts escaped in song,
       The worldly-wise derided,
    They cared not whether right or wrong,
       'Twas jealously decided;
    Though I ne'er marked another's thought
30   For servile imitation,
       Though ne'er another rill I sought
    To draw thence Inspiration,

    'Twas strange, in sooth, that scarce a lay
       That youthful Genius wove then
35   Found one a favouring word to say —
       Found one pure mind to love them;
    'Provincial merit', curse the cant
       Of city ostentation,
    That yields the fame for which men pant
40   To meaner Inspiration.

    I'll touch my wild harp's strings no more
       To themes of Fire and passion,
    My dreams of Fame, once bright, are o'er,
       The poor were ne'er in fashion;
45   Unvalued as the idle wind
       Is now the Bard's vocation —
    There are no honours now for Mind,
       No wreathes for Inspiration.

Song of the Ejected Tenant

WILLIAM PEMBROKE MULCHINOCK

I leave thee on the morrow, my old accustomed home,
In sadness and in sorrow the hollow world to roam,
Too old to be a ranger, with heart too full of pride
To crouch unto the stranger whom I have oft defied.
5 'Tis hard links should be riven that time and friendship wove,
'Tis hard power should be given to hearts that know not love,
'Tis hard when death is near me with certain step, though slow—
When nought is left to cheer me, 'tis hard from home to go.

I leave the chimney corner, the old familiar chair,
10 To lay before the scorner my aged bosom bare,
To stand at every dwelling, to catch the rich man's eye,
And with a heart high swelling, for some small pittance sigh.
My hope of joy is broken, my happiness is o'er,
The words of fate are spoke — 'Beg thou for evermore.'
15 Would that my life were over, my weary life of pain!
Would that the green grave's corner my aged form might gain!

With eye and heart delighted, my only child beside,
I heard her young vow plighted — I saw her made a bride.
In joy we knelt around her; but ere a year went by,
20 The demon, Sickness, found her — she sought her bed to die.
When Spring's night stars were paling, our *ululu* was loud,
With women's bitter wailing, we wound her in her shroud.
She left a child behind her — I reared him on my knee;
Alas! if man were kinder he need not beg with me.

25 Over the mighty mountain, and by the lone sea shore,
By ice-bound stream and fountain we'll wander evermore;
To us, like lamb that ranges, along a bleak hill side,
From all the season's changes a shelter is denied.
I will not wish disaster to him who did me wrong,
30 I leave him to a Master that's merciful as strong:
And when the dawn is breaking upon the land and sea,
I'll say, with bosom aching, 'Farewell, *old home*, to thee.'

From:

Ireland's Lament: A Poem
JEREMIAH O'RYAN

Famine and plague, what havoc have ye made?
And was it thus that stalwart men should die?
Beside the husband's corse the wife was laid:
Her quivering lip and coldly glazing eye
5   Told that not yet had life's expiring sigh
From out that fond and faithful bosom fled.
In vain for food her starving infants cry:
There's none — there's none within the squalid shed
Nor even a taper's light to watch the solemn dead!

10   Ye human victims, from existence swept,
In your last fearful throes of mortal pain,
While thus you sank unrited and unwept,
How many wail'd your fate, alas, in vain!
Upon the Moloch shrine of guilty gain
15   Was Erin's hapless race to death consigned,
Oh, ghastly sacrifice — how black to stain!
Chill creeps a shuddr'ing o'er the heart and mind,
To think that thus should die such numbers of mankind.

Shroudless and coffinless they thickly lie,
20   The famish'd dogs devour'd them in their graves,
Now vaunting Albion safely may deny
The rights of freemen to her stricken slaves!
Nor need she send her hirelings o'er the waves,
For Erin's factious sons are sever'd still,
25   When party feud a nation's mind depraves,
Despot never need use force, or skill —
They've native traitors then, and tools to work their will!

How often have I seen, with tearful eye,
Departing from our land the exile's sail,
30   As from the deck each wild and melting cry
Broke o'er the waters, like a funeral wail,
And manhood's cheek with streaming grief was pale
From the soul's flood gates gushing unconfin'd,
And women shriek'd aloud — oh, doleful tale!

35 As sped the bark before the reckless wind,
    Then homeward sadly turn'd the mourners left behind.

    Ah, thus they go, our hardy sons of toil,
    To find a briny grave, or happier home;
    By dire oppression forc'd to fly that soil,
40 Where once in infant days they lov'd to roam.
    Poor wanderers — haply now they watch the foam
    That breaks on distant shores, and kindly mourn,
    With the faint hope that yet the time may come
    When, from earth's dearest ties no longer torn,
45 They'll tread their native fields, nor sigh afar forlorn.

    Yet, why should they bewail? For nought is left
    To bind them to the Isle that gave them birth!
    Sad out-casts on the world, of all bereft,
    Quench'd is the fire upon their lovely hearth!
50 There — once was heard the voice of humble mirth,
    The rustic song — the legendary tale —
    But lo! a burning curse hath swarm'd the earth,
    With choking graves, and stalking spectres pale;
    Oh, dark the blight of heav'n come down on Innisfail.

55 Such woes were never seen, since Cromwell's horde
    Spread famine o'er this isle, which Heav'n spared;
    When thro' the land they swept with fire and sword,
    Wasting the grain our fruitful valleys rear'd
    In tracks where murder stalk'd what deeds they dared!
60 And left behind a raging waste of flame;
    The spoilage of the soil their nearest shared,
    When to this isle the foul barbarians came;
    And boastful records still their villainies proclaim!

    Their vile descendants long have held the land,
65 And reap'd in fields which they have never sown;
    They wreck'd the peasant's home with ruthless hand,
    And of his dwelling, left nor roof, nor stone —
    They sent him forth, amidst the tempest's moan,
    To beg the world, or fly his native shore;
70 With hearts that mock'd at pity's melting tone,
    When, child of misery, shall thy woes be o'er?
    Too long, remorseless men have shed thy tears to gore.

By gold, by force, and fraud, from us was torn
Our country's rights, her senate, wealth and trade!
75   And now, the spoilers hold in bitter scorn
The cringing serfs and beggars they have made!
Since first they came, this island to invade,
Their path, with gory ruin, oft was red:
Low in the dust our ancient shrines they laid,
80   Defac'd those aisles where saints have lov'd to tread,
Those stolen sacred tombs that held the hallow'd dead!

The Eviction

MICHAEL SEGRAVE

A wretched quilt, and bed of straw —
    A shrunken frame, and hoary hair;
Full eighty winters' snows she saw,
    Now famine's fever laid her there;
5   And Malachi, her boy, is gone
    Across the broad Atlantic wave:
A daughter of her eldest son
    Is left to see her in her grave —

A maiden purer than the glow
10   That tints the snow when Spring is bright;
Now down her cheeks the hot tears flow,
    And she has watched the dreary night.
Oft startled by the dismal croak,
    The raven's and the banshee's cry;
15   Nor tasted sleep till daylight broke —
    O God, what horror meets her eye!

A band of ruffians burst the door,
    With huge crowbar and torch in hand,
Sent by their ruthless lord to clear
20   The rightful owners off the land,
Whose muscles raised his fairy hall,
    Whose sweat increased his pampered pride;
Poor slaves! though they seemed happy all
    Before the former landlord died.

25 Now famine is the peasant's lot —
   And hear the hapless maiden pray,
  'For pity spare this humble cot
   Till that shrunk form be laid in clay!'
  But 'Fire the thatch, the birds will fly!'
30   That the landlord's cry, — she hears no more;
  The light has fled her once bright eye,
   And she sinks senseless to the floor.

    * * * * * * *

  The people fly from hill and vale,
   While flames illuminate the sky,
35 And learn grim oppression's tale
   With fiery vengeance in each eye;
  And foremost was a youth as brave
   As ever trod the earth before;
  He raised her in his arms — 'Oh, save —
40   She's breathing now — she is no more!

  'Oh, speak, Kathleen, my darling bright,
   My own adored Cushla-ma-chree!
  Ah, no, thy spirit's ta'en its flight!
   Revenge is all that's left to me.'
45 'Oh, patience, youth', a voice now spoke,
   'To-night, at ten, we meet to try
  The villain who has dealt death's stroke,
   And by God's light he'll surely die!'

  The pale moon issued from a cloud,
50   The earth received its murdered dead,
  And, paler than the victim's shroud,
   The lover o'er the mountain sped:
  A cavern reached — the jury there —
   The murderer is guilty found!
55 'Then ere tomorrow's sun, I swear
   To fell the tyrant to the ground!'

  Now daylight bounds with happy speed,
   The hounds are panting for the chase;
  His lordship on a prancing steed
60   Comes forth 'Ha!' who said, 'Villain base!'

The dreaded voice rings in his ear —
    'Vile murderer, thy day is o'er!'
The tyrant shakes with rage and fear —
    And groans — and falls to rise no more.

The Boreen Side

JAMES TIGHE

A stripling, the last of his race, lies dead
    In a nook by the Boreen side;
The rivulet runs by his board and his bed,
    Where he ate the green cresses and died.

5   The Lord of the plains where that stream wanders on,
    — Oh! he lov'd not the Celtic race —
By a law of the land cast out fellow man,
    And he feeds the fat ox in his place.

The hamlet he levell'd, and issued commands,
10   Preventing all human relief,
And out by the ditches, the serfs of his lands
    Soon perish'd of hunger and grief.

He knew they should die — as he ate and he drank
    Of the nourishing food and wine;
15   He heard of the death cries of the famish'd and lank
And fed were his dogs and his swine.

That Lord is a Christian! and prays the prayer,
    'Our Father' — the Father of all —
And he reads in the Book of wonderful care,
20   That marks when a sparrow may fall.

And there lies that youth on his damp cold bed,
    And the cattle have stall and straw;
No kindred assemble to wail the lone dead —
    They perished by landlord law.

25   He lies by the path where his forefathers trod —
        The race of the generous deeds,
    That shelter'd the Poor for the honour of God,
        And fed them with bread — not weeds.

    Unshrouded he lies by the trackless path,
30   And he died as his kindred died —
    And vengeance Divine points the red bolt of wrath,
        For that death by the Boreen side.

The Irish Mother's Lament

ELIZABETH WILLOUGHBY VARIAN

I'm kneeling by your grave, *aroon!* the autumn sun shines
    bright,
Flinging upon the grassy mound a flood of golden light;
The flowers I tended for your sake are drooping one by one,
Whilst I must weep in hopeless grief above your grave, my son.

5   The wither'd leaves are showering down, they cannot break
    your rest;
And fair and bright the gorgeous pall they've flung upon your
    breast!
I saw them bud and blossom forth, beneath the soft spring sky,
But little dream'd that you, my son, should be the first to die!

I knew that want had paled your cheek, that hunger cast its blight
10   Upon the crimson lip, and eye, whose very glance was light!
I knew the powerful arm grew weak, the sweet voice lost its
    tone;
Yet still watched on, in trembling fear, till death the struggle
    won.

I longed to yield with cheerfulness the treasure lent to me,
But vainly strove to bow the will, although I bent the knee!
15   Oh! terrible the inward strife that rends the mother's heart;
They only know who've felt the pang, how hard it is to part.

Was there not plenty in the land? the earth gave forth her store—
The glad and fruitful mother earth, with riches brimming o'er.
Not for the slave who till'd the soil the garner'd wealth was won;
20   Our tyrant masters gorged their fill, and murder'd thee, my son!

Were there not stately homes enough, that our roof tree must
    fall?
On the forsaken green hill-side I see the blackened wall;
Be calm, my heart, in faith abide, God will not still endure
That tyrant hands shall desecrate the dwellings of the poor!

25   The dwellings of the virtuous poor, the homes of poverty,
Are sacred in the sight of God, though humble they may be;
Beneath the holy cabin roof the truest prayers may rise,
And many a suffering spirit there is fashioned for the skies.

Mavoureen! Hark, the bitter winds are howling round your
    home,
30   Sleep on in peace, my own one, sleep, your mother soon will come;
The autumn leaves are showering down upon your place of rest,
And bright and beautiful the pall that wraps your gentle breast.

The Tabinet Weaver

ELIZABETH WILLOUGHBY VARIAN

Weary and care-worn, still he toils, whilst morning's struggling
    light
Dispels each dreamy phantasy, those mists of vanished night —
The famine-fever wastes his cheek, yet no rest for the stricken
    slave,
Till cold, and want, and wretchedness, have won for him the
    grave.

5   He sits by the loom with head bow'd down, for his eyes wax dim
    and worn,
And the feeble hand its task must ply, through the glimmering
    light of morn;
No solace for throbbing heart and brow, no peace for the
    labouring brain,

75

For hunger binds him to his task, with a firm o'ermastering
    chain.

On his oars the galley slave may rest, the miner may pause for
    breath,
10   But he must struggle through night and day, for an hour's respite
    were death;
He thinks of his starving wife and child, and faster the shuttles
    fly,
Like a martyr on the rack he seems, in his fearful agony.

Rich is the costly robe he weaves, fit garment for a queen,
With wreaths of golden shamrocks, entwined on the brightest
    green;
15   'Mid poverty, cold, and nakedness, strange sight it is to see,
In the artisan's rude dwelling — a robe for royalty.

There, bending now beside him, his young wife shivering stands,
Hark! to the moan of suffering, as she wrings her wasted hands;
Her thread-bare garments screen her not from the chilly
    morning's cold,
20   Yet her blistered fingers dare not touch the web of green and gold!

On with thy task, poor artisan — who cares for thy fleeting
    breath —
Who cares that thy life-blood's ebbing, a drop to each glittering
    wreath?
Though the feverish pulse beats quicker, and the strained eyes
    throb and burn,
Yet, on with thy task, poor toiler! there's no time for thee to
    mourn.

25   But the time will come, thou worn one, when the weary martyred
    band,
As guests in our Father's dwelling, in their wedding robes shall
    stand;
Then, strive on a little longer, thou that hast bravely striven:
For the path of woe and misery, remember, leads to Heaven!

Drimin Donn Dilis

JOHN WALSH

Oh! *drimin donn dilis!* the landlord has come,
Like a foul blast of death has he swept o'er our home;
He has withered our roof-tree — beneath the cold sky,
Poor, houseless, and homeless, to-night we must lie.

5   My heart it is cold as the white winter's snow;
My brain is on fire, and my blood's in a glow.
Oh! *drimin donn dilis*, 'tis hard to forgive
When a robber denies us the right we should live.

With my health and my strength, with hard labour and toil,
10   I dried the wet marsh and I tilled the harsh soil;
I moiled the long day through, from morn until even,
And I thought in my heart I'd a foretaste of heaven.

The summer shone round us above and below,
The beautiful summer that makes the flowers blow:
15   Oh! 'tis hard to forget it, and think I must bear
That strangers shall reap the reward of my care.

Your limbs they were plump then — your coat it was silk,
And never was wanted the mether of milk;
For freely it came in the calm summer's noon,
20   While you munched to the time of the old milking croon.

How often you left the green side of the hill,
To stretch in the shade and to drink of the rill!
And often I freed you before the grey dawn
From your snug little pen at the edge of the bawn.

25   But they racked and they ground me with tax and with rent,
Till my heart it was sore and my life blood was spent:
Today they have finished, and on the wide world
With the mocking of fiends from my home I was hurled.

I knelt down three times to utter a prayer,
30   But my heart it was seared, and the words were not there;
Oh! wild were the thoughts through my dizzy head came,
Like the rushing of wind through a forest of flame.

I bid you, old comrade, a long last farewell;
For the gaunt hand of famine has clutched us too well;
35   It severed the master and you, my good cow,
With a blight on his life and a brand on his brow.

Lament of the Ejected Irish Peasant

JOHN WALSH

The night is dark and dreary,
    A gradh geal mo chroidhe,
And the heart that loves you weary,
    A gradh geal mo chroidhe;
For every hope is blighted,
That bloomed when first we plighted
5   Our troth, and were united,
    A gradh geal mo chroidhe!

We had once a happy hearth,
    A gradh geal mo chroidhe,
None happier on earth,
    A gradh geal mo chroidhe;
Thy loved smile made it so,
And toil caused our store's o'erflow,
10   Leaving something to bestow,
    A gradh geal mo chroidhe!

Oft when the biting blast,
    A gradh geal mo chroidhe,
Sent the stranger shivering past,
    A gradh geal mo chroidhe;
Would thy beaming eye flow o'er,
As thy hand flung wide the door,
15   To bid welcome to the poor,
    A gradh geal mo chroidhe!

Still our homestead we behold,
    A gradh geal mo chroidhe;
But the cheerful hearth is cold,
    A gradh geal mo chroidhe;
And those around its glow,
Assembled long ago,
20   In the cold, cold earth lie low,
    A gradh geal mo chroidhe!

'Twas the famine's wasting breath,
    A gradh geal mo chroidhe,
That winged the shaft of death,
    A gradh geal mo chroidhe;

And the landlord lost to feeling,
Who drove us from our sheeling,
25   Though we prayed for mercy kneeling,
         A gradh geal mo chroidhe!

Oh! 'twas heartless from that floor,
         A gradh geal mo chroidhe,
Where our fathers dwelt of yore,
         A gradh geal mo chroidhe,
To fling our offspring — seven —
'Neath the wintry skies of heaven,
30   To perish on that even,
         A gradh geal mo chroidhe!

But the sleety blast blows chill,
         A gradh geal mo chroidhe,
Let me press thee closer still,
         A gradh geal mo chroidhe;
To this scathed, bleeding heart,
Beloved as thou art,
35   For too soon — too soon we part,
         A gradh geal mo chroidhe!

Oh! there's a God above,
         A gradh geal mo chroidhe,
Of mercy and of love,
         A gradh geal mo chroidhe;
May he look down this night
From his heavenly throne of light
40   On our sad forlorn plight,
         A gradh geal mo chroidhe!

The Itinerant Singing Girl
LADY WILDE

Fatherless and motherless, no brothers have I,
And all my little sisters in the cold grave lie;
Wasted with hunger I saw them falling dead —
Lonely and bitter are the tears I shed.

5   Friendless and loverless, I wander to and fro,
Singing while my faint heart is breaking fast with woe,
Smiling in my sorrow, and singing for my bread —
    Lonely and bitter are the tears I shed.

Harp clang and merry song by stranger's door and board,
10   None ask wherefore tremble my pale lips at each word;
None care why the colour from my wan cheek has fled —
    Lonely and bitter are the tears I shed.

Smiling and singing still, tho' hunger, want, and woe,
Freeze the young life-current in my veins as I go;
15   Begging for my living, yet wishing I were dead —
    Lonely and bitter are the tears I shed.

PART II

'A Land Become a Monument'

AUBREY DE VERE & THE RELIGIOUS RESPONSE

The Desolation of the West

AUBREY DE VERE

'Migravit Judah propter afflictionem'

Day after day, mile after mile,
I roamed a land that knew no smile
    With awe akin to dread:
The land remained: the hills were there:
5   The vales — but few remained to share
    That realm untenanted.

Far-circling wastes, far-bending skies,
Clouds as at Nature's obsequies
    Slow trailing scarf and pall: —
10   In whistling winds on creaked the crane:
Grey lakes upstared from moor and plain
    Like eyes on God that call.

Above the hoary main a bluff
Rose with unnumbered gables rough
15   Beneath a sky of lead;
Nearer I drew: the tale was told
Grim, roofless walls, and hearths lay cold; —
    The villagers were dead.

The race of old from Ulster driven
20   Once more — for ocean — a far heaven —
    Had rushed o'er Connaught bound:
Void were the homes: the churchyards full:
Ten years had passed; and many a skull
    Whitened the churchyard ground.

25   Turn where I might, no blade of green
Diversified the tawny scene:
    Bushless the waste, and bare:
A dusky red the hills, as though
Some deluge ebbing years ago
30   Had left but seaweed there.

Dark red the vales: that single hue —
O'er rotting swamps an aspect threw
    Monotonous yet grand:
Long feared — for centuries in decay —

35   Like a maimed lion there it lay,
        What once had been a Land.

    Yet, day by day, as dropt the sun,
    A furnace glare through vapours dun
        Illumed each mountain's head:
40   Old tower and keep their crowns of flame
    That hour assumed; old years of shame
        Like fiends exorcised, fled.

    That hour from sorrow's trance awaking,
    My soul, like day from darkness breaking,
45   With might prophetic fired,
    To those red hills and setting suns
    Returned antiphonal response
        As gleam by gleam expired.

    And in my spirit grew and gathered
50   Knowledge that Ireland's worst was weathered,
        Her last dread penance paid;
    Conviction that for earthly scath
    In world-wide victories of her Faith
        Atonement should be made.

55   Well rose to heaven the hosts who there
    Upbuild the omnipotence of prayer
        O'er depths of vanquished grief!
    Well breasted they the billows drear
    A western Ireland who uprear
60   Like some slow coral reef!

    Thus musing, in remote vision
    Of God's 'New Heaven' I had fruition,
        And saw, and inly burned:
    And I beheld the multitude
65   Of those whose robes were washed in blood,
        Saw chains to sceptres turned!

    And I saw thrones, and Seers thereon
    Judging, and tribes like snow that shone,
        And diamond towers high-piled,
70   Towers of that City theirs at last,
    Through tribulations who have passed,
        And theirs, the undefiled.

A Land become a Monument!
Man works: but God's concealed intent
75   Converts his worst to best.
The first of altars was a tomb —
Ireland! thy grave-stones shall become
        God's Altar in the West!

Ireland: 1851

AUBREY DE VERE

O Thou! afflicted and beloved, O Thou!
Who on thy wasted hands and bleeding brow —
Dread miracle of Love — from reign to reign,
Freshenest thy stigmata of sacred Pain:
5   Lamp of the North, when half the world was night;
Now England's darkness 'mid her room of light;
History's sad wonder, whom all lands save one
Gaze on through tears, and name with gentler tone:
O Tree of God! that burnest unconsumed:
10   O Life in Death! for centuries entombed;
That art uprisen, and higher far shalt rise,
Drawn up by strong attraction to the skies:
Thyself most weak, yet strengthened from above:
Smitten of God, yet not in hate, but love: —
15   Thy love make perfect, and from love's pure hate
The earthlier scum and airier froth rebate!
Be strong: be true! Thy palms not yet are won:
Thine ampler mission is but now begun.
Hope not for any crown save that thou wearest —
20   The crown of thorns. Preach thou that Cross thou bearest!
Go forth! each coast shall glow beneath thy tread!
What radiance bursts from heaven upon thy head?
What fiery pillar is before thee borne?
Thy loved and lost! They lead thee to thy morn!
25   They pave thy paths with light! Beheld by Man,
Thou walkest a shade, not shape, beneath a ban.
Walk on — work on — love on; and suffering, cry,
'Give me more suffering, Lord, or else I die.'

Irish Colonization: 1848

AUBREY DE VERE

England, thy sinful past hath found thee out!
    Washed was the blood-stain from the perfumed hand:
    O'er lips self-righteous smiles demure and bland
Flickered, though still thine eye betrayed a doubt,
When round thy palace rose a People's shout —
    'Famine makes lean the Helots' helpless land.'
What made them Helots? Gibbet, scourge, and brand,
Plaguing with futile rage a faith devout.
    England! six hundred tyrannous years and more
Trampling a prostrate realm, that strength out-trod,
    Which twenty years availed not to restore.
Thou *wert* thy brother's keeper — from the sod
    His lifeblood crieth. Expiate thou that crime,
    Or bear a branded brow throughout all time.

Fell the tall pines! — thou nobler Argo, leap
    Wide winged deliverer, on the ocean's floods;
    And westward waft the astonished multitudes
That rot inert, and hideous Sabbath keep:
Or, stung to madness, guiltier ruins heap
On their own heads. No longer fabled Gods
Subdue vext waves with tridents and pearl rods;
Yet round that bark heroic Gods shall sweep,
    And guard an infant Nation. Hope shall flush
With far Hesperean welcome billows hoary:
Valor and virtue, love and joy, and glory,
    A storm-borne Iris, shall before you rush;
And there descending, where your towers shall stand
Look back, full faced, and shout, 'Britannia, land!'

I heard, in deep prophetic trance immersed,
    The wave, keel-cut, kissing the ship's dark side —
    Anon men shouted, and the cliffs replied:
O what a vision from the darkness burst!
Europe so fair a city never nursed
    As met me there! It clasped in crescent wide
    The gulf, it crowned the isles, the subject tide
O'er-strode with bridges, and with quays coerced.
In marble from unnumbered mountains robed,

With altar-shaped acropolis and crest,
There sat the queenly City, throned and globed:
40 Full well that beaming countenance expressed
The soul of a great people. From its eye
Shone forth a second Britain's empery.

How looks a mother on her babe, a bard
On some life-laboured song? With humble pride,
45 And selfless love, and joy to awe allied: —
So should a state that severed self regard,
Her child beyond the waves. Great Nature's ward,
And Time's, that child one day, with God for guide,
Shall waft its parent's image far and wide;
50 Yea, and its Maker's, if by sin unmarked.
Conquest I deem a vulgar pastime: trade
Shifts like the winds; and power but comes to go:
But this is glorious, o'er the earth to sow
The seed of Nations: darkness to invade
55 With light: to plant, where silence reigned and death,
The thrones of British law and towers of Christian faith.

England, magnanimous art thou in name:
Magnanimous in nature once thou wert;
But that which oftimes lags behind desert,
60 And Crowns the dead, as oft survives it — fame.
Can she whose hand a merchant's pen makes tame,
Or sneer of nameless scribe; can she whose heart
In camp or senate still is at the mart;
A Nation's toils, a Nation's honours claim?
65 Thy shield of old torn Poland twice and thrice
Invoked: thy help as vainly Ireland asks,
Painting with stark, lean finger, from the crest
Of western cliffs plague-stricken, to the West —
Grey-haired though young. When heat is sucked from ice,
70 Then shall a Firm discharge a Nation's tasks.

Ode:
After One of the Famine Years
AUBREY DE VERE

The Golden dome, the Trian dye,
    And all the yearning ocean
Yields from red caves to glorify
    Ambition, or devotion —
5   I leave them — leave the bank of Seine,
    And those high towers that shade it,
To tread my native fields again,
    And muse on glories faded.

The monumented city stands
10   Around me in its vastness,
Girdling the spoils of all the lands
    In war's imperial fastness.
That Starry scroll of every clime
    Some record boasts or sample;
15   Cathedral piles of oldest time,
    Huge arch and pillared temple.

They charge across the field of Mars;
    The earth beneath them shaking
As breaks a rocket into stars
20   The columned host is breaking —
It forms: it bursts: — a new host succeeds:
    They sweep the Tuileries under:
The thunder from the Invalides
    Answers the people's thunder.

25   Behold! my heart is otherwhere,
    My soul these pageants cheer not:
A cry from famished vales I hear,
    That cry which others hear not.
Sad eyes, as of a moontide ghost,
30   Whose grief, not grace, first won me,
'Mid regal pomps ye haunt me most: —
    There most your power is on me.

Last night, what time the convent shades,
    Far-stretched, the pavement darkened,
35   Where rose but late the barricades

Alone I stood, and hearkened;
Thy dove-mote, O my country, thine,
    In long-drawn modulation,
Went by me, linked with words divine,
40   That stayed all earthly passion!

A man entranced, and yet scarce sad,
    Since then I see in vision
The scenes whereof my boyhood had
    Possession, not fruition.
45 Dark shadows sweep the landscape o'er,
    Each other still pursuing;
And lights from sinking suns once more
    Grow golden on the ruin.

Dark violet hills extend their chains
50   Athwart the saffron even,
Pure purple stains not distant plains:
    And earth is mixed with heaven:
One cloud o'er half the sunset broods;
    And from its ragged edges
55 The wine-black shower descends like floods
    Dawn-dashed from diamond ledges.

Through rifted fares the damp wind sweeps,
    Chanting a dreary psalter:
I see the bones that rise in heaps
60   Where rose of old the altar;
Once more beside the blessed well
    I see the cripple kneeling:
I hear the broken chapel bell
    Where organs once were pealing.

65 I come, and bring not help, for God
    Withdraws not yet the chalice:
Still on your plains by martyrs trod,
    And o'er your hills and valleys,
His name a suffering Saviour writes —
70   Letters black-drawn, and graven
On lowly huts, and castled heights,
    Dim haunts of newt and raven.
I come, and bring not song; for why
    Should grief from fancy borrow?

75   Why should a lute prolong a sigh,
           Sophisticating sorrow?
        Dull opiates, down! To wind and wave,
           Lethean winds I fling you:
        Anacreonites of the grave,
80   Not mine the heart to sing you!

        I come the breath of sighs to breathe,
           Yet add not unto sighing,
        To kneel on graves, yet drop no wreath
           On those in darkness lying.
85   Sleep, chaste, and true, a little while,
           The Saviour's flock, and Mary's:
        And guard their reliques well, O Isle,
           Thou chief of reliquaries!

        Blessed are they that claim no part
90   In this world's pomp and laughter:
        Blessed the pure: the meek of heart: —
           Blest here; more blest hereafter.
        'Blessed the mourners.' Earthly goods
           Are woes, the Master preaches: —
95   Embrace thy sad beatitudes,
           And recognize thy riches!

        And if, of every land the guest,
           Thine exile back returning,
        Finds still one land unlike the rest,
100   Discrowned, disgraced, and mourning,
        Give thanks! Thy flowers, to yonder skies
           Transferred, pure airs are tasting;
        And stone by stone, thy temples rise
           In regions everlasting.

105   Sleep well, unsung by idle rhymes, -
           Ye sufferers late and lowly;
        Ye saints and seers of earlier times,
           Sleep well in cloisters holy!
        Above your bed the bramble bends,
110   The yew tree and the alder:
        Sleep well, O fathers, and O friends,
           And in your silence moulder!

From:

The Sisters: Or, Weal in Woe

AUBREY DE VERE

Sudden fell
Famine, the Terror never absent long,
Upon our land. It shrank — the daily dole;
The oatmeal trickled from a tighter grasp;
Hunger grew wild through panic; infant cries
5   Madden'd at times the gentle into wrong:
Death's gentleness more oft for death made way;
And like a lamb that openeth not its mouth
The sacrificial People, fillet-bound,
Stood up to die. Amid inviolate herds
10   Thousands the sacraments of death received,
Then waited God's decree. These things are known:
Strangers have witness'd to them; strangers writ
The epitaph again and yet again.
The nettles and the weeds by the way-side
15   Men ate; from sharpening features and sunk eyes
Hunger glared forth, a wolf more lean each hour;
Children seem'd pigmies shrivell'd to sudden age;
And the deserted babe too weak to wail
But shook if hands, pitying or curious, raised
20   The rag across him thrown. In England alms
From many a private hearth were largely sent
As oftimes they have been. 'Twas vain. The land
Wept while her sons sank back into graves
Like drowners 'mid the seas. Who could escaped:
25   And on a ghost-throng'd deck, amid such cries,
As from the battle-field ascend at night
When stumbling widows grope o'er heaps of slain,
Amid such cries stood May, when the ship
Its cables slipp'd and, on the populous quays
30   Grating, without a wind, on the slow tide,
Dropp'd downward to the main.

Widowhood: 1848

AUBREY DE VERE

Not thou alone, but all things fair and good,
Live here bereft, in vestal widowhood,
Or wane in radiant circlet incomplete.
Memory, in widow's weeds, with naked feet,
Stands on a tombstone. Hope, with tearful eyes,
Stares all night long on unillumed skies.
Virtue, an orphan, begs from door to door.
Beside a cold hearth, on a stranger's floor,
Sits exiled Honour. Song, a vacant type,
Hangs on that tree, whose fruitage ne'er was ripe,
Her harp, and bids the casual wind thereon
Lament what might be, fabling what is gone.
Our childhood's world of wonder melts like dew;
Youth's guardian genius bids our youth adieu;
And oft the wedded is a widow too.
The best of bridals here is but a troth, —
Only in heaven is ratified the oath:
There, there alone, is clasped in full fruition
     That sacred joy which passed not Eden's gates:
For here the soul is mocked with dream and vision;
     And outward sense, uniting, separates.
The Bride of Brides, a maid and widow here,
Invokes her Lord, and finds — Comfort: —
Her loftiest fame is but a visible perch
To sealed Creation's omnipresent Church.

     Zealous that nobler gifts than earth's should live,
Fortune I praise — but praise her, fugitive.
The Roman praised her permanent; but we
Have learned her lore, (and paid a heavy fee),
Have tracked her promise to its brake of wiles,
And sounded all the shallows of her smiles.
Fortune not gives but sells, and takes instead
A heart made servile, and a discrowned head.

The Year of Sorrow:
Ireland — 1849

AUBREY DE VERE

SPRING.

Once more, through God's high will and grace
    Of hours that each its task fulfils,
Heart-healing Spring resumes its place,
    The valley throngs and scales the hills;

5   In vain. From earth's deep heart o'ercharged,
    The exulting life runs o'er in flowers; —
The slave unfed is unenlarged:
    In darkness sleep a Nation's powers.

Who knows not Spring? Who doubts, when blows
10   Her breath, that Spring is come indeed?
The swallow doubts not; nor the rose
    That stirs, but wakes not; nor the weed.

I feel her near, but see her not;
    For these with pain uplifted eyes
15   Fall back repulsed; and vapours blot
    The vision of the earth and skies.

I see her not — I feel her near,
    As, charioted in mildest airs,
She sails through yon empyreal sphere,
20   And in her arms and bosom bears

That urn of flowers and lustral dews,
    Whose sacred balm, o'er all things shed,
Revives the weak, the old renews,
    And crowns with votive wreaths the dead.

25   Once more the cuckoo's call I hear;
    I know in many a glen profound,
The earliest violets of the year
    Rise up like water from the ground.

The thorn I know once more is white;
  And far down many a forest dale
The anemones in dubious light
  Are trembling like a bridal veil.

30

By streams released that singing flow
  From craggy shelf, through sylvan glades,
The pale narcissus, well I know,
  Smiles hour by hour on greener shades.

35

The honeyed cowslip tufts once more
  The golden slopes; with gradual ray
The primrose stars the rock, and o'er
  The woodpath strews its milky way.

40

From ruined huts and holes come forth
  Old men, and look on yonder sky!
The Power Divine is on the earth:
  Give thanks to God before ye die!

And ye, O children worn and weak,
  Who care no more with flowers to play,
Lean on the grass your cold, thin cheek,
  And those slight hands, and whispering, say,

45

'Stern mother of a race unblest,
  In promise kindly, cold in deed! —
Take back, O Earth, into thy breast,
  The children whom thou wilt not feed.'

50

SUMMER.

Approved by works of love and might,
  The Year, consummated and crowned,
Has scaled the zenith's purple height,
  And flings his robe the earth around.

55

Impassioned stillness — fervours calm —
  Brood, vast and bright, o'er land and deep:
The warrior sleeps beneath the palm;
  The dark-eyed captive guards his sleep.

60

The Iberian labourer rests from toil;
    Sicilian virgins twine the dance;
Laugh Tuscan vales in wine and oil;
    Fresh laurels flash from brows of France.

65   Far off, in regions of the North,
    The hunter drops his winter fur;
Sun-stricken babes their feet stretch forth;
    And nest dormice feebly stir.

But thou, O land of many woes!
70   What cheer is thine? Again the breath
Of proved Destruction o'er thee blows,
    And sentenced fields grow black in death.

In honour of a new despair
    His blood-shot eyes the peasant strains,
75   With hand clenched fast, and lifted hair,
    Along the daily-darkening plains.

'Why trusted he to them his store?
    'Why feared he not the scourge to come?'
Fool! turn the page of History o'er —
80   The roll of statutes — and be dumb!

Behold, O People! thou shalt die!
    What art thou better than thy sires?
The hunted deer a weeping eye
    Turns on his birthplace, and expires.

85   Lo! as the closing of a book,
    Or statue from its base o'erthrown,
Or blasted wood, or dried-up brook,
    Name, race, and nation, thou art gone.

The stranger shall thy hearth possess;
90   The stranger build upon thy grave,
But know this also — he, not less,
    His limit and his term shall have.

Once more thy volume, open cast,
    In thunder forth shall sound thy name;

95   Thy forest, hot at heart, at last
          God's breath shall kindle into flame.

      Thy brook dried up a cloud shall rise,
          And stretch an hourly widening hand,
      In God's good vengeance, through the skies,
100   And onward o'er the Invader's land,

      Of thine, one day, a remnant left
          Shall raise o'er the earth a Prophet's rod,
      And teach the coasts of Faith bereft
          The names of Ireland, and of God.

AUTUMN.

105   Then die, thou Year — thy work is done:
          The work ill done is done at last.
      Far off, beyond that sinking sun
          Which sets in blood, I hear the blast

      That sings thy dirge, and says — 'Ascend,
110   'And answer make amid thy peers,
      (Since all things here must have an end),
          Thou latest of the famine years!'

      I join that voice. No joy have I
          In all thy purple and thy gold;
115   Nor in that nine-fold harmony
          From forest on to forest rolled;

      Nor in that stormy western fire,
          Which burns in ocean's gloomy bed,
      And hurls, as from a funeral pyre,
120   A glare that strikes the mountain's head;

      And writes on low-hung clouds its lines
          Of cyphered flame, with hurrying hand;
      And flings amid the topmost pines
          That crown the steep, a burning brand.

125   Make answer, Year, for all thy dead,
          Who found not rest in hallowed earth;

The widowed wife, the father fled,
    The babe age-stricken from his birth.

Make answer, Year, for virtue lost;
130   For courage proof 'gainst fraud and farce
Now waning like a noontide ghost;
    Affections poisoned at their source.

The labourer spurned his lying spade;
135   The yeoman spurned his useless plough;
The pauper spurned the unwholesome aid,
    Obtruded once, exhausted now.

The roof-tree fall of hut and hall,
    I hear them fall, and falling cry,
'One fate for each, one fate for all;
140   So wills the Law that willed a lie.'

Dread power of Man! what spread the waste
    In circles hour by hour more wide,
And would not let the past be past; —
    The Law that promised much, and lied.

145   Dread power of God! Whom mortal years
    Nor touch, nor tempt; Who sitt'st sublime
In night of night — O big thy spheres
    Resound at last a funeral clime!

Call up at last the afflicted race,
150   Who man, not God, abolished, — Sore,
For centuries, their strife; the place
    That knew them once shall know no more!

WINTER.

Fall, snow, and cease not! Flake by flake
    The decent winding sheet compose;
155   Thy task is just and pious; make
    An end of blasphemies and woes.

Fall flake by flake! by thee alone,
    Last friend, the sleeping draught is given:

96

Kind nurse, by thee the couch is strown —
160   The couch whose covering is from heaven,

Descend and clasp the mountain's crest;
  Inherit plain and valley deep:
This night, in thy maternal breast,
  A vanquished nation dies in sleep.

165 Lo! from the starry Temple Gates
   Death rides, and bears the flag of peace:
The combatants he separates;
  He bids the wrath of ages cease.

Descend, benignant Power! But O,
170   Ye torrents, shake no more the vale;
Dark streams, in silence seaward flow;
  Thou rising storm, remit thy wail.

Shake not, tonight, the cliffs of Moher,
  Nor Brandon's base, rough sea! Thou Isle,
175 The rite proceeds! From shore to shore,
  Hold in thy gathered breath the while.

Fall, snow! in stillness fall, like dew,
  On temple's roof and cedar's fan;
And mould thyself on pine and yew,
180   And on the awful face of man.

Without a sound, without a stir,
  In streets and wolds, on rock and mound,
O omnipresent Comforter,
  By thee, this night, the lost are found!

185 On quaking moor, and mountain moss,
  With eyes upstaring at the sky,
And arms extended like a cross,
  The long-expectant sufferers lie.

Bend o'er them, white-robed Acolyte!
190   Put forth thine hand from cloud and mist,
And minister the last sad rite,
  Where altar there is none, nor priest.

Touch thou the gates of soul and sense;
    Touch darkening eyes and dying ears:
195   Touch stiffening hands and feet, and thence
    Remove the trace of sin and tears:

And ere thou seal those filmed eyes,
    Into God's urn thy fingers dip,
And lay, 'mid eucharistic sighs,
200   The sacred wafer on the lip.

This night the Absolver issues forth:
    This night the Eternal Victim bleeds
O winds and woods — O heaven and earth!
    Be still this night. The Rite proceeds!

Sonnet: 1849

ELLEN FITZSIMON

'And sure 'tis a most fair and pleasant land,'
This hapless Erin, this sad isle of ours!
Though late fell Famine stalked throughout her bowers,
Though dense the crowds that daily leave her strand,
5   Lovely her valleys, and her mountains grand,
Fertile her fields, pure, clear, and bright her rills,
Green even each crevice of her rockiest hills!
Is then our Isle of Heaven accursed and banned,
That all desert her thus? Perish the thought!
10   Not in such spirit read we Erin's lot;
Full often is adversity's chill breath
More precious than the wealth of India's mine,
High is the comfort of the text divine:
'Whom the Lord loveth, them He chasteneth!'

PART III

'To Help Old Ireland in Another Rhyme'

SATIRES AND DIALOGUES

Dublin: A Poem
In Imitation of the Third Satire of Juvenal
[abridged]

SIR SAMUEL FERGUSON

Much though my friend's expatriation move
My grief, my old friend's purpose I approve,
To shift his dwelling to the tents of Penn,
And give Columbia one more citizen.
5   Fair sink her suns: her western glades unfold
Refulgent paths to Californian gold:
What though the dross not half repay the strife
Waged for't 'gainst hunger and the bowie-knife,
E'en San Francisco, when consignments come
10   From Birmingham, I'd now prefer to home!
For sure no hell-on-earth could well be worse
Than here to hear the alternate altar-curse
And pistol shot; the weakling infants' moans,
The mother's sobs, the maddened father's groans,
15   The evicted cottier's shrieks; the thousand cries
That swell the ruined nation's obsequies;
And, 'mid the hubbub of our woes and crimes,
The daily prate complacent of the *Times*.

So, while his goods are packed in Champion's van,
20   Beside King William stood our going man;
From the near College halls the rumour drank
Of jabbered formulas, and eyed the Bank;
Here, where Old Freedom once was used to wait
Her darling Grattan nightly at the gate,
25   Now little clerks in hall and colonnade
Tot the poor items of provincial trade;
Lo! round the walls that Bushe and Plunket shook,
The teller's desk, the runner's pocket-book,
The anxious trader for the board who fills
30   His little docket of three doubtful bills;
The trader, of his bills no more in doubt,
Whose little docket has been just thrown out;
So changed, alas! — since, sped by cruel fates,
Our three-per-cents expelled our three estates.

35 Thence passing quay-ward, ere we step on board,
   We reach the palace splendid Beresford
   Reared for his country's commerce; ah, how well
   The porch would rise, the graceful dome would swell,
   If the fair edifice could boast at all
40 Goods in its stores, or merchants in its hall;
   Nor the one consignee's one schooner mock
   The desolation of its empty dock.
   Here, then, my friend, 'Since now at home,' said he,
   'No labour yields return for industry;
45 Since property, with gradual decay,
   'S today worth less than 'twas worth yesterday,
   And each to-morrow with assured distress,
   That lessened little will make something less,
   Hoist and make sail! Beyond the Atlantic foam
50 The loyal exile, too, may crave a home
   Where cribbed Confederates stretch their aching backs,
   And weary D — doffs his nose of wax.
   So while as yet Time's hoar-frosts but begin,
   And Lachesis has still some thread to spin,
55 While, apt for labour still, with sinewy calf
   I plant my steps unconscious of a staff,
   Farewell to Ireland! Let Menenius here
   Thrive, and Sartorius, who can make it clear
   By mode synthetic, or, with equal ease,
60 By analytic method, which you please,
   That Ireland, after nature's lists were full,
   Was supplementalised in ease of Bull
   As servient tenement; Bull's Grange, in brief,
   Cum privilegio to raise his beef;
65 But, as for eating of the beef we rear,
   Or manufacturing the clothes we wear,
   (Pursuits and privileges such as these
   Pertaining but to nationalities),
   Enjoined perpetually, all and some,
70 *Sub prohibitione superûm.*
   Or show you by *sorites*, past dispute,
   That agitation is misfortune's root,
   (By agitation you're to understand
   Irishmen taking thought for Ireland),
75 And that, allowing only for some small
   Eventualities exceptional,

Of late occurrence, say some one or two
Millions of starved (a million too few)
Since agitation ceased, no men alive
80 Ere throve as we do, or we ought to thrive.
These are your stars aesthetic soirées boast,
These they who rule your literary roast,
And with official dialectics fix
Your social status by your politics.
85 What should I do in Ireland — I can't
Play cosmopolitan court-sycophant:
I, I admit, make not the least pretence
To frank the fallacies of 'Common Sense:'
Can't comprehend, and truly never could,
90 How absenteeism does any good;
Nor how, just now, if Court and Parliament,
Lords, ladies, commoners, and madams went
To live at Petersburgh, the Cockney folk
Should take it as an economic joke:
95 Though it beat cockfighting, I fail to catch
The rupturing raptures of the digging match:
Besides, I'm quite unable to explain
How this poor country's to get rich again
By ostracising, with repeal debates,
100 The willow pattern from her empty plates.
Worse still, I never yet could bear the jest
Would make me 'evil bird' in my own nest,
Nor simpering cry, 'How Irish!' when some fool
Has haply broken Hoyle's or Priscian's rule:
105 Therefore, I'm no man's eligible guest
On no commission, and in no request.

What! stay, where not a threadbare coat but draws
Some pert reflection on the country's cause;
Where not a law destructive does its work
110 Without the maker's aggravating smirk —
The blundering senate, and the brutal press
First causing, then insulting, our distress;
Where God himself can't lay His heavy hand,
In wrath mysterious on our sinful land;
115 But every Cockney sprig assumes the airs
Of privy councillor in heaven's affairs;
And while he dreams himself a mighty thane,

The Titmouse of some Irish earl's domain,
And for the splendid bargain counts his pence,
120 Applauds the policy of Providence.
Why waste your breath among them? You're too few
To stand the pressure of a single Jew;
Your strongest Irish vote would scarce be miss'd
Out of the proxies of one capitalist.
125 Sell out, and quit: 'twere better than be starved,
Cheesemonger's coming — notice duly served.

Who on the Alleghani's stony backs
Grows pale at rumour of an income tax,
Or 'neath the shade of Cincinnati's rock
130 Starts, sickening, at the tax-collector's knock?
Here we subsist, one half of us, by chance,
'Tother, on legislative sufferance;
Go rich to bed, and wake to-morrow morn,
To find ourselves of house and land forlorn.
135 The swift Triumvirs, while we slept, have sold,
Conveyed, made title, and disbursed the gold.
No, we must live, where property is spent
By those who own it — where no Parliament
Becomes the steward of a man's estate
140 To spend, to sell , to tax, to confiscate,
For other folks' behoof: — already, see
Your neighbour Callaghan's in jeopardy —
Drives off his stock; but keen collector now,
Makes swift distress of pig, and eke of cow;
145 You suffer last (if aught you profit by't),
Immediate lessor of the luckless wight.

Poor Codrus, or, vernacularly said,
Poor Paddy Cody had one feather bed;
And Mrs. Cody, on her freestoned shelf,
150 A decent show of glutinated delf;
These, with a chest replete with various trash,
And Patsey's breeches, recent from the wash,
Made all their wealth; and now Collector's call
Strips them and Patsey of that little all.
155 What's worse, alas! now driven to Pauper's door,
To share, themselves, their tribute to the poor,
Pauper must share them neither bite nor sup,

103

Till first the cropped half-acre's given up.
Ah, me, if he who penned the cruel clause,
160   Himself were fallen in this same dragon's jaws,
I fear 'twould pass my paraphrastic art,
To show the sequel by Arturius' part,
No press, I fear, would check the rising scoff;
No justice put the petty sessions off;
165   No shrewd philosopher surmise, that he
Distrained himself, to try men's sympathy.

Now, if inveterate habit don't refuse,
And you'll but leave your levees and reviews,
Content to settle where a virgin soil
170   Yields endless crops to honourable toil,
In green Arkansas, for less cash than here,
You'd pay for one poor doghole for a year,
You'll buy a property two miles about,
For ever, pure allodium, out and out.
175   There you may live in rural ease and wealth,
And court old age in happiness and health.
Here men of feeling, ere they yet grow old,
Die of the very horrors they behold.
'Tis hard to sleep when one has just stood by
180   And seen a strong man of sheer hunger die;
'Tis hard to draw an easy, healthful breath,
In fields that sicken with the air of death;
Or where relief invites the living throng
To see the withered phantoms flit along,
185   Hunger impelling, and exhaustion still
Leaving the weak limbs baffled of the will.
Who, without shortened days, could daily pass
The tottering, fluttering, palpitating mass,
Who gaze and gloat around the guarded dole,
190   That owned a heart of flesh, or human soul?
I pray you, further ask me not to draw
This dread, revolting *anti-sportula.*

Beware, besides, if here you drive abroad,
The yawning ruins of the mended road.
195   High as above the arching fences go,
So deep the black profound descends below.
If foundering in the chasm, you seek the ledge

That skirts the rugged basement of the hedge,
Beware; for, caved beneath, the treacherous floor
200   May drop where you'll ne'er see daylight more.
Frequent not such official paths until
You've made your soul, sir, or, at least, your will.

Why stay to see again the ancient grudge
Revived, of Ribbon and of Orange Lodge?
205   Ere three weeks pass, perhaps, by murmuring Bann,
Or placid Lagan, some drunk Orangeman,
Vexed to have sent no Papist soul to hell,
May think my head would serve his turn as well;
Perhaps the Ribbonman, with equal zeal
210   For Mr Orangeman's eternal weal,
Missing his mark, from sheltering hedge or tree,
For spite may take a cursive shot at me.
Sure for our wretched country's various ills,
We've got, a man would think, enough of bills —
215   Bills to make paupers, bills to feed them made;
Bills to make sure that paupers' bills are paid;
Bills in each phrase of economic slang;
Bills to transport the men they dare not hang;
(I mean no want of courage physical,
220   ''Tis conscience doth make cowards of us all;')
Bills, till the mills may haply soon refuse
Enough of paper for the printers' use;
And little boys the dreadful thought affrights,
That paper next shall fail them for their kites.
225   But one short bill that served so well before
To keep us quiet, we're to have more.

More I might say, but Mr. Champion's man
Signs with his whip, and onward drives the van.
Farewell; compelled perhaps by civic jars
230   To seek the shelter of the stripes and stars,
You yet may follow where I lead the way;
If so, expect a friend upon the quay,
Who, if your European muse permit
The rugged aid of homespun Yankee wit,
235   Shall bear a willing hand, some happier time,
To help old Ireland in another rhyme.

Inheritor and Economist:
A Poem
[*abridged*]
SIR SAMUEL FERGUSON

To Erin, once, ere yet disaster's list
Was quite filled up, sailed SIR ECONOMIST;
Spent in her survey certain days, and found
Her catallacticals were quite unsound:
5   Here saw the squire, a wealthy magnate made
By laws impolitic, that fettered Trade,
(That fettered England's dearest trade) and there
One asking alms, yet free to take the air:
'This land', quoth he, 'is in a piteous plight,
10   But haply I've been born to set it right'.

'First, then', he said — and, look you, he was one
With whom 'twas then no sooner said then done —
'You easy squires must go to Liebig's school,
And henceforth thrive by pharmaceutic rule;
15   For who would live, in careless ease, content
With crops deficient, though redundant rent,
When double crops, as good at half the price,
Would reinstate our workshops in a trice,
Would, with the loaf, bring wages down as well,
20   And, underbought, leave free to undersell;
Till spread o'er all the earth by steam and wind,
Our British calicos clothed all mankind,
And science hailed the spectacle sublime,
Of mighty England working double time':
25   But science first demands, as it befits,
That competition stimulate your wits;
Fair competition, to whose bland duress
Man owes in every art his last success:
Let, then, those rivals who from either sea
30   Yearn to confront you in our marts, be free!
Away with all the antiquated rules
Devised by tyrants, and obeyed by fools,
Which to fair nature's bounty shut your doors,
And mar the march of commerce round your shores;
35   Undo your selfish toll-bars with a grace,

And call the nations to your market-place;
So shall your hapless island soon be made
Great, glorious, free, and fruitful by Free Trade!'
'Sir', said INHERITOR, for such the name

40 By which our Irish squire is known to fame
'I bought this land, when beef and corn were high,
Assured by law of your monopoly;
And, trusting in your market still to set
Like preference, am something gone in debt.

45 My annual rental doubtless handsome sounds;
'Tis, in round numbers, say ten thousand pounds:
But then I call scarce half of that my own;
For, first, I pay for interest on a loan
Two thousand yearly; next, three thousand more,

50 In various items, go amongst a score
Of younger brothers, sisters, nephews, aunts,
Rent-chargers, dowagers, annuitants:
But still, I hope, the land itself secures
My mortgagee — a countryman of yours'.

55 'Yes', quoth ECONOMIST, 'tis justly said;
Your mortgagee must first of all be paid'.

'Then next to them', INHERITOR went on,
'I've got some little charges for my son,
TENANT-IN-TAIL, who, as I grieve to tell,

60 At Cambridge has outrun the constable:
Here, too, I've to support some five or six
Expensive foibles of INHERITRIX;
My daughter, sir, who makes us greybeards fools,
With lectures, classes, charities, and schools:

65 So that, should rents unhappily come down,
I'm not so rich but still to dread the frown
Of angry fortune; for, say rents should fall
Ten shillings in the pound, I lose my all'.

'Fear not for that', ECONOMIST replies,

70 'Repeal the corn-laws, and your rents will rise:
Doubt you the fact? by rule of algebra
I'll prove it plainly in a formula.
For, say our present export cotton trade
Is minus y, and call our imports z:

75 The minus y plus z, divided by

X squared (our increased exports), equal *y*,
Minus *x* squared by *z* divided — thus
Our *minus* export has become a *plus*'.

'Just so', rejoined INHERITOR: 'but these
80   Fine scientifical analyses
Quite pass our skill, who've only learned the rules
Of Bonnycastle in our country schools.
But, since I know that what you will you can,
And that protection, once put under ban,
85   Can now no more withstand your party's feud
Than the old exile, 'barred of salt and wood,
The social interdict; I'll turn my hand
To take an increased produce from the land;
And, since it may no better be, shall try
90   And learn Political Economy'.

There, INHERITOR drew out of bank
What ready cash he had, and, forthwith sank
His money by the perch, with mighty pains,
In Parkes's and in Smith of Deanston's drains:
95   To show what skill and capital could do,
Squared all his fields, and laid his roads anew;
Loosed from his threshing mill the weary team,
And set an engine there would thresh by steam.
The wondering farmers, when they saw the squire
100   On industry so hot, themselves took fire;
Retrenched their fare, and stead of roast and boiled,
More guana purchased, and fresh fields subsoiled.
ECONOMIST the prosperous work commends,
And, on his part, with ready bounty, sends,
105   At the state's charge, new valuators round,
To rate each acre at an extra pound;
Commissions, too, a scientific band,
To diagnose and analyse the land:
One lays the levels in fair contour lines,
110   The rivers one explores, and one the mines;
The Flora here, the Fauna there was seen,
Fossil and recent, land and submarine:
Could tell INHERITOR, when forth he went
To see how fast his capital was spent,
115   The birth-day date of each particular rock

That exercised his jumpers: name each dock
That choked his gripes, in Latin; by its trail,
Find him the pedigree of any snail
That crossed his cabbages: no dirt could grow
120   (Though only tadpoles might be thought to know
Or care for it) in any ditch, but pat
They'd tell its genus, species, habitat;
When first discovered upon Irish ground,
And who the wight the wondrous weed who found;
125   Whether in walks suburban, or afar,
And if on foot, or on a jaunting car.

INHERITOR imbibed the noxious trash,
Got rich in nomenclature, poor in cash;
Until at last, I grieve to tell, but must,
130   He grew a notable industrial *dust*;
In pseudo-scientific phrase would prate
Of silex, silica, and silicate;
In social hours, when songs of old were sung,
And jokes sent round, would dissertate on dung;
135   Show how cheap crops, reacting in a sweep,
By circumbendibus, make taxes cheap;
And how the cost of forcing the Chinese
For British calicoes to give their teas;
Of sale for thirty webs that Napier gets
140   At point of thirty thousand bayonets;
Of pin-markets, by broadsides open laid,
And such like items of Free (booting) Trade,
Pacific fleets and flagstaffs at Hong Kong,
Would pay the Irish farmer, before long.

145   Fair Muses, fairer none among the Nine,
Who clothed with grace Lucretius' learned line,
Mothers of arts and sciences, forgive
These scorns; they touch not your prerogative,
If ever I your altars dully deck'd
150   Pass without reverence; if ever act
Or word of mine impede the ingenuous youth
Who, in your paths, seeks philosophic truth,
Then let each sister Muse avenge the wrong,
Let cold Calliope deny me song,
155   And angry Clio, with averted face,

Refuse me knowledge of my name and race!
But, if intruders, gabbling in your schools,
Mad formulists and dialectic fools,
Who blush to own their land's historic name,
160   But call the paragraphs of —— fame,
And nobler occupations never crave
Than botanizing on poor Ireland's grave,
Incur contempts; let not the bard be blamed,
Nor slander say that Science is defamed!
165   Meantime, our tale resuming, let's attend
INHERITOR'S adventures to an end.

ECONOMIST and he, one day, espied
A certain PAUPER by the highway side:
Where the sun shone warm in the verdant gripe,
170   He sat among his bags and smoked a pipe:
His dog lay sleeping on the sunny ground;
The fragrant weed perfumed the air around.
INHERITOR, who'd been in youth imbued
With the humanities, in musing mood
175   Contemplating the little group, began —
'Saint Austin has a tale, how, at Milan,
He once espied a beggar in the street,
Had got belike his bellyful of meat.
Jesting and merry: Austin says he sighed
180   To think how mankind, for their empty pride,
The cares and pains of life exaggerate
And all to gain that beggarman's estate,
'For sure', says he, 'the beggar was full gay,
But I right heavy': even so today
185   Lies the same difference still 'twixt him and us,
So careless he, we so solicitous!'

'Take with you', said ECONOMIST, 'that we
Are living in the nineteenth century,
Not in the days of saints or anchorites;
190   Days did I say? — say rather in the nights!
When mendicancy in the state demands
A scientific treatment at our hands.
This vagrant now the countryside imbues
With idle habits and the love of news;
195   Pernicious tales from house to house imports

110

Of births, deaths, marriages, and country sports —
Seditious rumours, threats, and bulletins
O' the Ribbon-lodge, and smith's-forge magazines;
Idles the little schoolboys with his tricks,
200 The adult workers with his politics;
And so, at public charge, with little pains
Himself, his vermin, and his dog maintains.
Now, trust your Irish Poor-Reform to me,
And speedily (his terrier hanged) you'll see
205 How science shall economise your rogue,
And save society the keep of's dog;
Shall utilise him, sir, in such a sort,
That this one beggar haply shall support
Stead of the vermin who now suck his blood,
210 Of paid official bloodsuckers a brood
More numerous far, whose legions swarming thick
O'er all parts of the body politic,
Shall in a systematic way apply
Anti-phlogistics and phlebotomy;
215 Or, if the patient sigh for nobler wants,
A rousing course of counter irritants,
Till all the members of your Commonwealth
Are bled and blistered into perfect health.
No longer, then, your country's cure defer —
220 Make haste, appoint one Chief Commissioner
To supervise all Beggarland's concerns,
Fifty inspectors, chiefs, and subalterns;
Fifty collectors, with good sureties,
To gather in the dues: then add to these
225 Five hundred guardians, vice and volunteer —
Five hundred clerks at fifty pounds a-year;
Five hundred masters, and five hundred dames,
Five hundred Health-Board doctors of all names;
Five hundred builders from the Board of Works,
230 Five hundred chaplains, and five hundred clerks'.

'Sir', said INHERITOR, 'I'd not be rash,
But sure this cure would cost a deal of cash'?

'Not half so much', ECONOMIST replies,
'As now is spent on PAUPER'S luxuries.
235 For now, besides his pipe's expensive fumes,

111

Consider what his terrier consumes;
Sir, I'll demonstrate that that terrier
Costs the state more than a commissioner:
For, call the terrier x —'

                              'The terrier's name
240   Is Pincher',

              Well, my argument's the same:
Call Pincher x —'

                              'Admitted, sir; the brute
Eats greedily: 'tis idle to dispute
With one who, to your learning joins the weight
245   Of voices all potential in the state.
Assuming then, that 'tis the wiser way
To have a Poor-Law — pray, sir, who's to pay?'

'What! who support the land's neglected poor?
The land that breeds the beggars, to be sure!'

250   'Then', said INHERITOR, 'if that be so,
And if a portion of the rents must go
In poor-rate, still you'll lay the burden on
Proportionately as the rents are drawn;
Thus MORGAGEE who yearly skims away
255   The cream of mine, his quota, too, will pay'.

'What! charge the interest of MORTGAGEE?
Sir, let me tell you, that's flat burglary!
You promised MORTGAGEE his six per cent.,
Whether from greater or from lesser rent.
260   You share no profits if your rents go up,
He shares no losses, *contra*, if they drop'.

'But when the contract for this loan was made,
We neither of us dreamt the beggar's trade
Would thus be undertaken by the state,
265   Else we'd have bargained to divide the rate:
And sure on one the charge unjustly bears,
When both are purchasers at unawares'.

'No matter: twist and turn it as you will,
You are the borrower, he the lender still,
270   You, too, the Landlord; as such, understand
You represent the duties of the land,
Its charges, burdens, dangers, losses, blights,
As regularly as you do its rights.
When Science looks at land, her radiant eyes
275   Landlord and Tenant only recognise;
What hosts behind you of Incumbrancers
May crowd the rere, is no concern of hers.
You occupy the place, and can't refuse
The front-rank dangers, and the front-rank dues'.

280   'I fear me, sir, if this be so, indeed,
And these new corn-law changes don't succeed,
With falling markets and diminished rents,
Poor-rates will possibly breed discontents'.

Then, somewhat coldly, with polite 'good day',
285   Our interlocutors went each his way.
ECONOMIST (his measures ready planned)
Put PAUPER in commission out of hand.
Lodged and attended like a little lord,
His dues called in and managed by a Board;
290   Fed, clothed, inspected, doctored, chaplained, clerked,
Nor under-exercised, nor over-worked:
To morning prayers at six, to bed at ten,
PAUPER should, sure, be happiest of men!
But see the perverseness of human breasts;
295   PAUPER no more with matutinal jests
Will break his fast, nor with the ready joke
Preface the solace of the vesper smoke: —
No smoking here allowed, for great or small,
His pipe's locked up, tobacco-box and all.
300   PAUPER, within, soon grows as prone to pout
As ratepaying INHERITOR without;
He dreams of green lanes in the whited ward,
Longs for rough ditch-banks in the formal yard,
Frets for his pipe, and early mourns and late
305   Suspended Pincher's miserable fate.

In PAUPER's service now such crowds engage,
The workhouse yields good store of patronage:
To see the candidates for PAUPER's staff,
Might, mid his tears, make Heraclitus laugh;
310   Cadets of chiefs, and grandsons of grandees,
Thronging, each morn, ECONOMIST's levees,
Beard to the eyes, and rings to fingertips,
Humble expectants of inspectorships;
Such the aristocratic charms that dwell
315   Round rates struck promptly and collectable.

ECONOMIST now drives a thriving trade
In politics, and counts his fortune made:
The yard's remodelled, and the staff's increased
(Each new inspectorship's a vote at least),
320   He sits secure as Shere Sing in his trench,
And cries 'Ha, ha,' behind the treasury bench.

Such was the land's, and such the ruler's plight,
When heaven, at length, in anger sent the blight.
With silent swiftness, in a mildew blast,
325   O'er Erin, in one night, the mischief passed:
Where eve had sunk in shining emerald track,
Morn showed the green potato ridges, black;
And all the air, as with a sick man's breath,
Stunk o'er a waste of vegetable death.
330   Oh, God of Heaven! it was a dreadful sight,
To see the mighty multitude's affright,
Who'd gone to rest, secure of food, when dawn
Showed, at a glance, their year's subsistence gone.
But why despair? although the blighted plant
335   Was lost past help, the people need not want,
At least as much as life demands to eat,
For still the land had store of beef and wheat.

'Keep these, at least, at home,' the people said,
Or only barter them for coarser bread,
340   But suffer not the ships to take away
Food which is life, for luxuries to pay;
Still less permit the life's blood of the land,
To leave its shores for MORTGAGEE's demand'.

345 'Oh! unlearned rustics', cried ECONOMIST,
'Doth not the state's prosperity consist,
And are not nations civilized and made
Polite and rich, by commerce and by trade?
Yet, here, to satisfy your sordid wants
You'd stop your exports! Oh, ye ignorants!'

350 'Civilization, as it seems to me',
RUSTIC rejoined, 'implies Society;
And if my argument so far be good,
Society needs Life, and Life needs Food;
And if you take our Food, and Life be gone,
355 What's left to civilize, or trade upon?'

'Truth, sir, is left', ECONOMIST replies,
'And scientific law, that never dies!
The principle survives; and, just observe —
I'd sooner see you and your nation starve
360 Than compromise, infringe, impeach, evade,
Or bate one jot the doctrines of Free Trade.
Ship, then, your wheat and beef: importing fleets
Shall, in return, bring duly stamped receipts,
(I laugh the unlearned sophistry to scorn
365 That says your exports bring you no return!)
And, if you're patient till three months elapse,
You'll get some Indian corn, besides, perhaps'.

The wheat and beef went out: but out, alack!
'Twas long before the Indian corn came back;
370 And, when we're pleading in the stomach's court,
Behoves oft sittings and adjournments short,
Else ('tis the settled practice of the fates)
The best conducted suit ere long abates;
And from fate's office fast though pleas arrive,
375 No *scire facias* issues to revive:
So when ECONOMIST, as crier, bawled
'Celt *versus* Hunger', Celt had to be called:
The silent grave no Celt's complaint returned,
The suit abated, and the court adjourned.

380 Deem not, O generous English hearts, who gave
Your noble aid our sinking isle to save,

This breast, though heated in its country's feud,
Owns aught towards you but perfect gratitude.
For every dish retrenched from homely boards,
385 For every guinea from prudent hoards,
For every feast deferred, and jewel sold,
May God increase your stores a hundred-fold;
Grant to you health and wealth, and love's increase,
Here, and hereafter, Christ's eternal peace;
390 Long keep your realm from discord unembroiled,
Your arms triumphant, and your flag unsoiled!
But, frankly while we thank you all who sent
Your alms, so thank we not your Parliament,
Who, what they gave, from treasures of our own
395 Gave, if you call it giving, this half-loan,
Half-gift from the recipients to themselves
Of their own millions, be they tens or twelves;
Our own as well as yours; our Irish brows
Had sweated for them; though your Commons' House,
400 Forgetting your four hundred millions debt,
When first in partnership our nations met,
Against our twenty-four (you then twofold
The poorer people) — call them British gold.
No; for these drafts on our united banks
405 We owe no gratitude, and give no thanks,
More than you'd give to us, if Dorsetshire
Or York a like assistance should require;
Or than you gave us, when, to compensate
Your slave-owners, you charged our common state
410 Twice the amount: no, but we rather give
Our curses, and will give them while we live,
To that pernicious blind conceit, and pride,
Wherewith the aids we asked, you misapplied.
And to INHERITOR returning now
415 'Tis time that we resume the when and how.

ECONOMIST next found him at his door,
His ready cash exhausted, with a score
Of starving neighbours clamouring for aid,
And to their gaze the ruddy gold displayed.
420 'Oh, lend', exclaimed INHERITOR, 'I'll pledge
All in the great ring-fence, from hedge to hedge!
Had I but means, I've still enough to do

To give them work, and make a profit too:
This moor reclaimed would well repay my pains;
425   Much needful drainage incomplete remains;
Were not my credits so much overdrawn,
I'd had spade labour even in my lawn:
Lend! take my land; 'twill well secure the loan —'

'Sure', said ECONOMIST, 'your wits are flown,
430   To think the State, whose wealth belongs to all ,
Would so compete with private capital!
No; if you'd borrow, be it understood,
The public funds are lent for public good;
And public good requires what they produce
435   Shall be no kind of goods in public use,
Food, clothing, fuel, or aught else that lies
In manufacture, or in merchandize;
Else the fair trader, dealing on the square,
Would take his skill and capital elsewhere.
440   But if you must have money to expend,
Aud ask to borrow on your land, I'll lend;
Provided always that you spend the loan
On strictly unproductive lime and stone,
Or (for your carts must carry weightier loads
445   Before you prosper) on new public roads'.

'Sir', said INHERITOR, 'these country parts
Have got already more new roads than carts:
Would that we now had some new roads the less,
And I no balance due for county cess!'

450   'That balance for the present let's postpone,
And first consider how we'll spend your loan.
Your newest roads still, more or less, incline
At angles to the horizontal line:
Now, armed with hunger and exchequer bills,
455   Set briskly to, and cut me down the hills;
So shall your wagons smoothly go and come
With draught and friction at a *minimum*'.

'Mum!' said INHERITOR, 'for all I've sent
To market lately, I'd be well content
460   With any road would bear a low-backed car:

117

They're good enough — let's leave them as they are!'
'Let's leave them as they are!' — O Irish phrase!
'They're good enough!' — O slothful Irish ways!
Sir, against laws dynamical you've sinn'd,
465   Provoking friction, draught, and broken wind,
In laying down these roads: know, sir, the rate
Of friction is a ratio duplicate;
And 'tis demonstrable the saving gained
In locomotive faculties unstrained,
470   Will in five years the full expense repay
Of one in fifty lowered; as thus we'll say
The acclivity is x —'

                'Oh, worthy, sir,
No need to prove it!' cried INHERITOR:
'My rash objections and my doubts forgive;
475   Lend me the money; let the people live!'

The money lent, forth on the highway side
They went, worked, famished, spoilt the road, and died.

But still the grave enough of wretches spared
To fill the workhouse to the furthest ward:
480   PAUPER has now no lack of company:
He frets in file, and shares his bed with three:
The rates run up with frightful increments;
INHERITOR in vain demands his rents;
Oft as his bailiffs darken TENANT's door,
485   COLLECTOR'S bailiffs have been there before;
He sells his plate, his pictures, carriages
(His cellar long ago was on the lees),
TENANT-IN-TAIL, in middle terms, recalls.
Shuts up schools, kennels, stables, servants' halls,
490   But in spite of all the efforts of despair,
MORTGAGEE'S interest goes in arrear.
The bill goes on the file; there's no debate;
Next term RECEIVER's over the estate.
'From Custom-house and Castle, call me up
495   My Irish statisticians: ere I sup,
The full particulars in shape we'll set,
For advertising, in the next Gazette.
This best located, best economized,

118

Best Flora'd, Fauna'd, and geologized,
500 Best highwayed, bye-wayed (were they but restored),
Drained, green-cropped, guano'd, fallowed, — in a word,
This best (consistent with the *maximum*
Of produce, and consumption's *minimum*)
Depopulated estate in Christendom'.
505 So shall we speedily the land behold
Once more exchangeable for British gold;
And in its Castle-Rack-Rent mansions see
A bran-new Cheesemonger propriet'ry,
Able in all things, save alone thy grace,
510 Gentility, to fill a gentry's place.

He leaves INHERITOR his house and grounds,
Worth by the year, perhaps, a hundred pounds;
But soon, unable to defray the rate,
As tax on tax, charges accumulate,
515 He seeks the town, new fortunes there to seek,
And takes a lodging at a pound a week;
But slow to run the sycophantic race,
Is pushed aside, and fails to reach a place.
Of mind refined, too proud to intermix,
520 With blood plebian, fair INHERITRIX,
Whose schools for needlework, in happier days,
Won royal premiums and viceregal praise,
Herself a noble sempstress, daily earns
Her own and father's bread from Todd and Burns.
525 Oft as INHERITOR her form surveys,
Slow-wasting o'er the Free-trade shirts and stays,
And owns the pangs distracted fathers feel,
I envy not your spirit's burthen, Peel!

TENANT-IN-TAIL from college halls returned,
530 Saw the land's ruin, and indignant burned:
A mad exploit the hapless boy conceives,
At one good blow to overthrow the thieves,
To raise his bleeding country, and restore
Her Monarch, Lords, and Commons as of yore,
535 Joins, with rash zeal, a rude rebellious band,
Failing, escapes, and flies his native land.

Poor native land! poor withered breast of earth,
That once exuberant nourished love and mirth,
Now tugged at empty dugs by woe and hate,
540   Hungry and bare, how changed is thy estate!
Yet dry Jerusalem grew in an hour
A nursing mother by God's timely power;
And Christ, whose death should yet redeem the dead,
Like thee, had oft not where to lay his head;
545   And persecuting Diocletian showed
Christ prostrate under Jove, on medals broad,
Even when the heavens, to give mankind the sign,
Were labouring with the cross of Constantine.
Thy day prefixed in God's eternal doom,
550   May long be longed for; but the day will come
When heaven shall also give its sign to thee,
Thy Diocletians fallen, thy people free.

The Potato Commission
EDWARD FORBES

Have you heard the report — the last Edition —
Sent out by the Great Potato Commission,
Who crossed the water to find some new
Materials for an Irish stew?
5   For since 'twas vain to put the pot on
When every blessed root was rotten,
Sir Robert thought to improve the mess, sirs,
By a brace and a half of roast Professors!
        (Sich a row there's been of late, O!
10   All about a rotten potato!)

King Dan had said, 'the horrid cracks on
The skin were the work of the hoof of the Saxon!'
Back'd by Prince John and Smith O'Brien,
His word Repealers all rely on;
15   For when the Liberator takes a fancy,
Through the thickest millstone he will and can see,
'The rot,' says he, 'those fellows came fishin' here

120

Was fostered by the Times' Commissioner!'
                (Who say in return that the great O'
20   Connell's a rotten-hearted potato!)

The report is both a short and sweet one,
And if not profound, is at least a neat one;
It states — 'All ways that we could guess
We tried of praties to make a mess —
25   We tried them boiled — we tried them roasted,
We tried them fried, we tried them toasted,
All sorts and sizes, till *heu vanum,*
Nothing came out but smashed *Solanum.*
                (And wasn't that a dreadful fate, O!
30   To come of taking a rotten potato!)

Some say that grub is the cause of the rot:
But we, my Lords, affirm it is not;
For, isn't it plain, and there's the rub,
For such potatoes won't do for grub.
35   We've taken the matter feculaceous,
And tried to make it farinaceous.
'Twon't do for dinner, tea, nor tiffin,
For if fed on starch, you'll certainly stiffen,
                (And that would be a precious state, O!
40   Resulting from a rotten potato!)

Some cock their glasses up to their eye,
And mushrooms in the cells descry,
But we, my Lords, have looked as well,
And think such notions all a sell;
45   Decaine in France, in Germany Kutzing,
Have sought the rot all manner of roots in,
And proved that those have looked with a loose eye
Who said 'twas caused by fungi and fuci,
                (Sure never since the days of Plato
50   Was there such a row about a rotten potato!)

Now these, my Lords, are our opinions —
It's a bad look out for the British dominions.
We know as much as we did before,
And we don't think we shall know any more!
55   As for *Solanum tuberosum,*

121

It's a very bad job for them as grow 'em.
We think the weather has made them scurfy,
And we've proved the same by consulting Murphy!
(And if our report don't please debaters,
60   They must get some other common — taters!)

A Dialogue
between an Irish Agent and a Tenant
[abridged]

JAMES MARTIN

AGENT:
Come forward, farmer, what is your intent,
About those *arrears* and your half-year's rent?
I'll wait no longer —for the day's at hand,
When you must pay them or give up your land.

TENANT:
5   On an old tenant do not be so hard,
But have for industry some more regard.
You know my ancestors, an honest race,
For many ages occupied that place;
Till crafty Fowler, that base pander, came
10   To be the keeper of his lordship's game.
My simple father, whose true Irish heart
Was never tenanted by fraud or art,
Was circumvented by that worst of fiends,
Who still for lucre sacrificed his friends.
15   His present lordship, but a minor then,
Was still the dupe of such designing men,
By importunities and falsehoods tired,
Gave him our holding when the lease expired;
All but the spot which I at present hold,
20   Then almost worthless, rushy, wet and cold;
Till I by industry, expense and toil,
Cleared, subsoiled, sewered, and made it fertile soil.
And when reclaimed must I the whole forego,
And leave my labour to my greatest foe?
25   And quit the place that gave my fathers birth,

122

To be a friendless wanderer on earth?
Or in a workhouse throughout life confined,
And leave the fruits of all my toil behind!
Ah, no! much sooner would I suffer death,
30 Than leave the place where first I drew my breath.

AGENT:
How can I bear such insolence to get,
From such a tenant, and so much in debt?
Who tells an agent, in a fearless tone,
He'll keep possession, as if 'twere his own!
35 But know, my lord's the owner of the soil,
And cares but little for your sweat and toil —
The land's his own; and as a landlord may,
When leases drop, retain or put away —
And your's expired, and have no further claim,
40 But by resistance play the losing game.
His lordship, always lenient and humane,
Who gives no tenant reason to complain,
The present rent, providing you will pay,
Forgives the arrears but to go away —
45 And since that sum he's willing to remit,
So pay, be thankful, and in quiet quit.

TENANT:
I can't perceive what grateful thanks I owe
For paying rent, and then compelled to go!
And leave the land, which I reclaimed so well,
50 As all my neighbours and yourself can tell.
I made its value, nearly cent per cent,
And notwithstanding always paid my rent,
Till the potatoes through the nation failed,
And fleecing poor-rates and each tax assailed.
55 I starved my family, in hopes to clear
My little holding from all debts this year,
And God, who't seems my honest purpose knew,
Sent me the rent and all th'arrears too.
And while his lordship squandered cash away,
60 I toiled and starved, his gambling debts to pay.
The cash of Erin is thus yearly drained,
And wasted, where such riot is maintained —
Which leaves our husbandmen and swains in woe,

123

Fleeced, starved, ejected, without place to go —
65   Of native harpies the defenceless prey,
Who hurl us deeper in distress each day!

AGENT:
When of improvements tenantry complain,
Who subsoil, build, raise rocks, manure or drain,
And shelt'ring fences, such as you have made,
70   Are by their tillage for their labours paid;
And when their crops reward them in their day,
For such improvements why should landlords pay?
For of such profits landlords have the least —

TENANT:
Are not their rentals by such works encreased!
75   For many landlords, who have wisely planned,
Have rentals doubled by reclaiming land.
But hapless I, who have my time misspent,
When my reward is but a higher rent —
A higher rent, with money in advance,
80   Leaves the reclaimer but a slender chance;
For unrewarded for what he improved,
Is, by some pretext, speedily removed,
And sent to work on ruin's crowded ways,
To beg and starve, with thousands now-a-days!
85   And worse, my labours tamely to resign
To him, who basely ruined me and mine!
A cringing synchophant, vile, upstart knave,
Who God and *all* for worldly mammon gave.
A heartless land-jobber, to pity steeled,
90   Who grinds the poor, by adding 'field to field.'
Such men as he at present have their times,
But shall hereafter suffer for such crimes —
For God declared, that he cannot endure
These ruthless monsters that oppress the poor.

AGENT:
95   Desist from threats, for know the law is strict,
For their protection, who such men evict —
So mind, friend farmer, if you longer rail,
I'll do my duty, and hold you to bail!
The land's his lordship's — he's the owner still,
100   And by that *law* may let to whom he will.

TENANT:

The land's Jehovah's — but as tenures stand,
I grudge no landlord to possess his land,
Nor do I ask from whom they tenures draw,
For time converts all customs into law,
105 From God, from monarchs, or from statutes, they
Must hold th' estates, for which their tenantry pay.
And as such tenures landlords must immure —
Should not some tenure tenantry secure,
From all those evictions, at a landlord's will?

AGENT:

110 You have your answer — so no longer stay —
Give up possession — and at once away!
Go to your Clergy, as O'Connell's dead,
And they'll provide you in both land and bread.

TENANT:

Thro' the hypocrisy of many years,
115 The cloven member in the end appears!
The veil's removed, and visibly are seen
Much Party rancour and Sectarian spleen.
Aye, to the clergy! what can clergy do,
When now impoverished by folk like you?
120 For those from whom they could support procure,
Are, by evictions, sent from door to door!
Or starved, transported, or in work-house pent,
And if that system longer ye pursue,
Their flocks in short will number but a few!
125 For that curst system, in *some quarter* planned,
Already swept two millions from our land!
Had we no argument but that alone,
To prove we want a Senate of our own,
'Twould plainly show a native parliament
130 Would half the evils of our land prevent.
It would in season have provided bread,
As soon as famine reared her frightful head.
Ere killing hunger, with destruction's broom,
Had swept such numbers to a timeless tomb,
135 Or ere dread pestilence, with pois'nous breath,
Thro' town and hamlet, scattered woes and death,
Our country filled with terror and dismay,

And swept our people in whole crowds away!
Or if to the schoolhouse we direct our eyes,
140 And view the schemes some agents there devise;
Where well-paid bigots will the children press,
To hate the doctrine their sires profess!
In vain the pastors or the parent choose;
Their books, at school, the children dare not use!

AGENT:
145 Why not compelled to study well the whole,
Of what enlightened the benighted soul?
And in our schools to have the word of Truth,
Early instilled into the mind of youth —
For if *allowed* that sacred book to read,
150 Our land would shortly be from murders freed,
And pure religion speedily replace
The odious vices that our Isle disgrace.

TENANT:
Cease your whine and Bible-gasconade,
The Christian wants the *substance*, not the *shade*.
155 Take first the beam from your long hood-winked eye,
And then the mote in others' you'll descry.
Give me the man, who void of worldly gain
Will seek the truth, and in that truth remain,
And make religion his reward and stay,
160 Nor suffer wealth t'allure him from her way,
And shape his conduct on the Gospel plan —
And give the needy all the help he can;
From party, bigotry, and rancour freed —
I call him Christian in both word and deed.
165 Away with knaves and Pharisaic rant,
Fanatics, hypocrites with whining cant,
Who Bibles praise, and gospel maxims teach,
But are the last to practice what they preach.
By plunder, fraud, and peculation stained,
170 Groping for wealth, no matter how obtained.
For worldly honours, ever first to press,
But last, to make the poor man's burden less.
Their well-barred gates against the needy shut,
And hurl the peasant from his peaceful hut.
175 Their needy brother, of all else bereave,

126

But workhouse, want, and an untimely grave.
To worldly pleasures by their riches tied —
The pampered slaves of luxury and pride,
And, like all bigots, to rash judgement prone,
180   Exclude from bliss all parties but their own.
And like the Pharisee, with looks demure,
Think *faith* not *works* salvation can secure!
'Tis by his acts that the true Christian's known —
'By *works* we're saved, and not by *faith alone!*'
185   You talk of murders, but remove the cause,
By tenures long, and equitable laws.
Evictions quit, and let the tenant stand,
Who pays the rent, taxes, and improves the land.
Be just, and compensate — respect his rights —

AGENT:
190   The land each labour and expense requites.

TENANT:
Give us some law, the tenant to protect,
That landlords cannot, at their will, eject —
Without protection, like wild beasts of prey,
To starve, or plunder, or th'oppressor slay;
195   Or roam in misery, with babes and wives,
Till hardship, cold and hunger end their lives.
We ask but justice, and to live in peace,
And then shall all agrarian murders cease.
Remuneration for improvements give,
200   And in security let tenants live.

From:

The Mirror of Satire: A Rhapsody
JAMES MARTIN

May that Pow'r Supreme
Who was, Who is, and ever be the same!
Who to His servants, thro' the spacious earth,
Shewed special favour since creation's birth;
And gave them settlements, with will benign,
In fertile regions, blest with milk and wine,
Till their rebellions would His rage provoke,
Their crimes to punish, by a foreign yoke,
Or by the famine, pestilence or sword,
Till by repentance, to His grace restored,
Inspire our hearts, to join in one acclaim,
T'adore, praise, thank, that by sin no more
We bring fresh scourges on our native shore.
Our recent blight, from which a famine grew,
Our flagrant vices on our nation drew.
Our fertile Island, famous for its soil,
Deep, rich, and grateful to the tiller's toil,
Near half its crop by blight and mildew failed,
Which on our people misery entailed,
But as the Lord seems kindly to relent,
By the fine season which His goodness sent,
And that the prospects of our crop appear,
To promise plenty, and a happy year —
Why should not gratitude our people urge,
To cease from crime, t'avert another scourge?
And quit their drunkenness, that practice base,
Which would the worst of savages disgrace.
Desist from swearing, theft and quarrels vile,
Which bring contempt and odium on our Isle.
Abandon Party, and vile Party oaths,
Which a just God with indignation loathes —
For Christian charity can never dwell,
Where men are bound by Party's factious spell.
Avoid to figure in religious strife,
Which is, in Erin, recently so rife,
And inimical to Gospel's plan,
By sowing discord between man and man.

PART IV
'One Whom Some Have Called A Seer'

JAMES CLARENCE MANGAN

A Vision of Connaught
in the Nineteenth Century

ANONYMOUS

'Et moi, j'ai ête aussi aux enfers.'
'And I, I too, have been in the West of Ireland.'

— Orpheus (free translation)

I walked aghast
    Where the land was filled
With famine and death from morn to night;
    The Spring had passed
5   Over fields untilled,
And broken-up highways aleft and right.
    Even in the clime
        Where the wild wolf strays,
There is no such land as that land of woes;
10   For it was the time,
        We were in the days
Of Randolph Routh, of the wine-red nose.

    Being very dry,
        To mine host I ran
15   And called for a pint of port sublime;
    Him queried I,
        As I emptied the can,
What clime is this, and what shocking time,
    Said he — 'The clime
20   Is a clime to curse,
'Tis Erin's clime, and you may suppose,
    That it is the time
        (It can't be worse)
Of Randolph Routh, of the wine-red nose!'

25   Then I saw drones
        And all the *elite*
And a kitchen rose near me as by a spell;
    But neither of bones
        Nor of juicy meat
30   Could I ever the faintest perfume smell.
    A greasy slime
        The water appears

As Soyer, the great enchanter, knows;
        For it is the time —
35   These be the years
Of Randolph Routh, of the wine-red nose.

        I sought 'the Hall',
                And behold! the *change*
That weekly came in was getting low;
40   Clerks, chairman, all,
                Look'd aghast and strange
At the stubborn humbug 'wot *wouldn't go*';
        For in some dread crime
                In that Hell of *rays*
45 The red-flashing steel no longer glows.
                Ah! 'Twas then the time
                We were in the days
Of Randolph Routh, of the wine-red nose.

        For the wild dogs' feast
50   Where the corpses lie
O'er heaped up graves; and an alien sun
        Glares in the cast,
                And its beams fly
O'er the million homes of THE SKELETON!
55   It was reading the *Freeman* —
                An's page sublime,
That opiate speeches made me doze;
        And I dreamed this dream
                Of the terrible time
60 Of Randolph Routh, of the wine-red nose.

The Famine

JAMES CLARENCE MANGAN

It was a time when thoughts and violets bloomed —
        When skies were bright, and air was bland and warm,
And Pleasure every fleeting hour assumed
        A new and strange Camelion hue and form,

131

5   When, suddenly, that horrid cloud, once beheld
From Carmel by the Tishbite seer of Eld —
    Appeared, and foresayed coming storm.

All minds were called away. The slumberers who
    Had slept through years of Idleness awoke —
10   All felt a consciousness of somewhat new,
    The lightning prelude to the thunder stroke.
God struck on every heart, and men grew pale —
Their bliss was metamorphosed into bale.
    There was no Power they dared evoke!

15   Even as the dread Simoom of Araby
    Sweeps o'er the desert through the pathless air,
So came, 'mid Ireland's joy and revelry,
    That cloud of gloom above her visions fair.
The thoughtless wondered, and the thoughtful wept.
20   And those who through long years had dreamt and slept
    Arose — too many to Despair!

Despair? Yes! For a blight fell on the land —
    The soil, heaven-blasted, yielded food no more —
The Irish serf became a Being banned —
25   Life-exiled as none ever was before.
The old man died beside his hovel's hearth,
The young man stretched himself along the earth,
    And perished, stricken to the core!

O God! Great God! Thou knowest, seest, Thou!
30   All-blessed be Thy name! This work is Thine —
To Thy decrees, Thy law, Thy will, we bow —
    We are but worms, and Thou art the DIVINE!
But Thou wilt yet in Thine own day redeem
Thy Faithful; and this land's bright sun shall beam
35   To Earth a Pharos and a Sign!

Ye True, ye Noble, who unblenching stand
    Amid the storms and ills of this dark Day,
Still hold your ground! Yourselves, your Fatherland,
    Have in the Powers above a surest stay!
40   Though Famine, Pest, Want, Sickness of the Heart,
Be now your lot — all these shall soon depart
    And Heaven be yet at your command!

The Funerals

JAMES CLARENCE MANGAN

It was a vision of the night,
  Ten years ago —
A vision of dim FUNERALS that passed
  In troubled sleep before my sight,
5 With dirges and deep wails of woe,
  That never died upon the blast!

  Swiftly, — not as with march that marks
    The earthly hearse,
Each FUNERAL swept onward to its goal —
10   But oh! no horror overdarks
  The stanzas of my gloomsome verse
    Like that which then weighed down my soul!

    It was as though my Life were gone
      With what I saw!
15 Here were the FUNERALS of my thoughts as well!
    The Dead and I at last were One!
  An ecstasy of chilling awe
    Mastered my spirit as a spell!

    On, on, still on and on they swept,
20   Silently, save
When the long FUNERAL chant rose up to Heaven,
    Or some wild mourner shrieked and wept —
  Earth had become one groanful grave —
    The isles and lords were left bereaven.

25   And on each hearse there sat enthroned
      A skeleton!
The FUNERALS showed him by a lurid gleam,
    And round each stood, as 'twere, enzoned
  Others, the like, so many as one
30   They might have peopled worlds of Dream!

    Towards the West at first they marched,
      Then towards the South —
Those endless FUNERALS, till the sky o'erhead,
    As one vast pall, seemed over-arched

35 With blackness, and methought the mouth
　　　Of Hades had cast up its Dead!

　　　And one night passed, and there was day —
　　　　　So dreamt I there:
　　　The FUNERALS, then, had been but phantoms all —
40 　　　　How cheats Imagination's play!
　　　Given her illusions, thou, no care,
　　　　　O Man! but hearken Reason's call!

　　　But night fell dark on Earth once more,
　　　　　And many a night,
45 And still the FUNERALS knew nor pause nor change;
　　　　　And ever nightly, as before,
　　　I again felt dead to mark a sight
　　　　　So terrible, so dread, so strange!

　　　What was this mystery? Years would seem
50 　　　　To have rolled away.
　　　Before the FUNERALS halted on their path —
　　　　　Were they but mockeries of a dream?
　　　Or did the vision darkly say,
　　　　　That here were signs of looming wrath?

55 　　　I know not! but within the soul
　　　　　I know there lives
　　　A deep, a marvellous, a prophetic power,
　　　　　Far beyond even its own control —
　　　And why? Perchance, because it gives
60 　　　　Dread witness of a JUDGEMENT HOUR!

Lamentation of Jeremias over Jerusalem

(A paraphrase from Holy Scripture)

JAMES CLARENCE MANGAN

'And it came to pass, after Israel was carried into captivity, and
Jerusalem was desolate, that Jeremias the prophet sat weeping, and
mourned with this lamentation over Jerusalem, and with a sorrowful
mind, sighing and moaning he said': —

How doth she sit alone,
The city late so thronged; how doth she sit in woe,
        Begirt with solitude and graves!
Oh! how is she that from her Temple-throne
5   Ruled o'er the Gentiles, now become
        A widow in her dreary home!
How have her Princes fallen low,
        And dwindled into slaves!

She weepeth all night long,
10 Forsaken and forgot: her face is dusk with tears;
        Her heart is rent with many throes,
Not one of all the once-admiring throng
        That sued and wooed her night amd morn
        But looketh down on her with scorn
15 Her fondest friends of other years
        Have now become her foes!

Her dwelling-place is dark:
Her palaces lie waste: she feareth even to pass
        The bass-courts desolate and bare.
20 She hath become a byword and a mark
        Among the nations: lorn and lone,
        She seeketh rest and findeth none.
Her persecuting foes, alas!
        Have caught her in their snare!

25   Gloom shroudeth Sion's halls
And trodden in the dust lie silver lamp and bowl,
        Her golden gates are turned to clay,
Her priests are now the godless Gentiles' thralls.
        Her youths walk wan and sorrow-worn;
30   Her silent virgins droop and mourn,
In hopeless bitterness of soul
        She sigheth all the day!

Behold the sad Bereaven!
Her enemies have grown to be her pitiless lords,
35   And mock her in her sore disgrace!
Her sins have risen in black array to Heaven;
        Therefore the Lord Jehovah hath
        Rained on her head His chastening wrath;
Therefore her sons go bound with cords
40   Before the oppressor's face!

        How hath her glory fled!
The beauty is out-blotted as a fallen star
        Of her that whilom looked so fair!
Her stricken Princes cower for shame and dread!
45   Like wandering sheep, that seek in vain
        Their pasture ground o'er hill and plain,
Stray abroad, they flee afar,
        Guideless, and in despair!

        * * * * * * * * *

        Oh! lost Jerusalem
50 Where now be her mad hours of wantonness and wine?
        Her leprousness is on her hands,
So lately prankt with pearl and golden gem!
        A captive Queen she sits, cast down
        From Heaven to Earth, without her crown
55 O Lord, my God, what grief is mine
        To see her thus in bands!

        She lieth overthrown,
Smitten of Thee, O Lord! and shrinking in her fear
        Before the alien Gentile powers,
60 Since Thou hast cast away Thy Church, Thine own!
        They violate her sanctuary,
        Of whom command was given by Thee,
That they should ne'er adventure near
        Her Temple and its towers!

65   Woe for the fallen Queen!
Her people groan and die, despairful of relief.
        They famish and they cry for bread!
No more her nobles walk in silken sheen!

Their gauds and rings, their precious things,
70   Are pawned for food! O God! it wrings
My soul to see it! Through my grief
    I lie as one half dead!

    Oh, ye who travel by!
All ye who pass this way, stop short a while, and see
75   If Earth have sorrow like to mine!
Judea's dark iniquities belie
        The faith she vaunteth in her God;
        And therefore are her people trod
In dust this day, and men tread *me*
80   As treaders tread the wine.

    O, most mysterious Lord!
From Thine high place in Heaven Thou sendest fire and flame
    Into my dry and withered bones!
85   Thou searchest me as with an angry sword!
        Thou spreadest snares aneath my feet!
        In vain I pray, in vain entreat,
Thou turnest me away with shame,
        And heedest not my groans!

    Thus waileth she aloud,
90   The God-forsaken one, in this her day of dole: —
        'My spirit faileth me; mine eyes
Are filmed o'er with mist; my neck is bowed
        Beneath a yoke the livelong day,
        And there doth lie a weight alway,
95   An iron hand, on my spent soul
        That will not let it rise!

        * * * * * * * * * *

    'The Lord, the Lord is just!
His wrath is kindled fierce against me for my ways.
        I have provoked the Lord, my God,
100   Therefore I make my darkling bed in dust.
        Pity me, ye who see me, all!
        Pity my sons, who pine in thrall!
Their spirit wastes, their strength decays,
        Under the Gentile's rod.

137

105   'I sought my friends to tell
The story of my woes; alas! they would not hear!
      Disease drank up my princes' blood,
For Famine's hand lay black on them as well.
      My priests, too, fainted on their feet;
110   They feebly crawled from street to street,
Seeking all day, afar and near,
      A morsel of coarse food!

      'Behold, O Lord! — behold!
Behold my wretchedness! For I am overcome
115   By suffering — almost by despair
My heart is torn with agonies untold!
      The land expires beneath Thy frown,
      Abroad the red sword striketh down
Its tens of thousands; and at home
120   Death reigneth everywhere!

      'My groanings are not hid.
All they who hated me regard me with disdain!
      They see the darkness of my face,
And mock it, for they know Thou hast forbid
125   My nearest friends to help me now,
      But Thou wilt yet avenge me, Thou
They shall lie low where I have lain
      Who scoff at my disgrace!

      'Then shall their evil fall
130 On their own heads — for still 'tis evil in Thy sight,
      And they shall mourn as now I mourn;
And Thou, Lord, shalt make vintage of them all,
      And tread them down even as they see
      Thou, for my sins, hast trodden me,
135 They who to-day deride and slight
      The afflictions I have borne!'

The Peal of Another Trumpet

JAMES CLARENCE MANGAN

'Irlande, Irlande, rejouis toi! Pour toi l'heure de vengeance est sonne.
Ton tribun prepare ta deliverance.' — From the 'Derniers Mots' of
Mdlle. Lenormand, the celebrated French Pythoness.

Youths of Ireland, patriots, friends!
    Know ye what shall be your course
When the storm that now impends
    Shall come down in all its force?
5 Glance around you! You behold
    How the horizon of the Time
Hourly wears a duskier hue,
    From all else await we bold
Bearing, and Resolve sublime —
10   Youths of Ireland, what from you?

Will you bide irresolute?
    Will you stand with folded arms,
Purposeless, disheartened, mute,
    As men hopeless of escape,
15 Till the wildest, worst alarms
    Of your souls take giant shape?
Are you dastards? Are you dolts?
    Irishmen! shall you be seen
    With white lips and faltering mien,
20   When all on earth, when heaven above,
Torn by thousand thunderbolts,
    Rocks and reels which way you move?

Oh, no! no! forfend it, Heaven!
    Such debasement cannot be!
25   Pillaged of your liberty,
You are not as yet bereaven
Of that heritage of bravery
    Which descends to you through ages,
And ennobles all — save slavery.
30 Yours, thank God, are manhood still,
    And the inborn strength of soul,
    Which nought outward can control,
And the headlong chariot — Will,

Ever-bounding, never-bending,
35   Which alike with Sword or Song,
As befits the season, wages
  Unrelenting war with Wrong —
Unrelenting and unending.

Gentler gifts are yours, no less,
40   Tolerance of the faults of others,
  Love of mankind as your brothers,
Generous Pity, Tenderness,
Soul-felt sympathy with grief:
  The warm heart, the winged hand,
45 Whereso suffering craves relief.
Through all regions hath your fame
  For such virtues long gone forth.
  The swart slave of Kaffirland,
  The frozen denizen of the North,
50 The dusk Indian Mingo chief
  In his lone savannahs green,
  The wild, wandering Beddaween
Mid his wastes of sand and flame;
All have heard how, unsubdued
55   By long centuries of sorrow,
   You still cherish in your bosoms
  The deep Love no wrongs can slay,
  And the Hopes which, crushed to-day,
Rear their crests afresh, renewed,
60   In immortal youth, tomorrow,
   Like the Spring's rejoicing blossoms.

  And 'tis well you thus can blend
Softest moods of mind with sternest —
  Well you thus can temper earnest
65 Might with more than Feminine meekness,
Thus can soar and thus descend;
  For even now the wail of Want,
The despairing cry of Weakness,
  Rings throughout a stricken land,
70 And blood-blackening Plague and gaunt
  Famine roam it hand-in-hand!
To you, now, the millions turn
With glazed eyes and lips that burn —

To you lies their last appeal,
75   To your hearts — your feelings — reason!
  Oh, stretch forth your hands in season!
Soothe and solace — help and heal!
Rich in blessings, bright with beauty,
  Shine their names throughout all aeons,
80   Theirs who nobly consecrate
To self-sacrificing Duty
  Their best years — the new St. Leons,
  Who thus conquer Time and Fate!

But for more, far more, than this,
85   Youths of Ireland, stand prepared!
Revolution's red abyss
  Burns beneath us, all but bared —
And on high the fire-charged Cloud
  Blackens in the firmament,
90 And afar we list the loud
  Sea-voice of the unknown Event.
  Youth of Ireland, stand prepared!
For all woes the Meek have dree'd,
  For all risks the Brave have dared,
95 As for suffering, so for Deed,
  Stand prepared!
For the Pestilence that striketh
Where it listeth, whom it liketh,
For the Blight whose deadly might
100 Desolateth day and night —
For a Sword that never spared
  Stand prepared!
Though that gory Sword be bared
  Be not scared!
105   Do not blench and dare not falter!
  For the axe and for the halter
  Stand prepared!
  And give GOD the glory
  If, whene'er the WREATH OF STORY
110 Swathe your names, the men whose hands
  Brightly twine it,
  May enshrine it
In one temple with your lands!

Pompeii

JAMES CLARENCE MANGAN

The heralds of thy ruin and despair
    Thickened and quickened as thy time drew nigh.
What prodigies of sound convulsed the air!
    How many a death-flag was unfurled on high!
5   The sullen sun went down — a glove of blood,
    Rayless, and colouring every heart with gloom,
Till even the dullest felt and understood
    The coming of an overwhelming doom —
The presage of a destiny and fall,
10   A shock, a thundershock, for thee, for them — for all.

The sullen sun went down — a globe of blood,
    Rayless, and colouring every soul with gloom;
And men's imagination, prone to brood
    Over the worst, and summon from the womb
15 Of unborn Time, the Evil and the Dark,
    Launched forth in fear upon the shoreless ocean,
Whose whirlpool billows but engulf the bark —
    Conjectured Dread, and each fresh-felt emotion,
Like spectral figures on a magic mirror,
20 Seemed wilder than the last, and stronglier strung with terror.

We shrink within ourselves when Night and Storm
    Are darkly mustering; for, to every soul
Heaven here foreshadows character and form
    Of Nature's death-hour. Doth the thunder roll,
25 The wild wave boil, the lightning stream or strike,
    Flood, fire, and earthquake devastate, in vain?
Or is there not a voice which peals alike
    To all from these, conjuring up that train
Of scenes and images that shall be born
30 In living, naked might upon the Judgement morn?

If thus we cower to tempest and to night,
    How feltest thou when first the red bolt broke,
That seventeen suffocating centuries might
    Enshroud thine ashes in Time's midnight cloak?
35 Where wert thou in that moment? Was thy power
    All a funeral phantom? Thy renown

An echo? Thine the triumph of an hour?
      Enough! — I rave — when empires, worlds, go down
Time's wave to dissolution — when they bow
40   To Fate, let none ask *where*, but simply — *what* wert thou?

The desolated cities which of yore
      Perishing by flooding fire and sulphury rain,
Where sleeps the Dead Sea's immemorial shore,
      Lie, blasted wrecks, below the mortar plain.
45   They fell — thou fell — but, renounced of Earth,
      Blotted from being to eternal years,
Their image chills the lifeblood — *thine* gives birth,
      Even while we shudder, to some human tears.
Hadst thou less guilt? Who knows? The book of Time
50   Bears on each leaf alike the broad red stamp of crime.

Siberia

JAMES CLARENCE MANGAN

In Siberia's wastes
      The Ice-wind's breath
Woundeth like the toothed steel;
      Lost Siberia doth reveal
5   Only blight and death.

Blight and death alone.
      No Summer shines.
Night is interblent with Day.
In Siberia's wastes alway
10   The blood blackens, the heart pines.

In Siberia's wastes
      No tears are shed,
For they freeze within the brain.
Nought is felt but dullest pain,
15   Pain acute, yet dead;

Pain as in a dream,
      When years go by

143

Funeral-paced, yet fugitive,
When man lives, and doth not live,
    Doth not live — nor die.

In Siberia's wastes
    Are sands and rocks.
Nothing blooms of green or soft,
    But the snow-peaks rise aloft
And the gaunt ice-blocks.

And the exile there
    Is one with those;
They are part, and he is part,
For the sands are in his heart,
    And the killing snows.

Therefore in those wastes
    None curse the Czar.
Each man's tongue is cloven by
The North Blast, that heweth nigh
    With sharp scymitar.

And such doom each drees,
    Till, hunger-gnawn,
And cold-slain, he at length sinks there,
Yet scarce more a corpse than ere
    His last breath was drawn.

Song of the Albanian (1826)

JAMES CLARENCE MANGAN

Why, from the dawn till Day declines,
    Why hear we cries aloft and under
    Upon Albania's crested hills
And through her long ravines?
    Flood, war, destroy not now: — no thunder,
    No lightning, strikes and kills.

No! Fire and Flood appal not now!
    The dominant Moslem need not war on

This downtrod land of ours again.
10 Storm sleeps on Góvria's brow
But Charon comes — the ghastly Charon,
He comes with all his train!

Gaunt Famine rideth in the van,
And Pestilence, with myriad arrows,
15 Followeth in fiery guise: they spare
Nor Woman, Child, nor Man!
The stricken Dead lie without barrows
By roadsides, black and bare!

Down on the burnt up cottage roofs
20 The sick sun all the long day flashes.
In vain the old men seek the wood.
'Neath Charon's hot horse-hoofs
At every step a fresh corpse plashes
Into a pool of blood!

25 Yet there is food — but, take and eat,
And still thou diest: — the sharp sword slaughters
Thee, daring robber! So, by forest
And field, — or path, in street,
Amid the Blessed Living Waters,
30 Souls perish without count!

Oh God! it is a fearful sign
This fierce, mad wasting Hunger!
Were there a land that could at most
But sink and pine,
35 Infant-like when such Agony wrung her,
That land indeed were lost!

Were there a land whose people could
Lie down beneath Heaven's blue pavilions
And gasp, and perish, famished slaves!
40 While the ripe golden food
That might and should have fed their millions
Rotted above their graves —

That land were doomed! . . . But, glorious Greece,
Not such art thou! Even now thou risest

145

45   Reborn from that drugged Sleep of Death
And soul-embruting Peace
      Which all-too-long thy Bravest, Wisest,
        And Best lay sunk beneath!

Upon thy hills methinks I see
50   Flashing like light and fire, the *khandjers*
         Worn by our godlike sires of old! —
I hear that shout of jubilee
      Which tells that neither Death nor Dangers
        Avail to daunt the Bold!

55 Come, Charon, then, and crown thy work!
      The few heroic souls thou leavest
        Surviving still are strong to wrest
Their birthright from the Turk!
      Slay on! Perchance the task thou achievest
60   Is one Heaven's powers have blessed.

A Vision: A.D. 1848

JAMES CLARENCE MANGAN

In the vastness of Night,
      In the Valley of Dreams,
      When our thoughts, like a stream
      That in vain seeks the light,
5 Yet rolls onward in might,
      Sweep in legions along
      The lone paths of the soul,
      Dark, chainless and strong,
A chariot-like throng,
10   That mocks our control! —
In that spectralest hour,
      In that Valley of Gloom,
        Fell a Voice on mine ear,
Like a wail from the tomb,
15   Or that dread cry which Fear

Gives our Angels of Doom
But of world-waking power.
What it spake ye shall hear.

The Anointing: 1839-1842

Thus the Oracle saith:
20   'The land long had lain bound
        As in fetters of Death.
In the soul-killing cup
                Her despairing sons drowned
Half the sense of their woe,
25   Half the life of their shame,
Till the Great God rose up,
And sent a Man forth,
        Who enkindled a flame
Of celestial glow
30   East and west, south and north.
At the Man's high command,
There woke life through the land,
        As God had forespoken,
And the red bowl was broken,
35   And the chain fell asunder
Which — worst bondage of all! —
Had held Mind in its thrall
        Through long ages. This wonder,
Of Heaven's own appointing,
40   Was IRELAND'S ANOINTING.

The Muster: 1842-1845

Thus the Oracle saith:
        'The great God once again
Cast a glance down beneath,
And, behold! there uprose
45   A Man among men,
With a soul stern and warm,
        And a voice like the storm
When through midnight it blows.

147

And the people by millions
    At the Man's call assembled,
Under Heaven's blue pavilions,
    And they heard from him words
That pierced them like swords,
For the Man spake with might
    Of Strength, Freedom, and Right,
And the powers in high places
    Looked on; and some trembled,
And more hid their faces.
This marvel of story —
    This sunburst of glory —
Unmatched for its lustre, —
Was Ireland's GRAND MUSTER'.

The Famine: 1845-1848

Thus the Oracle saith:
    'The ANOINTED must fall —
The Weak Ones must yield
Up in silence their breath
    Ere the Last Scene of all.
For that scene must behold
But stern spirits and bold,
    When the Lord takes the field.
Therefore Famine first came
And then Pestilence came,
    And careered through the Land
Like twin giants of Flame —
And men's hearts were updried,
    And a seventh of that Band,
Who were still to be tried,
Fell in death, mute, unmanned,
And with names writ in sand.
There fell One for each Seven — .
    Pray thou peace for their souls
In the homesteads of Heaven!
    Hark! *another* Bell knolls
        Than for *their* vanished souls.
It sounds from afar

With an omenful peal —
With a clangor most like
That ye hear when men strike
With sharp steel upon steel.
90   'Tis the Tocsin of War!'

The End: 1848-1850

So THE ORACLE SPAKE,
        And was silent once more.
        Then medreamt I turned round,
        For I felt the earth quake,
95   And I saw in the West
                A cloud lurid with gore,
        Looming shoreward and seaward,
        And nearing to me-ward;
        And I heard, as I guessed.
100   The far-echoing sound
Of a trumpet, with tones,
        And lightnings and thunders,
As ye read of in John's
        Revelation of Wonders.
105 What meant they? I trow not,
        What next might befall?
        And how ended ALL?
This, too, friends, I know not —
For here were my cords
110   Of Sleep suddenly broken
                The bell booming Three;
But there seemed in mine ears,
                As I started up, woken,
A noise like fierce cheers,
115 Blent with clashings of swords,
And the roar of the sea!

A Voice of Encouragement —
A New Year's Lay

JAMES CLARENCE MANGAN

Youths! Compatriots! Friends! Men for the time that is nearing!
Spirits appointed by Heaven to front the storm and the trouble!
You, who in seasons of peril, unfaltering still and unfearing,
Calmly have held on your course of the Just and the Noble!
5   You, young men, would a man unworthy to rank in your number,
Yet with a heart that bleeds for his country's wrongs and
    affliction,
Fain raise a voice to, in song, albeit his music and diction
Rather be fitted, alas! to lull to, than startle from, slumber.

Friends! the gloom in our land, in our once bright land grows
    deeper.
10   Suffering, even to death, in its horriblest forms, aboundeth;
Thro' our black harvestless fields, the peasants' faint wail
    resoundeth.
Hark to it, even now! . . . The nightmare oppressed sleeper
Gasping and struggling for life, beneath his hideous bestrider,
Sëeth not, drëeth not, sight or terror more fearful or ghastly
15   Than that poor paralysed slave! Want, Houselessness, Famine,
    and lastly
Death in a thousand-corpsed grave, that momently waxeth wider.

Worse! The great heart of the country is chilled and throbbeth
    but faintly!
Apathy palsieth *here* — and *there*, a panic misgiving:
Even the Trustful and Firm, even the Sage and the Saintly,
20   Seem to believe that the Dead but foreshow the doom of the
    Living.
Men of the faithfullest souls all but broken-hearted
O'er the dishonoured tombs of the glorious dreams that have
    perished —
Dreams that almost outshone Realities while they were
    cherished —
All, they exclaim, is gone! The Vision and Hope have departed!

25   Worst and saddest! As under Milton's lowermost Tophet
Yawned another yet lower, so for the mourning Million

Still is there deeper woe! Patriot, Orator, Prophet,
Some who a few years agone stood proudly in the Pavilion
Of their land's rights and liberties, gazing abroad thro' its
    casement
30   On the fair Future they fondly deemed at hand for their nation,
Now not alone succumb to the change and the Degradation,
But have ceased even to feel them! God! *this* indeed is
    abasement!

Is the last hope then gone? Must we lie down despairing?
No! there is always hope for all who will dare and suffer;
35   Hope for all who surmount the Hill of Exertion, uncaring
Whether their path be brighter or darker, smoother or rougher;
No! there is always hope for those who, relying with earnest
Souls on God and themselves, take for their motto, 'Labour.'
See the rainbow's glory where Heaven looms darkest and
    sternest;
40   Such in the storm wind hear but the music of pipe and tabor.

Follow your destiny up! Work! Write! Preach to arouse and
Warn, and watch, and encourage! Dangers, no doubt, surround
    you —
But for Ten threatening you now, you will soon be appalled by
    a Thousand
If you forsake the course to which Virtue and Honour have
    bound you!
45   Oh, persevere! persevere! Falter not! — faint not! — shrink not!
Hate and Hostility serve but as spurs to the will of the Zealous;
Tho' your foes flourish awhile, and you *seem* to decline, be not
    jealous,
'Help from the Son of Man cometh in such an hour as you think
    not!'

Slavery debases the soul; yea! reverses its primal nature;
50   Long were our fathers bowed to the earth with fetters of iron —
And, alas! we inherit the failings and ills that environ
Slaves like a dungeon wall and dwarf their original stature.
Look on your countrymen's failings with less of anger than pity;
Even with the faults of the evil deal in a manner half tender;
55   And like an army encamped before a beleaguered city,
Earlier or later you must compel your foes to surrender!

Lo a New Year! a year, into whose bosom Time gathers
All the past lessons of ages — a mournful but truth-teaching
    muster;
All the rich thoughts and deeds, and the marvellous lore of our
    fathers;
60   All the sun-light experience that makes men wiser and juster.
Hail it with steadfast resolve — thankfully, if it befriend you;
Guardedly, lest it betray without either Despair or Elation,
Panoplied inly against the sharpest ills it may send you,
With a high hope still for yourselves and the Rise of your
    Nation.

65   Omen full, archèd with gloom, and laden with many a presage,
Many a portent of woe, looms the Impending Era
Not as of old, by comet — sword, Gorgon, or ghastly Chimera,
Scarcely by Lightning and Thunder, Heaven today sends its
    message,
Into the secret heart — down thro' the caves of the spirit,
70   Pierces the silent shaft — sinks the invisible token —
Cloaked in the Hall, the Envoy stands, his mission unspoken,
While the pale, banquetless guests await in trembling to hear it.

The Warning Voice

JAMES CLARENCE MANGAN

Ye Faithful — ye noble!
    A day is at hand
Of trial and trouble,
    And woe in the land!
5   O'er a once greenest path,
      Now blasted and sterile,
        Its dusk shadows loom —
It cometh with Wrath,
      With Conflict and Peril,
10   With Judgement and Doom!

False bands shall be broken,
    Dead systems shall crumble,
      And the haughty shall hear

Truths never yet spoken,
  Though smouldering like flame
   Through many a lost year
In the hearts of the Humble;
For hope will expire
As the terror draws nigher,
  And, with it, the Shame
Which so long overawed
  Men's mind by its might —
And the Powers abroad
  Will be Panic and Blight,
And phrenetic Sorrow —
  Black Pest all the night,
And Death on the morrow!

Now, therefore, ye True,
Gird your loins up anew!
By the good you have wrought,
By all you have thought,
  And suffered, and done!
  By your souls! I implore you
   Be leal to your mission —
  Remembering that *one*
   Of the *two* paths before you
    Slopes down to Perdition!
To you have been given,
  Not granaries and gold;
But the Love that lives long,
  And waxes not cold;
And the Zeal that has striven
  Against Error and Wrong,
And in fragments had riven
  The chains of the strong!
Bide now, by your sternest
Conceptions of earnest
Endurance for others,
Your weaker-souled brothers!
  Your true faith and worth
   Will be History soon,
  And their stature stand forth
   In the unsparing Noon!

You have dreamed of an era

55 Of Knowledge, and Truth,

And Peace — the *true* glory!

Was this a chimera?

Not so! — but the childhood and youth

Of our days will grow hoary,

60 Before such a marvel shall burst on their sight!

On *you* its beams glow not —

For *you* its flowers blow not,

You cannot rejoice in its light,

But in darkness and suffering instead,

65 You go down to the place of the Dead

To *this* generation

The sore tribulation,

The stormy commotion,

And foam of the Popular Ocean,

70 The struggle of class against class,

The Dearth and the Sadness,

The Sword and the War-vest;

To the *next*, the Repose and the Gladness,

'The Sea of clear glass',

75 And the rich Golden Harvest.

Know then, your true lot,

Ye faithful, though few!

Understand your position,

Remember your mission,

80 And vacillate not,

Whatsoever ensue!

Alter not! Falter not!

Palter not now with your own living souls,

When each moment that rolls

85 May see Death lay his hand

On some new victim's brow!

Oh! let not your vow

Have been written in sand!

Leave cold calculations,

90 Of Danger and Plague,

To the slaves and the traitors

Who cannot dissemble

The dastard sensations

That now make them tremble .

95   With phantasies vague! —
The men without ruth —
     The hypocrite haters
Of Goodness and Truth,
Who at heart curse the race
100   Of the sun through the skies;
And would look in God's face
     With a lie in their eyes!
To the last do your duty.
     Still mindful of this —
105   That Virtue is Beauty,
        And Wisdom, and Bliss;
So, howe'er, as frail men, you have erred
     Your way along Life's throngéd road,
Shall your consciences prove a sure guerdon
110   And tower of defence,
     Until Destiny summon you hence
To the Better Abode!

When Hearts Were Trumps

JAMES CLARENCE MANGAN

O! the days when HEARTS were Trumps!
     Then the soul made *great* way —
With slight leaven and largest lumps,
     Man marched forward straightway —
5   God revealed His lightning face
     That time unto Moses —
O, my life on't! Adam's race
     Slept not then on roses!

Praise the days when HEARTS were Trumps
10   Ere yet Heads were talked of —
Ere yet Gall 's and Spurzheim's bumps
     Were mapped out and chalked off!
When men yet could laugh and quaff,
     When Hope's Tree bore blossoms,
15   And the Electric Telegraph
     Spoke from living bosoms!

Clubs were Trumps in 'Ninety three —
  With the gaunt Parisians, —
And with Us too, while yet we
20   Had our dazzling visions.
Our CLUBS — all remembered there: —
  Wide and well we held them,
Till the Castle-Hercules
  Raised *his* club, and felled them!

25 Spades are *now* Trumps: far and near
  All seek out the sexton,
What with Cholera, Famine, Fear,
  Men ask what comes next on.
No more marryings, no more cheer;
30   All is dark and lonely;
Town and country both appear
  One wide churchyard only.

Praise the days when HEARTS were Trumps!
  Those couleur-de-rose days,
35 Brummell's gloves and D'Orsay's pumps
   Made no MAN in those days!
Then the Heart, as Nature's bark,
  Both with oar and sail rowed —
Science then but lost her mark
40   On fresh *FEELING'S* railroad!

But, will HEARTS be Trumps again?
  That they will, I fancy.
Love will yet abolish Pain,
  As by necromancy;
45 And, friends, trust me; your — (not *my*) —
  Offspring will have wondered
Much at myriad changes — by
  ANNO NINETEEN-HUNDRED!

Lament for Clarence Mangan

RICHARD D'ALTON WILLIAMS

'Oft with tears I've groaned to God for pity.
  Oft gone wandering till my way grew dim,
Oft sang unto Him a prayful ditty,
Oft, all lonely in this throngful city,
  Raised my soul to Him;
And from path to path His mercy tracked me,
  From many a peril snatched He me.
When false friends pursued, betrayed, attacked me,
When gloom overdarked, a sickness racked me,
  He was by to save and free.'
                              — Clarence Mangan.

Yes! happy friend, the cross was thine; 'tis o'er a sea of tears
Predestined souls must ever sail to reach their native spheres.
May Christ, the crowned of Calvary, who died upon a tree,
Bequeath His tearful chalice and His bitter cross to me.

5   The darkened land is desolate — a wilderness of graves —
Our purest hearts are prison-bound, our exiles on the waves;
Gaunt Famine stalks the blasted plains — the pestilential air
O'erhangs the gasp of breaking hearts or stillness of despair.

The ebbing blood of Ireland is shed by foreign streams,
10 Where our kinsmen wake lamenting when they see her in their
        dreams.
Oh! happy are the peaceful dead — 'tis not for them we weep
Whose troubled spirits rest at length in calmly laurelled sleep.

No chains are on thy folded hands, no tears bedim thine eyes,
But round thee bloom celestial flowers in ever tranquil skies,
15 While o'er our dreams thy mystic songs, faint, sad, and solemn,
        flow,
Like light that left the distant stars ten thousand years ago.

How sweet thy harp on every string — wild, tender, mirthful,
        grand,
Of fairy pranks, of war, or love, or bleeding Fatherland;
And long the mournful caoina of Tyrconnell and Tyrone
20 Like midnight waves on caverned coasts around their tombs
        shall moan.

157

Still 'boating down the Bosphorus,' with thee we gaily go,
And still the 'elfin mariners' o'er tiny brooklets row,
The phantom 'Lady Agnes' still roams in awful woe,
And Irish hearts o'er 'Cahal Mor' and 'Roisin Dubh' shall glow.

25   Thou wert a voice of God on earth — of those prophetic souls
Who hear the fearful thunder in the Future's womb that rolls,
And the warnings of the angels, as the midnight hurried past,
Rushed in upon thy spirit, like a ghost o'erladen blast.

Then the woes of coming judgement on thy trancèd vision burst,
30   To call immortal vengeance on an age and land accurst;
For where is Faith, or Purity, or Heaven in us now?
In power alone the times believe — to gold alone they bow.

If any shade of earthliness bedimmed thy spirit's wings,
Well cleansed thou art in sorrow's ever-salutary springs;
35   And even bitter suffering, and still more bitter sin,
Shall only make a soul like thine more beautiful within.

For every wound that humbles, if it do not all destroy,
Shall nerve the heart for nobler deeds, and fit for purer joy;
As the demigod of fable-land, as olden legends say,
40   Rose up more strong and valorous each time he touched the clay.

And wisely was a weakness with thine ecstasies allied —
Thus Heaven would save a favourite child from God-dethroning
      pride,
And teach the star-land dreamer that his visioned Milky Way
Is but the feeble reflex of his Sire's transmitted ray.

45   As aforetime the apostle wept to bear an earthly thorn,
While his raptured spirit floated through the portals of the morn;
For bards, like saints, have secret joys none other mortals know:
And He who loves would chasten them in weakness and in woe.

Tears deck the soul with virtues, as soft rains the flowery sod,
50   And the inward eyes are purified for clearer dreams of God:
'Tis sorrow's hand the temple-gates of holiness unbars;
By day we only see the earth, 'tis night reveals the stars.

Alas! alas! the minstrel's fate! — his life is short and drear,
And if he win a wreath at last, 'tis but to shade a bier;
His harp is fed with wasted life — to tears its numbers flow —
And strung with chords of broken hearts is dream-land's
    splendid woe.

But now — a cloud, a cloud transfigured, all luminous
    auroral —
Thou joinest the Trisagion of choired immortals choral,
While all the little discords here but render more sublime
The joybells of the universe from starry chime to chime.

O Father of the harmonies eternally that roll
Life, light, and love to trillioned suns, receive the poet's soul!
And bear him in Thy bosom from this vale of tears and storms
To swell the sphere-hymns thundered from the rushing starry
    swarms.

In sacred lustre rolling where the constellated throngs
Peal down through Heaven's chasmata unutterable songs,
And myriad-peopled systems — beneath, around, above —
Resound with admiration — reverberate with love —

Sleep, happy friend! The cross was thine — 'tis o'er a sea of
    tears
Predestined souls must ever sail to reach their native spheres.
May Christ, the crowned of Calvary, who died upon a tree,
Vouchsafe His tearful chalice and His bitter cross to me!

PART V
'The Bright-Eyed and the Bold'

THE NATIONALIST CHALLENGE

Be Free

ANONYMOUS

Be free! across the broad, bright waves that wash our Western
    shores,
Distinct as silver trumpet call, above old ocean's roar,
That heart-awelcoming, thrilling cry, has reached our ears at last!
Oh! that our souls could breath it, as our bodies breathe the
    blast!
5   Oh! that we all inhaled its life and pow'r-fraught spirit — then,
Our famine-blighted brethren were no longer beasts, but men!

Be free! look up, my countrymen! — that star-bespangled dome!
Was it spread out, by Freedom's GOD, to roof a bondsman's
    home? —
The glorious 'sun to rule the day, the moon to rule night' —
10   Were they design'd that tyrants should for their dark deeds have
    light?
That slaves should see to count the links, that chain them to
    Despair? —
Should only see to number them, and not to break them dare?

Be free! look down, my countrymen, our own unequalled land!
Behold it laden with the gifts of His unsparing hand!
15   'The hills are standing thick with corn; with joy, the valleys sing!'
Doth Nature, from her storehouses, for slaves such treasures
    bring?
The LORD himself declared it, in his just and loving plan,
That Earth's abundance was bestow'd, not on some men, but on
    MAN.

Be free! we see, and hear it, in the broad and brilliant sky —
20   In the voice of rushing tempests — in the soft breeze
    murm'ring by!
Be free! 'tis sweetly whispered by the rustling ears of corn!
We see it written on our fields, in gems, each dewy morn!
And shall we — dare we — suffer, still, such counsellings to
    pass,
As unproductive of results as breathings upon glass?

25   Be free! if only to throw off that hideous nightmare, 'Law!'
That Law, which, in the good old days — the Penal days — we
    saw; —

That Law which makes it Felony, our thoughts to speak or
      write—
That Law, hallooing man against his countryman, to fight —
That Law, which farms out Church and State to coronetted
      knaves —
30   That Law, whose just awards behold, in yet pest-teeming graves!

Be free! if it be but to stop our thousands being sent,
Again to rot, in the shroudless heaps, 'by Act of Parliament':
To cause to cease Law murdering. — What! has it not been so?
Was it not murder under which our millions were laid low?
35   Aye! heartless thieves that 'Law' allowed, protected, even woo'd,
To buy for groats, and sell for gold, our starving peasants' food!

Be free! be not affrighted by their slogan 'right divine'!
'Twere difficult to name the date 'twas granted, I opine:
(1) *Perhaps* it was that harvest day — that day of awe and
      pain—
40   JEHOVAH showed his ire, in fearful thunderings and rain!
(2) 'I gave a king in anger, and I took him in my wrath';
Heaven's chancery stamp, approving it, perhaps that licence
      hath?

Be free! that we may be released from England's robber-right —
The 'right' of treaties broken by the red right hand of Might —
45   The 'right' of parchment victories, by perjured caitiffs seal'd,
Whose souls in Treason's deepest, darkest furnace were
      anneall'd;
That all that long, dark, dread account, to England's debit
      placed,
May from our Lord's polluted books be for ever erased!

How Shall We Hail the Spring?
ANONYMOUS

How shall we hail the bright-eyed Spring?
    Shall we sing of opening flowers,
    Rosy buds and scented leaves?
    Shall we prate of leaves and streams,

5   Silver dews and violet gleams,
       Gladness, mirth, and blossoming?
       No! Let those whose arms are free
            Hail the Summer's visitings;
       Or those who love their slavery
10   Wreathe their fetters' clatterings,
       Darker, wilder is our doom —
       Taint and thraldom, crime and gloom,
            Brood wide, with ghastly wings.

       What songs shall hail the bright-eyed Spring?
15   Shall we sing of love and pleasure;
       Eyes that outblaze Golconda's treasure;
       Stolen hours, through green lanes straying,
       With kisses sweet our path delaying,
            Heart to heart soft fluttering?
20   No! Let those whom freedom blesses
            Proffer hearts without a stain;
       But to him whom wrong oppresses
            Passion's tale is cold and vain.
       Sterner, bolder, be our words.
25   Strains that shall nerve the spirit's chords —
       Brace the arms and whet the swords
            That reap revenge or break the chain.

       Welcome *thus* the rose-lipped Spring:
            Swear by every ruined hearth,
30   Where grass will soon peer forth;
            Swear by every stricken bosom.
            Where no Spring shall ever blossom;
            Swear by years of suffering —
       Swear by every nameless grave,
35   O'er whose famine-wasted clay
       Pale-eyed flowers of Spring shall wave
            With mournful blazonry —
       Swear by your country's tear-dimmed eye —
       By her mighty heart run dry
40   By natal soil and natal sky,
       That Spring's frail flowers shall not die
            Ere you strike at foreign sway.

The Plucking of the Shamrock

ANONYMOUS

Since one short year,
My Shamrock dear,
I sorrowfully said,
A million men,
Who loved thee then,
Are numbered with the dead.
A million more
May sink before
Another year rolls by,
If we don't band
Head, heart, and hand,
To succour thee or die.

Thanatos, 1849

ANONYMOUS

'Him that dieth of Baasa in the city, the dogs shall eat; and him that
dieth of this in the country, the fowls of the air shall devour' — *Kings*

God sent a curse upon the land, because her sons were slaves;
The rich earth brought forth rottenness, and gardens became
        graves;
The green crops withered in the fields, all blackened by the
        curse,
And wedding gay and dance gave way to coffin and hearse.

God hung a cloud before the sun — a gloomy, ominous cloud;
The cloud came down and wrapped the land, as in a dusky
        shroud;
It was a regal robe that swathed the giant monarch — Death,
Whose voice was in the famine-scream, who breathed the fever-
        breath.

The wondrous things foretold by JOHN were realized at last,
And APOLLYON came on earth, to blacken and to blast;
The People withered one by one, from off the stalk of Life —
The woman meek and sturdy man — the husband and the wife.

The maiden's springy step grew dull — the rose-hue fled her
    cheek,
For Famine gnawed the Beautiful, and left her worn and weak.
15   The child's bright eye grew dim and dark; he fell, like blighted
    bud —
The Fever-breath was in his veins, and blasted his young blood.

A mother's heart was marble-clad, her eye was fierce and wild—
A hungry Demon lurked therein, while gazing on her child.
The mother-love was warm and true; the Want was long
    withstood —
20   Strength failed at last; she gorged the flesh — the offspring of her
    blood.

Fond lover! lip your youthful bride — it is not sinful now,
For pulseless is that loving heart, and clammy that fair brow.
God's curse was over her and you; God loves to curse a slave;
Starve, wither, die the coward's death; then wed her in the
    grave!

25   It was a ghastly sight to see the land within its pall,
Without a groan, without a moan — so grim and silent all.
And CHRIST! 'twas sickening to inhale the death-smell which
    has birth,
When flesh is melting off from bone, and earth rots back to
    earth.

God darkened then the hanging cloud, and spread a deeper
    gloom —
30   The days rolled by; Death plied his trade, and garnered for the
    tomb;
He was the only reaper there, whose harvest was not marred —
Who gathered in a plenteous crop — whose labour met reward.

And day and night, and night and day, the boneyard was
    increased
Like Sennacherib, legions fell, and Death was unappeased;
35   And GOD made darker still the cloud, because the men were
    slaves,
And heavier still the curse became; the land was strewed with
    graves.

Present and Future

J.W. BOURKE

Still comes thy piteous wail,
> Erin aroon,
Borne on the moaning gale,
> Erin aroon,
Pale Famine's feeble cries,
> Dread Fever's wasting sighs,
5   Fond watcher's agonies,
> Erin aroon.

Deep in thy misery,
> Erin aroon,
Too madd'ning sight to see,
> Erin aroon,
From thy breast sorrow sown,
Spring grief and woe alone,
10   Hope after hope o'erthrown,
> Erin aroon.

And shall thy brave and true,
> Erin aroon,
Be still the loving few,
> Erin aroon,
When will thy sons combine,
Scorning to weep and whine
15   Sworn to make Freedom thine,
> Erin aroon.

When 'neath thy banner blent,
> Erin aroon,
Shall their proud vow be sent,
> Erin aroon,
Echoing from shore to shore,
Mocking the billow's roar,
20   'Thou shalt be Queen once more.'
> Erin aroon.

Then, on thy peerless brow,
> Erin aroon,
Drooping with anguish now,
> Erin aroon,

167

Joy shall sit throned in light,
Smiles ever new and bright,
Tok'ning dark thraldom's flight,
Erin aroon.

A Song of Ulster
FRANCIS DAVIS

And, Ulstermen, is this the soil
    Our fathers loved so dearly well?
And shall we 'mid their ashes toil,
    And not the same proud feeling tell?
Forbid it, honour, truth, and pride!
    The gems unsold their bosoms bare;
And let us prove, if rightly tried,
    We're all the Ulstermen of yore.
      Sing, oh! the land,
      The blooming land,
The land our fathers loved so dear:
      May sorrow crush
      The wretch who'd blush
His father's love of home to hear!

And Ulster, thou hast seen a day
    When tales of pride were thine to tell;
But discord cleared the Dutchman's way,
    And we from all our glory fell:
And groaning only to her God
    Our country wore a double chain;
But fifty years of stripes and fraud
    Have surely raised a soul again.
      Sing, oh! the land,
      The groaning land,
The land our fathers loved so dear;
      May *blushing* crush
      The wretch who'd blush
His father's love of home to hear!

Shall alien courts, or foreign crowns,
    Have merchandize in honest hearts,

And buy or ban our smiles or frowns,
  As suit their own unholy arts?
No! from the unpolluted veins
  That clothed the graves we gaze upon,
We'll prove no father scorned his chains
  That did not leave as proud a son!
   Sing, oh! the land,
   The lovely land,
The land our fathers loved so dear;
   May sorrow pale
   The wretch who'd quail
His father's love of home to hear!

Too long have we the truant played,
  And slept or waked as tyrants taught;
Too long, unthinking, lent our aid
  To rear a foreign Juggernaut:
Nor claimed nor owned a native land;
  Mere birds of passage, homeless guests;
We only loved the alien hand
  That wrung the manhood from our breasts.
   Sing, oh! the land,
   The slighted land,
The land our fathers loved so dear:
   May feeling crush
   The wretch who'd blush
His father's love of home to hear!

How wrong we were our homes declare!
  How mad exclaims the seedless earth!
Where maniac famine rends her hair,
  Or huddles o'er the fireless hearth:
Ah, men might melt their eyes like rain,
  But *men* have nobler work to do;
Nor shall we halt till every vein
  The fire of freedom rushes through.
   Sing, oh! the land,
   The awakened land,
The land that holds our fathers' clay,
   May love of sire
   Each soul inspire
To cheer her on her glorious way!

What, what were ours but milky blood,
　　　If tame and coldly we could stand,
When lightning-limbed young Nationhood
　　　Is more than midway with her hand:
75　　She comes, she comes, and we've delayed!
　　　　Up, factious folly! from our shore;
For, true as truth, thine upas shade
　　　Must mantle Ulster's soul no more!
　　　　　Sing, oh! the land,
80　　　　　The infant land,
The growing Isle of bounding soul;
　　　　May sorrow wet
　　　　His cheek who'd fret
To see her in at glory's goal.

The Artisan's Apology for Emigrating
JOHN DE JEAN FRAZER

The vision has faded that cheered us so long
In our wilderness journey thro' suffering and wrong;
We dreamt of a freedom akin to the wind's
For the skill of our hands, and the strength of our minds;
5　But we wake to a chain that confounds and controls,
With its amulet circle, our limbs and our souls —
To the cold chain of poverty — binding us all
In the fathomless depth of our national fall:
And blest o'er his brothers is he who can shape
10　By the force of despair — not ascent — but escape!

The artisan swelters, the husbandman delves,
To stall feed the idle, and famish themselves!
And still, as the gloom of the country grows blacker,
The bond between classes grows slacker and slacker!
15　The Saxon oppressor the land has o'erspread
With tyrants, like tribes from a patriarch head;
Who, plundered, must plunder — who trampled, will trample;
Some swayed by necessity — some by example!
The Saxon extorts from the Kingdom at large;
20　And the humblest the least is exempt from the charge;
The landlord and labour-lord filch and secure

The tribute they pay from the bones of the poor:
So tyranny falls with the deadliest weight,
By a natural law, on the lowest estate;
25   And strong hearts and spirits, o'erpowered at last,
Despair of the future, surveying the past.

The fine springs of action that move men to deeds,
Of semi-divinity, broken like reeds,
Sustain no endeavour — inspire no deep vow,
30   For single or aggregate excellence now!
No vigorous thoughts start, like leaves on the bough,
To life, when the fresh air is bathing the brow;
As forth from our chambers of woe and ill-health,
We creep in the twilight, like culprits, by stealth:
35   But a sense, all pervading, of pain and more pain,
Enfeebles the hand, and distempers the brain;
Till, fevered in mind, we internally rave,
Of poorhouse and prison, of famine and grave!

Day and night we are wrapped in a desperate strife,
40   Not for national glory, but personal life;
And our hair raineth sweat, like the clouds on the soil;
Yet the ass, with his thistle, has more for his toil!
Or, lacking employment, our energies rust;
Our ambitions decay into ashes and dust;
45   And we crave, like lame beggars, permission to *strive*,
Oh! when this is our lot, in life's manliest stage,
What horror of horrors awaits our old age!
What marvel we sternly extinguish our fires,
When our hopes are extinct in the home of our sires;
50   And fly from the soil, where oppression has nursed
Mankind into classes — the cursers and curst —
The taskers who rob, and the toilers who rot
In suffering, so deep that it murmureth not:
And where blasphemous prayers are sent up for bliss
55   And long life to the tyrants who crushed us to *this*!
What marvel we gaze from the desolate floor,
To the world-in-the-west, where no millions of poor,
'Neath the hoof and the heel of aristocrat drones,
Keep each other in place, like the pavement stones!
60   It is not *one* fruit of this Eden we call
Our land, that, to us, is forbidden — but all;

No flame-armed angel of GOD we obey;
'Tis dark spectres of death compel us away!

65 The flower of the meadow, the way-fringing weed
Must be deep in decay, ere they throw off their seed;
And seared must the state be that flings the brave *minds*,
Hearts and hands of its citizens on the wild winds:
To sway a young rival, in new-world climes,
With purpose to punish its old-world crimes;
70 Be it so — it is something of joy after all,
That the victor, at last, by the victim shall fall:
And albeit we now rush in flight from the foe,
We may wreak full revenue from the whither we go!
At least the resolve can be never so vain,
75 In us, who depart — as in you, who remain,
Expecting the murderer's hand to renew
The pulse of the Being he purposely slew!

Extermination

JOHN DE JEAN FRAZER

Loud wailing loads the winds of heaven!
      Is it loud wailing for the dead?
Is it the burst from hearts new-riven
Of pent-up grief that long had striven
5   For utterances o'er the dying bed?
Its wild and weird, unearthly tones —
      Its passionate, impetuous strain —
Deep supplication, curses, groans,
      Might pierce thro' hearts, if hearts were stones,
10   And leave a sense of pain!

It is not for the dear, and dead,
      Nor live, and lost, that wailing loads
The winds of Heaven — nor yet for bread —
Not for high hopes that failed and fled,
15   But ruined roofs, and wrecked abodes!
An all-embracing evil flings
      Despair around the outcast poor,

172

Massing all dead and living things
    In one small picture when it brings
20   The roof-tree to the floor.

The household altar of the hearth —
    The Sabbath rest each evening gave —
The holiest holy things of earth —
The mother's love — the father's mirth —
25   The bridal bed — th' ancestral grave —
All soothing memories of the past —
    The present hour — the future day —
Are into hideous darkness cast,
    When men are homeless in the blast
30   That whirls their thatch away.

Saw ye a forest when the shower
    And storm of winter sweep the sky —
Swaying and writhing in that hour
As if their roar had not a power
35   To tell their mighty torments by?
The number of those forest forms
    Is here by human forms o'erstepped.
Wilder the swaying of the arms!
    Louder the wail! and o'er them storms
40 More terrible have swept!

Their lives were one long draught of gall,
    Even from their infant breath;
And prematurely they should fall,
Poisoned by tyranny — for all
45   Its elements work early death!
This were, at best, their brightest doom —
    But it is now a potent joy —
Of tyranny's, thro' denser gloom,
    To hunt them to a sudden tomb —
50   To ruin, and destiny.

The land is parcelled as a spoil
    Among a robber gang; and they
To whom God's fiat gave the soil,
Even with the great degree of toil,
55   Are chased to death like beasts of prey! —

Homeless and hungry — and denied
        The rights of beasts to prowl at need!
Their tyrants have high Heaven defiled,
        Perverted God's sentence and lied
60   To Adam and his seed!

The earth was made for all — or none;
        And Kings and Queens might dare
To grant estates of air — of sun —
To favoured minions, till were gone
65   The plundered people's share,
As well as to bestow the land —
        Or brook the rich man's gold
To buy the soil into his hand;
        The primal right is far too grand
70   To be bestowed — or sold!

To what high deeds can men aspire,
        Whom tyrants, without fear or shame,
Can cast like wood upon the fire,
And their out-gushing woe or ire
75   Be but its spewing on the flame?
See homesteads levelled far and nigh!
        What refuge does the world afford
The stricken crowds driven out to die?
        If there be mercy in the sky
80   The soil must be restored!

The Harvest Pledge
JOHN DE JEAN FRAZER

The Lord of the Manor with musket and sabre
Went forth overlooking his serfs at their labour;
For their loud harvest prayer to the God of the Season
Disturbed his repose like an outburst of treason;
5   Yet it merely invoked Heaven's grace on their pledge,
'Now a grave in the furrow, or feast from the ridge!'
A prayer so humble seems manifest token,
The pride of the people was blasted and broken.

Ah! When fatal success plumes a tyrant's endeavour,
10   How the mark of the blaster remaineth for ever!

He had crushed to his brow, till it fitted him quite,
The sovereign crown of the people's right —
He had reaped the graveyard, and wealth had flowed
From the human crop his famine sowed.
15   The strong winds of winter he tired with the groans,
Of wretches, flung off from his roadstead like stones;
But the spring, while it mottled with king-cup and daisy
His meadows of emerald, made him uneasy —
It whispered abroad of a mighty new-comer,
20   A spirit to speak to men's souls through the summer!

And the spirit came, in the freshness and beauty
Of truth, to proclaim the imperative duty
Of man to himself is, not only to labour
With sickles and spade, but to hold with the sabre!
25   That slaves changed their tyrants from bats into eagles,
And their packs of pursuers to lions from beagles!
That each grain of the harvest with weapons should bristle,
'Gainst the hand of oppression, like hedgehog or thistle!
That the shyest of birds took his share from the spoiler,
30   And that courage alone was the want of the toiler.

So the serfs, in the face of the Lord of the Manor,
Set a spear for shaft and a sheaf for banner;
And said: 'If we chose, from the sward to the sky
From centre to shore, thou shouldst yield — or die!
35   It is ours — by the gift of the glorious Creator!
It is thine — by the grip of the robber and cheater!
But we seek only bread — we! — the wronged from the
          wronger —
Let us eat — and thy burdens may bind us yet longer!'
Ah! when fatal success crowns a tyrant's endeavour,
40   How the mark of the blaster remaineth for ever!

Soon he lowered his weapons, remembering how
The soft hand, in milking, gets most from the cow;
He saw even serfs must be fed after toil,
Ere the olive of peace could strike root in the soil;
45   That he need not unchain them, but lengthen their tether,

And the dupes and himself might live happily together.
In that spirit made answer the Lord of the Manor!
And they broke off the spear-head, and pulled down the
      banner—
They crushed not the crusher, nor freed themselves then!
50   May he load them, and scourge them, and starve them again!

The Lost Labour

JOHN DE JEAN FRAZER

My soul is dark with double gloom: —
     The sufferings of the past,
Like cypress in perpetual bloom
Around a lone and sunken tomb,
5   My spirit overcast: —
And with the past is present woe,
     Like undergrowth, entwined,
Too close for future bliss to glow
Upon the cold remains below: —
10   Oh! would I were resigned!

It is a mortifying loss
     To lose the hopes of life: —
To slide on — on — o'er bar and cross,
Tho' storms distract, and rocks emboss
15   Life's stream with foamy strife!
To hear the hiss of serpent's tongue!
     To see the slander cast!
Yet stand in spirit o'er the throng,
     For one good end — to punish wrong —
20   And find all vain at last!

Yes — yes — it is a fearful doom: —
     But one that he must brave,
Who cometh from his country's womb,
And fain would go not to his tomb,
25   A slave —a slave — a slave.
Man's mind — and man — are robbed of dower,
     Where tyrant feet have trod: —

Submit to chains — and in that hour,
Will tyranny's perverting power
30   Debase the gifts of God.

Behold man's nature — is it not,
  In this our fair, old land,
A hideous and revolting blot?
The weed and briar usurp the spot
35   Where flower and tree should stand!
The famished peasant dies a fool!
  The honest rob for bread!
The tyrant peer's a tyrant's tool!
And patriots jabber calm and cool,
40   While dogs devour the dead!

The slave-born sons of slave-born sires
  Speed off thro' fire and foam,
To save or seize, as need requires;
Aiding the plunderer till he tires,
45   Who plundered them at home!
We strike down freedom to the dust,
  In every clime and zone;
With native swords we dare not trust
To smite the smiter, in the just,
50   Forced quarrel of our own!

The heartless sneer — the hollow cant —
  The brutal threat — the scorn —
The solemn mockery of our want
The boasted boons, cold, sour, and scant —
55   The promises, stillborn —
Fraud — insult — falsehood — and, still worse,
  Proud taunts, like living coals —
Famine and Death, without remorse,
Have we not borne, without a curse
60   Upon our coward souls?

For me, the mastery of bad laws
  (Those cold impassive chains,
That drag the victim, without pause,
Into the victor's crimes and cause)
65   Was fire within my veins!

177

Skill, learning, mind were filched away;
    Yet spat upon, and spurned;
And my great dream was of a day,
Whose these would be — who will say 'nay' —
70   Deemed precious — yet returned.

True men the lofty vision shared,
    And fell, self-sacrificed:
Because the craven herd despaired,
When standard flew, and blade was bared,
75   Once more to be despised;
One scalding truth alone was learned: —
    That freedom to the few
Is never paid, tho' nobly earned,
Until the million mass has yearned,
80   And struck for freedom, too!

And those true men, who, like a soul,
    Had quickened the dull clay,
That slavery made us, when it stole
Our kingdom out of history's scroll —
85   Brave spirits! where are they?
God of Nations! — in the power
    Of Thy defiers pine
Those stern demanders of man's dower!
To smash their chains is not in our
90   Red wrath — but 'tis in Thine!

My soul is dark with double gloom —
    I toiled in hidden tears,
And still forgot them — for my doom,
Methought, would bring an honoured plume
95   For chainless after-years —
A righted land, at any cast,
    Was guide and goal combined.
And now, when guide and goal are lost
The mearn of my whole hope is crossed;
100   Oh! would I were resigned.

The Spring Flowers

JOHN DE JEAN FRAZER

The spring flowers are peeping
    From hedge, bank, and brake;
Oh! God, what wild weeping
    Those flowers would awake,
If grief could be cherished
    'Mid famine and pain,
For the dear ones who perished
    By the doomed who remain!

The kindly spring weather
    With balm once beguiled
To the hedge-row together
    The primrose and child;
But clay is now crushing
    The child in the tomb!
And the primrose is blushing!
    But blushing for whom?

And the violet once lifted
    Its blue eyes to greet
Young eyes that were gifted
    With azure as sweet;
But sealed in their lashes
    Past April's deep power
Those blue eyes are ashes!
    Why bloometh the flower?

Let it bloom for its season
    Gaunt Famine has dried
From the bosoms it preys on
    Humanity's tide —
Life's lingering embers
    To strength must be fed;
Ere the living remembers
    What had charmed the dead.

No quaint epitaph
    The fond parent now weaves,
In the lost child's behalf,

Of fresh flowers and green leaves;
Each pure, fireside feeling
      Is wrapped in a strife,
All tenderness steeling —
      The struggle for Life!

For careless and callous
      As grey-bearded men,
Of the crow's beechen palace,
      Or moss hut of the wren —
Of the fair flowers waving
      By wayside and wood,
Shrunk children are craving
      Food — nothing but food!

For mother — for father
      No wail to the sky!
The orphans must gather
      Some garbage, or die!
The famine-fiend blighted
      The chaplets of love
And a vulture has lighted
      Where nestled the dove.

Oh! Command us not, Heaven,
      For a future of bliss,
That the foes be forgiven
      Who crushed us to this!
Though angels were beckoning,
      How could we forgive?
A day of dark reckoning
      Must come — if we live.

The Three Angels

JOHN DE JEAN FRAZER

Then I looked — and I saw the proud angel of war,
    With the mien of a mighty king; —
He rode in a high, triumphal car —
His brow was a dazzling, meteor star —
5   And his advent thrilled through the earth, as far
    As the tempest spreads its wing! —
And shaken and searched by his chariot roll,
Were the depths of the heart, and the heights of the soul!
Swords, banners, brave music and grand parade,
10   Such a halo of glory around him made,
It mingled with all things — the oak and the reed —
It kindled the heroic breast to flame —
It withered the coward's heart with shame —
15   The pastor sent forth his pure son — to slay!
And blest the flags, ere they flew in the fray —
The widow felt her pride restored,
When she girt her boy with his father's sword; —
The timid maiden half raised her eyes,
20   Ashamed to syllable forth her sighs,
When breathed her lover a soldier's vow,
To weave her a bower of laurel bough; —
The very children mimicked bands
Of warriors wielding conquering brands: —
25   Oh! like wind in the forest — or light in the wave —
That angel's presence an energy gave,
And a gladness, full as if mortal strife
Were a grander element added to life: —
And millions followed through fire and steel,
30   The track of his terrible iron wheel;
Mid wrecks and triumphs — mid cheers and groans —
O'er plundered shrines — and o'er ruined thrones —
O'er famished towns and o'er harvests burned —
O'er mansions to crumbling monuments turned —
35   O'er foundered fleets that coffined their dead,
Where line of an epitaph never was read: —
And many a fire was quenched with blood;
And many a hamlet roofless stood;
And weeds on many an altar grew;
40   And many a host had shrunk to few;

And many a brow bore fearful token,
Of hope, and heart, and spirit broken;
Ere that emblazoned angel passed
And the silence woke the world at last.

45 *Then* nations and powers, that had heeded not
Their bleeding wounds, while the blood was hot,
And men, who had scorned to count the cost
Till final triumph were won or lost,
Beheld the clouds that proud angel's track
50 Had made all-gorgeous, lower all-black!
As rain in the spring time had blood been spilt,
And the national harvest was grief and guilt;
And they who, in striking for triumphs and thrones,
Had sharpened the sword upon human bones;
55 Setting wrong in the honoured place of right —
Treading weakness down with the heel of might —
Whether victors or victims at the close of the fight —
Found the fruit was black — if the blossom was white! —
Then cursed the castle its first-born's plume,
60 For it hearsed him featly from tent unto tomb;
And served the blind worm to scare away
From his own dark banquet the bird of prey! —
Then the cottage cursed the hot victor's tread,
For trampling its darling down to the dead; —
65 (Like a nest in a thicket the cottage had been;
And tho' humble the youth, he had stood between
His mother and want — till, in evil hour,
O'er his spirit the spells of war had power: —
He went — and she suddenly languished alone, —
70 An insect unsheltered by turn of a stone!) —
Then grief prevailed o'er the stern — and the bland —
It dripped from the rock — it welled up from the sand! —
From the rustic chair to the regal throne,
All mourned — tho' each but missed his own —
75 Deeming the honours that crowned the brave,
Mere flowers they gathered to deck the grave: —
(And what are tomb-flowers — or fresh or faded —
When living hearts with thorns are braided?) —
Yea — the guilty gathering left a brand
80 Of dishonour, perhaps, on some gallant land!
High minds were debauched — and brave bodies maimed —

The matron was widowed — the virgin was shamed —
Lust, rapine and murder — extortion and fraud
Were suffered at home — were inflicted abroad —
85   And the hardest heart, like the hardest knife,
Took the keenest edge —cut the best thro' life —
While morals and manners rose higher in price,
The lower they fell to the standard of vice! —
Poor comfort it seemed, that the cup of gall —
90   Yet comfort it was — had been drunk by all; —
So the angel of war that all-gloriously passed,
Became, in men's eyes, a dark fiend at last!

* * * * * * * * *

Slowly — but visibly — came with time,
A flow of virtue — and an ebb of crime; —
95   But never one hour was a land on earth
Entirely the empire of sorrow or mirth; —
The fountain streamed — tho' the sun was glowing —
And the sunbeam glanced — tho' the fount was flowing.

* * * * * * * * *

When behold! — the fell angel of pestilence furled
100   His wing o'er the yet-unrecovered world;
And a shudder, like agony, struck thro' the frame
And spirit of men, when he uttered his name:
For — no strength could fell him — no speed could fly —
No skill could baffle — no bolts defy! —
105   His mission was writ on his morbid brow,
To slay! — to slay! — but no man knew how! —
No flag, save the pall, did he deign to wave;
Yet his lightest footfall hollowed a grave:
Deep midnight and noon were the same to him; —
110   He marched — he encamped — as it were by whim —
Now bending aside from the dens of the poor,
To smite the rich of the marble floor!
Now seizing the beggar before he could dine!
Now clutching the reveller after his wine!
115   Now weeding the workshop in alley and lane!
Now scaling the fortress, and thinning its train,
Now sparing the sickly sons of the town,

Yet striking the stalwart rustics down!
Now setting the homes of one kith and kin,
120   Apart from their neighbours, to massacre in!
Now falling on hamlet and city at once,
And the hearth that escaped him by chance!
Anon he swept off with the speed of the wind,
With the horror before him — and havoc behind,
125   And aged or young he forbore not to strike;
But thro' blossom and bough he went crashing alike!
Anon he tarried from day to day,
And wandered thro' crowds he refused to slay!
At eve lay hid in some by-lane or bawn,
130   Yet was leagues away ere the grey of the dawn;
And waters of bitterness sprung without stint,
In palace — or prison — his foot's deep print! —
Oh! he might be traced by the homes bereft,
To the sport where he lighted from that he left; —
135   He entered the church with the bridal train,
And tore the fresh bridal bond in twain!
He boarded the ship on the ocean foam,
And it came unmanned to its harbour home! —
The steed returned with a slackened rein;
140   And the rider ne'er stood in the stirrup again!
The pilgrim's prayer waxed faint — and more faint —
Till a corse encumbered the shrine of the saint!
As a frost breeze to the buds of spring,
A blight to mankind was that angel's wing!
145   To a blackened mass —to a shrivelled scroll! —
It blasted the body — it withered the soul —
The captive clung to his dungeon gloom,
Lest stepping forth free he step into his tomb! —
The soldier who nobly had rescued — or died —
150   His comrade in battle — now slunk from his side!
In highways and byways was death — but the wail
Of man — or of woman — scarce rippled the gale!
For if no o'er-mastering fear had spread
A reckless indifference for the dead
Yet love itself would have shrunk estranged
155   From features and forms so blackened and changed:
No vigil — no pomp — no funeral crowd! —
With cerecloth for both a coffin and shroud;
The dead were laid in their ghastly lair,

And the living prayed with a secret prayer,
160   That, even in the clay, they should not sleep
With hideous remains, that defied them to weep!
Still — one cold gleam of comfort shone —
The rich — the poor — had not fallen alone, —
As onward the angel of pestilence passed,
165   A dark, dark fiend from the first to the last.

* * * * * * * * *

The children of men in their specified parts,
Were working out *Fate* again — heads and hearts —
The loss of some loved ones had made the breast
Of many a mourner — a ruin at best —
170   But the ruins were built in — 'tis nature's kind law —
Perhaps, some by the Cushat dove — some by the daw —
And the world went on between folly and reason,
With gladness and sorrow by turns in season.

* * * * * * * * *

Till lo! — the gaunt angel of famine burst,
175   From the teeming soil he had poisoned first;
But with haughty defiance and scornful hiss,
He was hunted from earth's every land, save this,
Where a strange ubiquity made him felt
In every nook, as if there he dwelt —
180   Foreshown in his sunken and haggard eye
Were the pangs the famished should perish by;
Yet meekly he bore him, awaiting his time,
In the people's folly — and the ruler's crime;
He saw the millions whose brawny arms
185   Might circle for ever their shores and their farms,
With an ocean belt — or a bloody fosse,
No angel of famine could stalk across: —
They drank of no cup where some venomous toad
Of tyranny had not a leasehold abode;
190   Yet they came in their raws to oppressors in silk,
Like kine, to be spanselled and drained of their milk;
Albeit they prated of shackles and shame,
As hotly as if they had fed upon flame!
He beheld them stare in his own dread face! —

195　He heard them shriek out, as he hastened his pace!
　　　He saw them for help to a tyrant kneel,
　　　Whose heart was a slimy and cold as an eel;
　　　Who had hate in his bosom — and love on his brow —
　　　Like the snake at the root —and the bird in the bough —
200　And he saw that tyrant for strangers carve
　　　The food of those millions he destined to starve!
　　　But he promised of hunger they should not die,
　　　And the angel grinned at the juggling lie!
　　　So the prayers — the false promise —and time — went on —
205　Till the strangers were served — and the food was gone;
　　　And the angel took such a multiplied shape,
　　　Not help itself could secure an escape: —
　　　Still the tyrant's mind would receive no light,
　　　Beyond what suited his purpose of sight!
210　But which was more guilty —the wretch who ruled —
　　　Or the braggarts who brooked to be famished and fooled?
　　　He listened — and heard not one masculine voice
　　　Speak out for the sword, as the manlier choice;
　　　No — they *trusted!* — they *waited!* — the suicide slaves!
215　Tho' patience, they knew, was the spade in their graves —
　　　Or they praised the oppressor! still stranger to see,
　　　Than the parasite plant round the upas tree —
　　　Then the angel waved slowly his skeleton hand,
　　　And touching the masses from centre to strand,
220　By sunlight or starlight, they could not win
　　　One hour from that howl of the wolf within:
　　　Then that spider — whose web alike is laid
　　　At bridal and burial — in sunshine and shade —
　　　The usurer! — hoarded up grain — and sold,
225　When the grains of corn were as grains of gold;
　　　And when rural cabins and city rooms
　　　Had floors — walls — and tenants as naked as tombs;
　　　Still deepened the want to a keen dispute,
　　　For offal and weed with the reptile and brute;
230　The tame, pet hare from the floor was shorn —
　　　The fondled bird from the cage was torn —
　　　The team was blooded — and blooded in vain —
　　　The ploughman still hungered —the horses were slain —
　　　The matron suckled her children's sire —
235　He had no strength — he could earn no hire —
　　　They all died that night with the sparks of the fire —

And the price of a process was saved to the squire!
And thus the spirits, too fondly linked
To struggle apart, were the first extinct: —
240   At the open grave of one child would lie
The widow, till one in her breast would die!
The betrothed by charnel rites were wed,
And they never woke from the bridal bed!
Friendless and coffinless — strange and well-known
245   Were gathered and carted, and flung down — like stone!
Scarce knew the Priest any face in his flock!
And a nook of the chapel would fold the stock!
Some lost all power to love — or hate —
Some wildly raved at themselves — and fate —
250   Some wandered, like spectres, too weak to complain
Of the hollow breast and the wasted brain: —
Some gathered their kith to a fugitive band,
And sought the stars of a happier land; —
Themselves and their kindred, thro' sheer despair,
255   Some slew, in belief that *to slay* was *to spare!* —
A cannibal fierceness but ill-suppressed
In many — made some — we must veil the rest!
Some bolted and earthed the doors from within,
That vermin or brute, no quick entrance might win,
260   And lay down with nerves over-humanly steady,
To rot with the group that lay rotting already!
Some left the dead in their dark abodes,
And crawled forth to perish in ditches and roads!
And the Priest and Coroner tried in vain,
165   To shrive the dying — or to count the slain!
But a murmur went up with the dying moan
That the poor — the poor — had been victims alone!
That the angel of famine, to rich men a friend —
To the humble — a foe — was the darkest fiend! —
270   And the breathings of God, ere the famine-fiend passed,
Sent abroad his high promise of justice at last.

The Queen's Visit

J.

Rise, wretched Erin, from thy children's graves,
    No longer, prostrate, let thy sorrows flow;
Thy grief offends — it is not meet that slaves
    Should thus indulge 'the luxury of woe';
5   Up, and obey the brutal Whig's behest,
    Thy guerdon cool contempt, or sneers but ill supprest.

Wipe from thy pallid brow the damps of death;
    Conceal thy garb of wretchedness and woe;
Exchange the cypress for a rosy wreath,
10   And o'er thy squalor festal garments throw —
    Suppress the bursting sod, and clothe, the while,
    Thy ghastly features with a hollow smile.

Then, while gaunt famine decimates thy sons —
    Famine, thy masters could, but would not, stay —
15   Go, join the pageant of the mighty ones,
    Shine at their revels, gayest of gay;
    And show a shuddering world, with what disgrace,
    Contented slavery stamps the human race.

Rhymes for the Landlorded

WILLIAM JAMES LINTON

1. Eviction

Long years their cabin stood
    Out on the moor;
More than one sorrow-brood
    Passed through their door;
5   Ruin them over-cast,
Worse than the wintry blast;
Famine's plague followed fast:
    God help the poor!

Dying, or living here —
10   Which is the worse?

Misery's heavy tear,
　　　　Back to thy source!
Who dares to lift her head
Up from the scarcely dead?
15 Who pulls the crazy shed
　　　　Down on the corse?

What though some rent was due,
　　　　Hast thou no grace?
So may God pardon you,
20 　　　　Shame of your race!
What though that home may be
Wretched and foul to see —
What if God harry thee
　　　　Forth from His face?

2. Revenge

The leaves are still; not a breath is heard;
　　　　How bright the harvest day!
'Tis the tramp of a horse; the boughs are stirred:
　　　　The agent comes this way.
5 Was it an old gun-muzzle peeped
　　　　Behind yon crimson leaf?
　　　　A shot! — and murder's bloody sheaf
　　　　　Is reaped.

Who sold the farm above his head?
10 　　　　Who drove the widow mad?
Who pulled her dying from her bed?
　　　　Who robbed the idiot lad?
Who sent the starved girl to the streets?
　　　　Who mocked grey sorrow's smart?
15 　　　　Yes! listen in thy blood! — His heart
　　　　　Yet beats.

Not one has help for the dying man;
　　　　Not one the murderer stays;
Tho' all must see him where he ran,
20 　　　　Not even the child betrays.
O wrong! — thou hast a fearful brood!
　　　　What inquest can ye need
　　　　Who know Revenge but reaped the seed
　　　　　Of Blood?

189

A Mystery

DENIS FLORENCE MAC CARTHY

They are dying! they are dying! where the golden corn is growing,
They are dying! they are dying! where the crowded herds are lowing;
They are gasping for existence where the streams of life are flowing,
And they perish of the plague where the breeze of health is blowing!

5   God of Justice! God of Power!
                  Do we dream? Can it be?
            In this land, at this hour,
                  With the blossom on the tree,
            In the gladsome month of May,
10   When the young lambs play,
            When Nature looks around
                  On her waking children now,
            The seed within the ground,
                  The bud upon the bough?
15   Is it right, is it fair,
            That we perish of despair
            In this land, on this soil,
                  Where our destiny is set,
            Which we cultured with our toil,
20   And watered with our sweat?

            We have ploughed, we have sown,
            But the crop was not our own;
            We have reaped, but harpy hands
            Swept the harvest from our lands;
25   We were perishing for food,
            When, lo! in pitying mood,
            Our kindly rulers gave
            The fat fluid of the slave,
            While our corn filled the manger
30   Of the war-horse of the stranger!

            God of Mercy! must this last?
                  Is this land pre-ordained
            For the present and the past,
                  And the future, to be chained,
35   To be ravaged, to be drained,
            To be robbed, to be spoiled,

To be hushed, to be whipt,
Its soaring pinions clipt,
And its every effort foiled?

40 Do our numbers multiply
But to perish and to die?
Is this all our destiny below,
That our bodies, as they rot,
May fertilise the spot
45 Where the harvests of the stranger grow?
If this be, indeed, our fate,
Far, far better now, though late,
That we seek some other land and try some other zone;
The coldest, bleakest shore
50 Will surely yield us more
Than the store-house of the stranger that we dare not call our
own.

Kindly brothers of the West,
Who from Liberty's full breast
Have fed us, who are orphans, beneath a step-dame's frown,
55 Behold our happy state,
And weep your wretched fate
That you share not in the splendours of our empire and our
crown!

Kindly brothers of the East,
Thou great tiara'd priest,
60 Thou sanctified Rienzi of Rome and of the earth —
Or thou who bear'st control
Over golden Istambol,
Who felt for our misfortunes and helped us in our dearth,

Turn here your wondering eyes,
65 Call your wisest of the wise,
Your Muftis and your ministers, your men of deepest lore;
Let the sagest of your sages
Ope our island's mystic pages,
And explain unto your Highness the wonders of our shore.

70 A fruitful teeming soil,
Where patient peasant's toil

191

ath the summer's sun and the watery winter sky —
Where they tend the golden grain
Till it bends upon the plain,
reap it for the stranger, and turn aside to die.

Where they watch their flocks increase,
And store the snowy fleece,
ey send it to their masters to be woven o'er the waves;
Where, having sent their meat
80   For the foreigner to eat,
Their mission is fulfilled, and they creep into their graves.

'Tis for this they are dying where the golden corn is growing,
'Tis for this they are dying where the crowded herds are
  lowing:
'Tis for this they are dying where the streams of life are
  flowing,
85 And they perish of the plague where the breeze of health is
  blowing.

A Very Old, Old Man

MARTIN MAC DERMOTT

'I must be very old' — I keep
Repeating o'er and o'er;
And yet, by the Bible page,
(Where my good father marked my age),
5   My years are twenty-four.
What, twenty-four! Life's sunny prime!
  Life's early Age of Gold!
When thoughts are warm, when hopes are bright
And hearts still bathed in young delight —
10   Ah no! *my* heart is cold.
  I must be very, very old —
   A very Old, Old Man.

They say my hairs are thick and brown —
  I *feel* them thin and grey;
15 They say my cheek — though pale — still bears
No furrowed trace of tears or cares —

I care not what they say.
Does my step totter? No, I pace
Erect and firm, and bold!
What then?— Deep underneath the lid
Of my strong heart, the worm is hid —
The worm that's keen and cold;
Ah, me! I must be very old —
A very Old, Old Man.

For why? The glad sun's genial rays
Fail to make my heart glad;
And strangely as a thing foregone
Striketh youth's soaring, joyous tone
Upon my soul so sad,
I love the night time more than day —
The night, with stars so cold;
And better quiet thought than mirth,
Though it were round a Christmas hearth
Where tales of love are told.
In sooth I must be very old —
A very Old, Old Man.

I know not now (I am so old)
How long it is ago,
But, sure, it must be very long!
Since I beheld a Nation, strong
In hope and valour grow.
Her voice was loud, her bearing proud,
And glorious to behold!
And now where is she? What is she?
A beggar upon bended knee,
A slave that's bought and sold!
Indeed, I must be very old —
A very Old, Old Man.

Besides, doth not the good God give
Life its appointed span?
Some more, some less, but still enow
To let sweet flowers and green grass grow
Upon the graves of man.
But I have seen death strike so fast
That churchyards could not hold —

Though torn into one yawning grave —
The remnants of the young, the brave,
The bright-eyed and the bold
I must be very, very old —
60   A very Old, Old Man.

The Famine in the Land

THOMAS D'ARCY MC GEE

Death reapeth in the fields of Life, and we cannot count the
    corpses;
Black and fast before our eyes march the busy biers and hearses;
In the laneways, and in highways, stark skeletons are lying, ✗
And daily unto Heaven their living kin are crying —
5   'Must the slave die for the tyrant — the sufferer for the sin —
And a wide, inhuman desert be, where Ireland has been;
Must the billows of oblivion over our hills be rolled,
And our Land be blotted out, like the accursed lands of old?'

Oh! hear it, friends of France —hear it, our cousin Spain,
10   Hear it, our kindly kith and kin across the western main —
Hear it, ye sons of Italy — let Turk and Russian hear it —
Hear Ireland's sentence registered, and see how we can bear it—
Our speech must be unspoken, our rights must be forgot;
Our land must be forsaken — submission is our lot —
15   We are beggars, we are cravens, and vengeful England feels
Us at her feet, and tramples us with both her iron heels.

These brothers of Gonsalvo, these cousins of the Cid —
They are Spaniels and not Spaniards, born but to be bid;
They of that Celtic war-race who made the storied rally
20   Against the Teuton lances in the lists of Roncesvalles —
They, kindred to the Mariner, whose soul's sublime devotion
Led his caravel like a star to a new world, through the Ocean.
No! No! they were begotten by fathers in their chains,
Whose valiant blood refused to flow along the vassal veins.

194

25   'Ho! Ho!' the Devils are merry in the farthest vaults of night,
        This England so out-Lucifers the prime arch-hypocrite;
        Friend of Peace, and friend of Freedom — yea, divine
            Religion's friend,
        She is feeding on our hearts like a sateless nether fiend —
        'Ho! Ho!' for the vultures are black on the four winds —
30   No purveyor like England that foul camp-following finds —
        Do you not mark them flitting between you and the sun?
        They are come to reap the booty, for the battle has been won.

        Lo! what other shape is this self-poised in the upper air,
        With wings like trailing comets, and face darker than despair?
35   See! See! the bright sun sickens into saffron in its shade,
        And the poles are shaken at their ends, infected and afraid —
        'Tis the Spirit of the Plague, and round and round the shore
        It circles on its course, shedding bane for evermore —
        And the slave falls for the tyrant, and the suff'rer for the sin
40   And a wide inhuman desert is, where Ireland has been.

        'Twas a vision — 'tis a fable — I did but tell my dream —
        Yet twice, yea thrice, I saw it, and still the same did seem.
        Ah! my soul is with this darkness, nightly, daily overcast —
        And I fear me, God permitting it, it may fall out true at last.
45   God permitting, man decreeing! What, and shall man so will,
        And our sealed lips be silent and our unbound hands be still?
        Shall we look upon our fathers, and our daughters, and our wives
        Slain, ravished, in our sight, and be paltering for our lives?

        Oh! countrymen and kindred, make yet another stand —
50   Plant your flag upon the common soil — be your motto,
            Life and Land!
        From the charnel shore of Cleena to the sea-bridge of the Giant
        Let the sleeping souls awake — the supine rise self-reliant —
        And arouse thee up, oh! City, that sits furrowed and in weeds
        Fair and pallid as a Sphinx o'erthrown amid the sad Nile's
            reeds—
55   Up, Mononia, land of heroes, and bounteous mother of song —
        And Connaught, like thy rivers, come unto us swift and strong.
        Oh! countrymen and kindred, make yet another stand —
        Plant your flag upon the common soil — be your motto, Life
            and Land!

A Harvest Hymn

THOMAS D'ARCY MC GEE

God has been bountiful! Garlands of gladness
Grow by the wayside exorcising sadness,
Shedding their bloom on the pale cheek of slavery,
Holding out plumes for the helmets of bravery,
5   Birds in them singing this sanctified stave —
'God has been Bountiful — Man must be Brave!'

Look on this harvest of plenty and promise —
Shall we sleep while the enemy snatches it from us?
See where the sun on the golden grain sparkles!
10   Look where behind it the pauper's home darkles!
Hark the cry ringing out — 'Save us, oh save!
God has been Bountiful — Man must be Brave!'

From the shore of the ocean, and farther and hither,
Where the victims of famine and pestilence wither,
15   Lustreless eyes stare at the pitying Heaven,
Arms, black, unburied, appeal to the levin —
Voices unceasing shout over each wave —
God has been Bountiful — Man must be Brave.

Would ye live happily, fear not nor falter —
20   Peace sits on the summit of Liberty's altar;
Would ye have honour — Honour was ever
The prize of the hero-like death-scorning Liver;
Would ye have glory! She knows not the slave.
God has been Bountiful, you must be Brave!

25   Swear by the bright streams abundantly flowing,
Swear by the hearths where wet weeds are growing,
By the Stars and the Earth, and the four winds of Heaven,
That the Land shall be saved, and its tyrants outdriven.
Do it! and blessings will shelter your grave.
30   God has been Bountiful — will ye be Brave?

The Living and the Dead

THOMAS D'ARCY MC GEE

Bright is the springtime, Erin, green and gay to see;
But my heart is heavy, Erin, with thoughts of thy sons and
    thee—
Thinking of your dead men lying thick as grass new mown —
Thinking of your myriads dying, unnoted and unknown —
5   Thinking of your yeoman flying, beyond the impassable waves,
And to think of your magnates sighing and stifling their
    thoughts, like slaves.

Oh! for the time, dear Erin — the fierce time long ago,
When your men felt, sad Erin, and their hands could strike a
    blow!
When your Gaelic Chiefs were ready to stand in pass or
    breach —
10   Danger but made them steady — they struck and saved their
    speech.
But where are the men to head ye, and lead your face to face —
To trample the powers that tread ye, men of the fallen race?

The corn and wheat, oh! Erin, wave green along the plain;
But where are the hands, dear Erin, to gather in the grain?
15   The sinewy man is sleeping in the crowded churchyard near,
And his young wife is keeping lonesome company there;
His brother shoreward creeping, has begged his way abroad,
And his sister — tho', for weeping, she scarce could see the
    road.

No other nation, Erin, but only you would bear
20   A yoke like yours, oh! Erin, a month, not to say a year;
And will you bear for ever, writhing and sighing sore,
Nor learn — learn now, or never, to dare, not to deplore —
Learn to join in one endeavour your creeds and people all —
So only can you sever your tyrants' iron thrall.

25   Then call your people, Erin — call with a prophet's cry —
Bid them link in union, Erin, and do like men, or die —
Bid the hind from the loamy valley, the miller from the fall —
Bid the craftsman from his alley, the lord from his lordly hall —
Bid the old and the young man rally, and trust to work, not
    words —
30   And thenceforth ever shall ye be free as the forest birds.

The Three Dreams

THOMAS D'ARCY MC GEE

Borne on the wheel of night, I lay
 And dream'd as it softly sped —
Toward the shadowy hour that spans the way
 Whence spirits come, 'tis said:
And my dreams were three; —
 The first and worst
 Was of a land alive, yet 'cursed,
 That burn'd in bonds it couldn't burst —
And thou wert the land, Erie!

A starless landscape came
 'Twixt that scene and my aching sight,
And anon two spires of flame
 Arose on my left and right;
And a warrior throng
 Were marching along,
 Timing their tramp to a battle song,
 And I felt my heart from their zeal take fire,
But, ah! my dream fled as that host grew nigher!

Next, methought I woke, and walk'd alone
 On a causeway all with grass o'ergrown,
That led to ranks of ruins wan,
 Where echo'd no voice or step or man;
Deadly still was the heavy air,
 Horrible silence was everywhere —
 No human thing, no beast, no bird
 In the dread Death-land sung or stirred:
Saint Patrick's image up in a nook
Held in its hand a Prophecy Book,
And its mystic lines were made plain to me,
And they spoke thy destiny, loved Erie!

The skene and the sparthe,
The lament for the dearth,
The voice of all mirth,
Shall be hush'd on thy hearth,
 O Erie!
And your children shall want earth

When they bury!
Till Tanist and Kerne
Their past evils unlearn,
40 And in penitence turn
To their Father in Heaven;
Then shall wisdom and light,
Then manhood and might,
And their land and their right
45 To the sons of Milesius be given.
But never till then —
'Till they make themselves men —
Can the chains of their bondage be riven!

The Woeful Winter:
Suggested by Accounts of Ireland in December 1848

THOMAS D'ARCY MC GEE

They are flying, like northern birds over the sea for fear,
They cannot abide in their own green land, they seek a resting
here;
Oh! wherefore are they flying, is it from the front of war,
Or have they smelt the Asian plague the winds waft from afar?

5 No! they are flying, flying, from a land where men are sheep,
Where sworded shepherds herd and slay the silly crew they
keep;
Where so much iron hath pass'd into the souls of the long
enslaved,
That none was found by fort or field, or in Champion's right
hand waved.

Yea! they are flying hither, breathless and pale with fear,
10 And it not the sailing time for ships, but winter, dark and drear;
They had rather face the waters, dark as the frown of God,
Than make a stand for race and land on their own elastic sod.

Oh! blood of Brian, forgive them! oh, bones of Owen, rest!
Oh, spirits of our brave fathers, turn away your eyes from the
West!

15   Look back on the track of the galleys that with the soldiers came —
          Look! look to the ships of Tyre, moor'd in the ports of Spain.

          But look not on, dread fathers! look not on the shore
          Where valour's spear and victory's horn were sacred signs of
               yore.
          Look not toward the hill of Tara, or Iveagh, or Ailech high!
20   Look toward the East and blind your sight for they fly at last,
               they fly!

          And ye who met the Romans behind the double wall,
          And ye who smote the Saxons as mallet striketh ball,
          And ye who shelter'd Harold and Bruce — fittest hosts for the
               brave —
          Why do you not join your spirit-strength, and bury her in the
               waves?

25   Alas! alas! for Ireland, so many tears were shed,
          That the Celtic blood runs palely, that once was winy red!
          They are flying, flying from her, the holy and the old,
          Oh, the land has alter'd little, but the men are cowed and cold.

          Yea! they are flying hither, breathless and pale with fear,
30   And it not the sailing-time for ships, but winter dark and drear;
          They had rather face the waters, dark as the frown of God,
          Than make a stand for race and land, on their own elastic sod.

Patrick's Day, 1847

MIRO

It is our own lov'd Patrick's day, and, glory be to God,
The sun is bright, the breeze is fresh, and green the shamrock
     sod;
The churches ring their holy peals that call to sacrifice,
And fervent souls the altars seek where prayer and incense rise;
5   But o'er the face of young and old whom I have met today
There hangs a cloud of settled grief, whose low'ring seems to
     say,
Where are the hearts so fond and true that made this festal smile?
Oh! Answer them, ye grassless graves, thick strewn throughout
     the isle.

I've heard the drunken revel's voice that cursed the peaceful
    hearth —
10   I've seen the blessed banner wave that told of sober mirth;
And yet a sight more glorious still that time won't wear away —
I've seen the strength of Ireland in one proud calm array,
And heard the booming cheer that from a million voices went!
Oh! how its thunder rent the clouds and shook the firmament!
15   To-day there is no sound of joy — no keen above the dead;
One faint despairing wail is heard — it is the cry for bread.

Like other years, our Island Saint has brought the bounding
    spring —
Like other years, the 'passage birds' shall come on gladsome
    wing —
The cuckoo's voice, distinct and soft, shall pierce the deep
    wood through,
20   But none shall watch its earliest tone, as they were wont to do;
The creak may sound his jarring note, from ev'ry danger freed—
There are no laughing children now to chase him through the
    mead;
No! — child and matron, man and maid, are hastening on to
    death,
The victims of black famine, or fever's burning breath.

25   Our Island Saint! — our glorious Saint! — oh! lift thy hands
    on high,
And pray for us, thy children, who in thousands daily die;
And if the woe be still to last, and if the autumn sun
Shall see no other harvest home but what the grave has won,
Obtain for us at Mercy's throne that, as we sink in death,
30   We still shall raise our hearts to Heaven in love and living faith—
We still shall bow submissively beneath the scourging rod,
And still shall pray our Father's prayer, of 'Glory be to God!'

Pro and Con

MIRO

There is a curse upon us; everywhere
      'Tis visible — the green, far-noted soil —
Fat in its nature, by sun, show'r, and air,
Cherished alike — yields to our heart-spent toil
5   No recompense, save for its foreign lord—
A blasted crop the toilers' sole reward.

Of want we die in millions, yet too slow
      We give to earth its marrowless manure.
A plague comes for dispatch. This eastern woe
10   Befits the iron harness we endure —
And if, with saving blood, one hand be red,
'Tis his who robs and eats the people's bread.

We have our exports, too — the strong and fair,
      Now weak and worn, crowd departing decks,
15   Or die in holds for want of common air,
Or sink like ballast with unheeded wrecks,
While *their own land* — their father's land of old —
Is speculation meet for Cockney gold.

Do some stand up to tell the world that they
20   Will not, like helots, yield to wrongs so fell —
They're blasted like our harvest — not a day
Of theirs, worth naming, history can tell;
Failing — they seek to die in Europe's face;
In vain — they're hulked and chained by special grace.

25   You ask, what aggravation can there be,
      Of murders manifold like these — and I
Say 'tis to drive the car of victory,
Clogg'd in our gore, across us as we die—
To find among us starving serfs who reel
30   To fling themselves beneath its carnaged wheel.

There *is* a curse upon us! Know ye, then,
      Whence, and what is it? Heav'n is merciful:
Talk not of blighted harvests, blighted men,
Of plague or exile, hunger or misrule;
35   These are effects thrown up to show an evil
As deep as hell, and black as hell's worst devil.

If GOD chastises us, ours, alone, the fault;
    If bad men slaughter, charge it not on GOD —
'Twere blasphemy. Our only hope of aught
40   Is in the great Omnipotent, whose rod
Can smite the proud, the guilty, crumble thrones,
And call up sinewy men from withered bones.

The curse is from ourselves; 'tis murderous strife,
    Fostered among us seven hundred years,
45   That slays the brother, father, sister, wife —
Grows fat on misery — quaffs down blood and tears;
That poisons and betrays, bullies, lies,
And cares for nought but human sacrifice.

We kill each other. Irish *blood*, on high,
50   Cries out 'gainst Irish *men* from ev'ry hill,
And hell gloats over it, and angels sigh,
And dogs may lap it till they have their fill —
While ruthless fiends, in human shape disguised,
Clutch fast the soil thus squandered — fertilised.

55   Men! Let this cease — beg, council it, command —
    For CHRIST'S deep love, who suffered for us all,
Be sure no curse from GOD'S avenging hand,
Or man's seared heart, shall longer on us fall.
Oh, Christians! let us kneel before heav'n's throne,
Embrace, forgive — the land is then our own.

Famine and Exportation
JOHN O'HAGAN

Take it from us, every grain,
We were made for you to drain;
Black starvation let us feel,
England must not want a meal!

5   When our rotting roots shall fail,
When the hunger pangs assail,
Ye'll have of Irish corn your fill —
We'll have grass and nettles still!

We are poor, and ye are rich;
10 Mind it not, were every ditch
Strewn in Spring with famished corpses,
Take our oats to feed your horses!

Heaven, that tempers ill with good,
When it smote our wonted food,
15 Sent us bounteous growth of grain —
Sent to pauper slaves, in vain!

We but asked in deadly need:
'Ye that rule us! Let us feed
On the food that's ours' — behold!
20 Adder deaf and icy cold.

Were we Russians, thralls from birth,
In a time of winter dearth
Would a Russian despot see
From his land its produce flee?

25 Were we black Virginian slaves,
Bound and bruised with thongs and staves,
Avarice and selfish dread
Would not let us die unfed.

Were we, Saints of Heaven! were we
30 How we burn to think it — FREE!
Not a grain should leave our shore,
Not for England's golden store.

They who hunger where it grew —
They whom Heaven had sent it to —
35 They who reared with sweat of brow —
They or *none* should have it now.

Lord that made us! What it is
To endure a lot like this!
Powerless in our worst distress,
40 Cramped by alien selfishness!

Not amongst our rulers all,
One true heart whereon to call;

Vainly still we turn to them
Who despoil us and contemn.

45   Forced to see them, day by day,
Snatch our sole resource away;
If returned a pittance be —
Alms, 'tis named, and *beggars*, we.

Lord! thy guiding wisdom grant,
50   Fearful counsellor is WANT;
Burning thoughts will rise within,
Keep us pure from stain of sin!

But, at least, like trumpet blast,
Let it rouse us all at last;
55   Ye who cling to England's side!
Here and *now*, you see her tried.

The Battle of Antioch

JOHN THOMAS ROWLAND

'Twas in the holy Crusade long ago
    That Antioch city fell —
Betrayed to midnight massacre and spoil —
    Save a strong citadel,
5   That on a northern peak defied the power
    Of half a million men.
Thence o'er th' Orontes look'd, and look'd again,
Each Infidel for help — and not in vain —
    Soon came the Saracen.

10   Keerboga, favorite of the Kalif, came
    With his bright banners spread;
Long lances glistening in the noon-day sun
    Over each turbaned head;
War-horses neighed — the beasts of burden groan'd
15   Beneath their load of bread,

And broad pavilions, rang'd in showy line,
Adorned with all the arts of Palestine,
    Echoed the martial tread.

Whilst plunder rioted within the walls,
20   The enemy without
Extends his lines around the captured town;
    And when the piercing shout
Of some poor pagan reach'd their ears, they curst
    The Christian fanatics,
25 Who deem'd their war an incense sweet to God
Arising from each broken heart they trod,
    From blood of heretics!

Folly hath its destruction in itself.
    The Soldiers of the Cross
30 Expended soon, in waste, all proper food,
    And felt their direful loss
As feels the drunkard, when the wine has left
    And aching pain behind,
Gnawing his vitals. O, the horrid fate
35 Of those pent up in famine desolate!
    There was no corn to grind —

No beasts to slay — the horses all had served
    The table of the chiefs;
All noisome animals supplied their wants.
40   Who can recount their griefs?
Those looks that once breath'd love now terrified —
    Friendships had ceased to be;
And skeletons gaunt, the spectre of Want,
Stalked through the streets with unearthly chant,
45   A saddening sight to see.

And ever from the walls of Antioch
    The Latins saw their foes
Enjoying all the luxuries of life —
    All that could yield repose,
50 Flaunted the silken roof'd Seraglio:
    The very breezes bore,
To starving men, such incense from the feast
As would have forced the most religious priest
    To keep his fast no more.

55	And day by day the soldier's martial eye
	Retired beneath his brow;
	Night after night such visions came to him
	As were a mockery now,
	Of battles fought, and wassail glee, and Fame
60	Wreathing her chaplets rare,
	All dreams! The morning flash'd upon a sight
	Of dying men, and universal blight;
	Starvation everywhere!

Then, as it were by famine purified
     Men 'gan to see strange sights
Of Paradise, and angels radiantly
     Surrounded by rich lights,
Such as the morning throws upon the sea.
     The saints appeared on high,
And beckoned to the way of Victory —
'Till all exclaimed a battle fought should be:
     'Twere sweet even thus to die!

A Clerke had seen a vision. 'Twas a Lance
     Sacred by impious use:
That which the soldier pierced our SAVIOUR with:
     And RAYMOND of Toulouse
Vouch'd for the holiness and truth of him
     That thus revealed the sign:
Nor was the vision void. The Lance was found
Deep in a grave beneath a sacred mound,
     The troops form'd into line.

A Bishop bore the relic o'er the host
     Of starved men, that now
Issued with desperate valour from the gates —
     Urged on by holy vow:
And from the mountain tops were seen descend
     Warriors clothed in white,
Such as Earth never saw before. There rose
The cry, 'God wills it!' till their startled foes
     Quaked in the deadly fight.

There died that day, of Persian Infidels,
     Sixty-nine thousand men.

Laden with spoils, the conquerors returned
Within the town agen [*sic*].
95   Never was battle better waged on earth.
Thus starving men can fight:
Nor all the allied powers of earth and hell
The righteous struggle ever yet could quell,
Who feel they arm for Right.

The Leaves Are Blighted

JOHN THOMAS ROWLAND

Air — 'The Wild Geese'

Now the leaves are blighted,
O'er the land benighted,
Trampled on and slighted
    Flow'rs bestrew the vale,
5   Youth and age are weeping,
Foes are never sleeping,
Death (great harvest reaping)
    Loads the peasant's wail,
Every strength decaying,
10   Still for mercy foraying —
O! the old praying
    In the hated Pale.

Foes were thickly falling,
Or in servile crawling,
15   Were for mercy calling —
    On the proud Ard Righ.
Once the southern flowers
Adorned my queenly bowers,
Now the Gallic powers
20   Fell'd and withered lie.
Friendly words that charm'd me,
Spainish wine that warm'd me,
Gallant hearts that arm'd me,
    Oh, that all should die!

25   See you peasant standing,
                Beggars alms demanding;
                Once his brow commanding
                      Had no mark of woe.
                Not by fate surrounded,
30   Nor by sorrow bounded,
                Nor in battle wounded
                      Nobly by the foe;
                Safe from fire and ocean,
                Tossed by no commotion,
35   Hunger's bitter potion
                      Strikes the fated blow!

                Winter draweth nigher;
                Chill'd is each desire;
                Hope will soon expire
40   In my darling child.
                Give him consolation;
                Raise the fallen nation;
                Freedom brings salvation,
                    Let each chain be fil'd
45   Or rudely snapped asunder;
                    Oh, for mountain thunder!
                Oh, for magic wonder!
                    Be no longer mild.

                Deadly provocation
50   Stings my ancient nation.
                Up. Each to his station.
                    Guard the passes well.
                North and South, awaken!
                Haste. Your stand be taken.
55   East and West are shaken
                    Like a warning bell.
                Hark! the murmur spreading,
                Angry hosts are treading,
                Foeman's blood is shedding.
60   Loud the tyrant's knell.

                Grief from me is flying;
                No more I hear the crying
                Of my children lying

<pre>
           In a deep despair.
65   Leaves on trees are coming
           Bees are sweetly humming,
           Glorious is the summing
              Of the heroes there!
           Lo, the hills are blazing
70   See my banner's raising,
           Worth all poet's praises,
              Is the joy I bear.
</pre>

'Tis Evening Now

JOHN THOMAS ROWLAND

'Tis evening now in fair Ireland; upon a hill I stand,
Beneath me rolls the murmuring tide upon the shelly strand,
Basaltic rocks rise, pillar-like, to meet the wondrous sea
That in its space, and depth profound, emblems eternity.

5   The sun is hiding in the waves as he would penetrate
The ocean caves o'er which his beams a sea of gold create;
But not into the old sea-halls, for all the mermaids there,
Will he descend, though Neptune's hosts the fatal wish might
    dare.

Since morning he has travelled, o'er fair lands and cities high,
10   Where men are slaves and nature's gifts drop fruitless from the sky;
The sun is sick of blasted scenes of famine-stricken bands,
He goes to visit other zones — to garnish other lands.

He never stays his onward course: perfection needs no rest;
While now, departing from our shores, he's rising *in the west*;
15   There manly hearts receive his rays and glow with living fire.
How pale the twilight on our shores! How soon may hope
    expire!

'Tis long since on this olden land the fires have all gone out;
In shrines and hearts the embers sleep. What are the priests
    about?
Unwatchful priests — in other times you served your altars well:
20   Why are those altars broken down in forest, mount, and dell?

Great fire of Greedan, kindle in our hearts thy lightning flame;
Great God of light; illuminate, and bless the Celtic name;
Ye powers of strength make strong our arms to battle for the
    right!
Oh! what a joy is morn to him that watches through the night:

25   What joy to see the early sun with saffron hues arise.
The glory of the universe — the monarch of the skies!
Away fly mists: the dull grey clouds are chang'd to liquid gold;
No fairer sight on earth is seen; — 'tis heaven o'er earth
    unroll'd.
But dearer far to gods above, and brave men on the earth,
30   The first faint light of Freedom, when it startles into birth;
'Tis this when into glory spread that makes the world look
    bright;
Then moral mists, and darker gloom, take instantaneous flight.

Cry out, ye sleepless watchmen — cry out the hour of morn;
Already is the mantle broad of right to flutters torn!
35   I see the true light glimmer through the rents of broken clouds;
Come — climb the ark of liberty — we'll watch it from the
    shrouds.

The Famished Land

C.S.

Hark to the sound!
    Without a trump, without a drum,
The wild-eyed hungry millions come,
    Along the echoing ground.

5   From cellar and cave, from street and lane,
Each from his separate place of pain,
    In a blackening stream,
Come sick and lame, and old and poor,
And all who can no more endure;
10   Like a demon's dream!

211

Starved children with their pauper sire,
And labourers with their front of fire,
   In an angry hum;
And felons hunted to their den,
15   And all who share the name of men,
   By myriads come.

The good, the bad, come hand in hand,
Linked by that law which none withstand;
   And at their head,
20   Flaps no proud banner, flaunting high,
But a shout, sent upwards to the sky,
   Of *Bread! — Bread!*

That word their ensign — That the cause
Which bid them burst their social laws,
25   In wrath, in pain!
That the sole boon for lives of toil,
Demand they from their natural soil!
   Oh, not in vain!

One single year, and some who now
30   Come forth, with oaths and haggard brow
   Read prayers and psalm,
In quiet homes; their sole desire,
Rude comforts near their cottage fire,
   And Sabbath calm.

35   But Hunger is an evil foe:
It striketh Truth and Virtue low,
   And pride elate.
Wild Hunger, stripped of hope and fear!
It doth not weight, it will not hear,
40   It cannot wait.

For mark, what comes! — To-night the poor
(All mad) may burst the rich man's door,
   Till wine run
In floods, and rafters blazing bright
45   Will paint the sky with crimson light,
   Fierce as the sun!

And plate carved round with quaint device
And cups all gold will melt, like ice
    In Indian heat!
And queenly silks from foreign lands
50   Will bear the stamps of bloody hands,
    And trampling feet!

And Murder, from his hideous den,
Will come abroad and talk to men,
    'Till creatures born
55   For good (whose hearts kind pity nursed)
Will act the direst crimes they cursed
    But yester-morn.

Advice

AN ULSTERMAN

Listless sons of dark Ierne
    Brood still calmly o'er your wrongs;
Erin's patient daughters mourn ye!
    Plaint and wail beseem your songs.

5   Wail ye! wail for millions starving;
    Ay, and wail for millions dead —
But leave rampant lords carving
    Of those millions rightful bread.

Never dare to raise your voices —
10   Never dare to raise a hand
While ramp luxury rejoices
    On the fat things of your land.

Toil, and starve, and die 'in order',
    Nor give pain to lordly ears;
15   Lowly mourn the wholesome murder
    That has roused your dastard fears.

Lowly, mourn, not think of action;
    Or, ye craven sordid slaves,
Join the idiot wars of faction —
20   Flash your venom, not your glaives.

213

Recreant serfs! ye lauded Mitchel's
    Davis', Meagher's, Duffy's lore —
Who tried, 'mid eager, lab'ring vigils,
    To rouse ye 'gainst the thrall ye bore.

25   While ye lauded, while ye flouted
    With grov'ling passions wild extremes;
Ye cheer'd and hiss'd, confirmed and doubted,
    Shrunk and dispell'd their noblest dreams.

Traitors! 'dark ships' are on the ocean,
30   There hearts, once proud and daring pine;
Had you display'd time, stern devotion,
    No 'Felon' yet had crossed the brine.

Traitors! true hearts still labour near you;
    While you — and yes! you labour, too.
35   Pour soulless worms, 'twere vain to cheer you —
    Alas! you'd rather die than do.

Plod on, poor toil worn, peaceful dastards,
    The rights of property respect the while:
Nor question why proud, 'high-born' bastards
40   Hunt starving menials off their soil.

Bow your necks, ye hungry varlets,
    Meekly ply your supple knees,
Toil — to surfeit lordling's harlots,
    Die — pert statesmen's whines to please.

Our Welcome

ELIZABETH WILLOUGHBY VARIAN

We dare not bid thee welcome, to ourselves and Ireland true;
Ungrudgingly, we freely yield the homage that is due:
For love, unbounded gratitude, for hatred, bitter scorn,
For every gift of good or ill, a just and fair return.

5   They mocked thee with their sophistry who bid thee pause to hear
The paeans of the plundered slaves, meet music for thine ear;

Was there not one amid that band who dared the truth disclose?
That not for thee, but for thy pomp, the people's shouts arose.

Doubtless it was a goodly sight to see thy vessel's prow
10 Speed through the gleaming path of foam, a proud and gallant
        show.
And England's crimson banner, as it floated from the lea,
In honour of the captive host, lowered to the very sea!

Aye, 'twas a goodly sight to see the captive nation bow
Before the jewelled sceptre and the crown upon thy brow:
15 Offering the heart's vain homage to the glittering array
Of courtly knights, and gentle dames, the actors of the play!

We dare not bid thee welcome! hark to that mad appeal, —
Our brothers' blood for vengeance calls, whilst we ignobly
        kneel.
'Twere fitting work for rugged hand to strew with flowers thy
        way
20 And tattered rags would well befit a nation's holiday!

Hark! to the famine cries, the shrieks of stalwart men struck
        down,
Crushed in their manhood's noble prime, in all their fair renown;
Thy helpless sister's wailing the moan of infancy!
Then ask thy conscience, lady, what welcome waits for thee?

25 Hark! o'er the thunders crashing, across the stormy main,
It comes — oh, God! I know *that* sound, the clanking of a chain.
We swear before high heaven, until the martyr's free,
Free on the soil that gave him birth, no welcome waits for thee!

Must *thou* obey the savage will of men, so lost to shame?
30 They plot and scheme, like dastard knaves, and murder in thy
        name;
If crime, in all its blackest dyes, a royal robe may screen,
This is to be undoubtedly a *slave*, and not a queen!

A slave? ah, worse than slavery, to fashion thought and speech
To suit their base designs who dare the tyrant's creed to preach!
35 What are thy glittering baubles, the gems on breast and brow,
That we before their brilliant rays in mock obeisance bow?

No doubt it was a gallant sight to see thy fleet ship glide,
Fast through the opening waters, in all her stately pride;
But a nobler sight awaits us, and a welcome, warm and free,
For the convict-ship, and felon band — no welcome waits for thee!

Come, if thou wilt, or stay, to us, to ours it is the same —
No hand is raised to bless or curse, no tongue shall praise or
    blame;
It were a venal deed in us, too abject, base, and mean,
To swell the chorus of the slaves, and shout God save the
    Queen!

40

Proselytizing

ELIZABETH WILLOUGHBY VARIAN

Poor lonely wanderers! wherefore do ye pause
Before the rich man's dwelling? will your woes
Avail to move his pity, or to touch
One chord of feeling in his hardened heart?
What care he for the worn and pallid face,
The fleshless arm, the weary bleeding feet,
That thus ye plead, with untaught eloquence,
The cause of suffering virtue? What to him
The lips so blenched by hunger's awful power,
Or the strained glance of love and agony,
As the dim eyes regard each other's woes?
And even the wail of childhood dies away
Without an echo in his pulseless heart.

Again the knee is bent, the outstretched hands
Are wildly clasped, the starting eye-ball glares,
And, with a fearful strength, the mother's cry
Ascends to heaven — 'Oh! give us food, or else
We perish! give us from the store
Which God hath lent to thee, or we must die!'
The bowed head sinks yet lower, for no hand
Is stretched to aid her, but the tyrant's voice
Falls like a weight upon her tortured ear: —
'Thou shalt have food, but first thou most renounce
Thy erring faith, and yield these children up

25   To the pure guidance of our holy church;
           Thou must forsake the dark and fearful creed
           To which thy fathers clung. Now, answer me?'
           And he was answered by the flashing eye,
           The quivering lip, and burning cheek and brow:
30   The drooping head was proudly raised, and scorn
           And stern defiance gave those lips a voice: —
           'Keep thou thy proffered help, we will not crave
           A pittance at thy door, we will not stain
           Our souls with poisoned food — for what is death
35   That we should fear him? Death! our only friend,
           The messenger which bids us hasten home.
           Is not this outraged land one burial-place?
           And we who tread amidst our kindred's graves
           But long to share their rest.' She turned away,
40   And, crawling from the spot, lay down to die;
           And soon *that* door was opened unto her
           Where tyrant foot shall never enter in!

The Enigma

LADY WILDE

Pale victims, where is your Fatherland?
Where oppression is law from age to age,
Where the death-plague, and hunger, and misery rage,
And tyrants a godless warfare wage
5   'Gainst the holiest rights of an ancient land.

Where the corn waves green on the fair hillside,
But each sheaf by the serfs and slavelings tied
Is taken to pamper a foreigner's pride —
      There is our suffering Fatherland.

10 Where broad rivers flow 'neath a glorious sky,
And the valleys like gems of emerald lie;
Yet, the young men, and strong men, starve and die,
      For want of bread in their own rich land.

And we pile up the corses, heap on heap,
15 While the pale mothers faint, and the children weep;

217

Yet, the living might envy the dead their sleep,
    So bitter is life in that mourning land.

Oh! Heaven ne'er looked on a sadder scene;
Earth shuddered to hear that such woe had been;
Then we prayed, in despair, to a foreign queen,
    For leave to live on our own fair land.

We have wept till our faces are pale and wan;
We have knelt to a throne till our strength is gone;
We prayed to our masters, but, one by one,
    They laughed to scorn our suffering land;

And sent forth their minions, with cannon and steel,
Swearing with fierce, unholy zeal,
To trample us down with an iron heel,
    If we dared but to murmur our just demand. —
    Know ye not now our Fatherland?

    What! are there no MEN in your Fatherland,
To confront the tyrant's stormy glare,
With a scorn as deep as the wrongs ye bear,
With defiance as fierce as the oaths they sware,
With vengeance as wild as the cries of despair,
    That rise from your suffering Fatherland?

    Are there no SWORDS in your Fatherland,
To smite down the proud, insulting foe,
With the strength of despair give blow for blow
Till the blood of the baffled murderers flow
    On the trampled soil of your outraged land?

Are your right arms weak in that land of slaves,
That ye stand by your murdered brothers' graves,
Yet tremble like coward and crouching knaves,
    To strike for freedom and Fatherland?

    Oh! had ye faith in your Fatherland,
    In God, your Cause, and your own right hand,
Ye would go forth as saints to the holy fight,
Go in the strength of eternal right,
Go in the conquering Godhead's might —
    And save or AVENGE your Fatherland!

The Exodus

LADY WILDE

'A million a decade!' Calmly and cold
    The units are read by our statesmen sage;
Little they think of a Nation old,
    Fading away from History's page;
5
        Outcast weeds by a desolate sea —
        Fallen leaves of Humanity.

'A million a decade!' — of human wrecks,
    Corpses lying in fever sheds —
Corpses huddled on foundering decks,
10
    And shroudless dead on their rocky beds;
        Nerve and muscle, and heart and brain,
        Lost to Ireland — lost in vain.

'A million a decade!' Count ten by ten,
    Column and line of the record fair;
15
Each unit stands for ten thousand men,
    Staring with blank, dead eyeballs there;
        Strewn like blasted trees on the sod,
        Men that were made in the image of God.

'A million a decade!' — and nothing done;
20
    The Caesars had less to conquer a world;
And the war for the Right not yet begun,
    The banner of Freedom not yet unfurled:
The soil is fed by the weed that dies;
    If forest leaves fall, yet they fertilise.

25
But ye — dead, dead, not climbing the height,
    Not clearing a path for the future to tread;
Not opening the golden portals of light,
    Ere the gate was choked by your piled-up dead:
        Martyrs ye, yet never a name
30
        Shines on the golden roll of Fame.

Had ye rent one gyve of the festering chain,
    Strangling the life of the Nation's soul;
Poured your life blood by river and plain,
    Yet touched with your dead hand Freedom's goal;

35   Left of heroes one footprint more
     On our soil, tho' stamped in your gore —

   We could triumph while mourning the brave,
     Dead for all that was holy and just,
   And write, through our tears, on the grave,
40   As we flung down the dust to dust —
       'They died for their country, but led
       Her up from the sleep of the dead.'

   'A million a decade!' What does it mean?
     A Nation dying of inner decay —
45   A churchyard silence where life has been —
     The base of the pyramid crumbling away:
       A drift of men gone over the sea,
       A drift of the dead where men should be.

   Was it for this ye plighted your word,
50   Crowned and crownless rulers of men?
   Have ye kept faith with your crucified Lord,
     And fed His sheep till He comes again?
       Or fled like hireling shepherds away,
       Leaving the fold the gaunt wolf's prey?

55   Have ye given of your purple to cover,
     Have ye given of your gold to cheer,
   Have ye given of your love, as a lover
     Might cherish the bride he held dear,
       Broken the Sacrament-bread to feed
60   Souls and bodies in uttermost need?

   Ye stand at the Judgement-bar to-day —
     The angels are counting the dead-roll, too;
   Have ye trod in pure and perfect way,
     And ruled for God as the crowned should do?
65   Count our dead — before Angels and Men,
       Ye're judged and doomed by the Statist's pen.

The Famine Year (The Stricken Land)

LADY WILDE

Weary men, what reap ye? — Golden corn for the stranger.
What sow ye? — Human corses that wait for the avenger.
Fainting forms, hunger-stricken, what see you in the offing?
Stately ships to bear our food away, amid the stranger's scoffing.
5   There's a proud array of soldiers — what do they round your door?
They guard our masters' granaries from the thin hands of the
      poor.
Pale mothers, wherefore weeping — Would to God that we
     were dead;
Our children swoon before us, and we cannot give them bread.

Little children, tears are strange upon your infant faces,
10   God meant you but to smile within your mother's soft embraces.
Oh! we know not what is smiling, and we know not what is
     dying;
We're hungry, very hungry, and we cannot stop our crying.
And some of us grow cold and white — we know not what it
     means;
But, as they lie beside us, we tremble in our dreams.
15   There's a gaunt crowd on the highway — are ye come to pray to
     man,
With hollow eyes that cannot weep, and for words your faces
     wan?

No; the blood is dead within our veins — we care not now for
     life;
Let us die hid in the ditches, far from children and from wife;
We cannot stay and listen to their raving, famished cries —
20   Bread! Bread! Bread! and none to still their agonies.
We left our infants playing with their dead mother's hand:
We left our maidens maddened by the fever's scorching brand:
Better, maiden, thou were strangled in thy own dark-twisted
     tresses —
Better, infant, thou wert smothered in thy mother's first caresses.

25   We are fainting in our misery, but God will hear our groan:
Yet, if fellow-men desert us, will He hearken from His Throne?
Accursed are we in our own land, yet toil we still and toil;
But the stranger reaps our harvest — the alien owns our soil.

O Christ! how have we sinned, that on our native plains
30   We perish houseless, naked, starved, with branded brow,
        like Cain's?
Dying, dying wearily, with a torture sure and slow —
Dying, as a dog would die, by the wayside as we go.

One by one they're falling round us, their pale faces to the sky;
We've no strength left to dig them graves — there let them lie.
35   The wild bird, if he's stricken, is mourned by the others,
But we — we die in Christian land — we die amid our brothers,
In the land which God has given, like a wild beast in his cave,
Without a tear, a prayer, a shroud, a coffin or a grave.
Ha! but think ye the contortions on each livid face ye see,
40   Will not be read on judgement-day by eyes of Deity?

We are wretches, famished, scorned, human tools to build your
      pride,
But God will yet take vengeance for the souls for whom Christ
      died.
Now is your hour of pleasure — bask ye in the world's caress;
But our whitening bones against ye will rise as witnesses,
45   From the cabins and the ditches, in their charred, uncoffin'd
      masses,
For the Angel of the Trumpet will know them as he passes.
A ghastly, spectral army, before the great God we'll stand,
And arraign ye as our murderers, the spoilers of our land.

Foreshadowings

LADY WILDE

Oremus! Oremus! Look down on us, Father!
Like visions of Patmos Thy last judgements gather;
The angels of doom, in bright, terrible beauty,
Rise up from their thrones to fulfil their stern duty.
5   Woe to us, woe! the thunders have spoken,
The first of the mystical seals hath been broken.

Through the cleft thunder-cloud the weird coursers are rushing—
Their hoofs will strike deep in the hearts they are crushing;

And the crown'd and the proud of the old kingly races
10   Fall down at the vision, like stars from their places:
Oremus! Oremus! The pale earth is heark'ning;
Already the spirit-steeds round us are dark'ning.

With crown and with bow, on his white steed immortal,
The Angel of Wrath passes first through the portal;
15   But faces grow paler, and hush'd is earth's laughter,
When on pale steed comes the Plague Spirit after.
Oremus! Oremus! His poison-breath slayeth;
The red will soon fade from each bright lip that prayeth.

Now, with nostrils dilated and thunder hoofs crashing,
20   On rushes the war-steed, his lurid eyes flashing;
There is blood on the track where his long mane is streaming,
There is death where the sword of his rider is gleaming.
Woe to the lands where that red steed is flying!
There tyrants are warring, and heroes are dying.

25   Oh! the golden-hair'd children reck not but their playing,
Thro' the rich fields of corn with their young mothers straying;
And the strong-hearted men, with their muscles of iron,
What reck they of ills that their pathway environ?
There's a tramp like a knell — a cold shadow gloometh —
30   Woe! 'tis the black steed of Famine that cometh.

At the breath of its rider the green earth is blasted,
And childhood's frail form droops down pallid, and wasted;
The soft sunny hair falleth dank on the arm
Of the mother, whose love shields no longer from harm:
35   For strength is scarce left her to weep o'er the dying,
Ere dead by the loved one the mother is lying.

But can we only weep, when above us thus lour
The death-bearing wings of the angels of power;
When around the arrows of pestilence flying —
40   Around, the pale heaps of the famine-struck lying —
No, brother of sorrow, when life's light is weakest,
Look up, it is nigh the redemption thou seekest.

Still, work, though the tramp of the weird spirit-horses,
Fall dull on the ear, like clay upon corses;

45   Still Freedom must send forth her young heroes glowing,
               Though her standard be red with their life-current flowing;
               Still the preacher must cast forth the seed, as God's sower,
               Though he perish like grass at the scythe of the mower.

               Still do the Lord's work through life's tragical drama,
50   Though weeping goes upward like weeping at Rama;
               The path may be thorny, but Spirit eyes see us;
               The cross may be heavy, but Death will soon free us:
               Still, strong in Christ's power we'll chant the Hosanna,
               Fling down Christ's defiance — *'Hypage Satana!'*

55   I see in a vision the shadowy portal,
               That leadeth to regions of glory immortal;
               I see the pale forms from the seven wounds bleeding,
               Which up to God's Throne the bright angels are leading;
               I see the crown placed on each saint bending lowly,
60   While sounds the Trisagion — Holy, thrice Holy!

               I have Paradise dreams of a band with palm-branches,
               Whose wavings give back their gold harps' resonances,
               And a jewelled-walled city, where walketh in splendour
               Each one who his life for God's truth did surrender.
65   Who would weep their death-doom, if such bliss we inherit,
               When the veil of the human falls off from the spirit?

               The Christian may shrink from the last scenes of the trial,
               And the woes yet unknown of each mystical vial;
               But the hosts of Jehovah will gather beside him,
70   The rainbow-crowned angel stoop downward to guide him;
               And to him, who as hero and martyr hath striven,
               Will the Crown, and the Throne, and the Palm-branch be given.

France in '93:
A Lesson from Foreign History

LADY WILDE

Hark! the onward heavy tread —
   Hark! the voices rude —
'Tis the famished cry for Bread
   From a wildered multitude.
5   They come! They come!
       Point the cannon — roll the drum;
Thousands wail and weep with hunger —
Faster let your soldiers number.
Sword, and gun, and bayonet
10 A famished people's cries have met.

Hark! the onward heavy tread —
   Hark! the voices rude —
'Tis the famished cry for Bread
   From an *armed* multitude.
15   They come! They come!
       Not with meek submission's hum.
Bloody trophy they have won,
Ghastly glares it in the sun —
Gory head on lifted pike.
20 Ha! they weep not now, but *strike!*

Ye, the deaf to their cries —
Ye, who scorn'd their agonies —
'Tis no longer prayers for Bread
Shriek in your ears the famishèd —
25 But wildly, fiercely, peal on peal
Resoundeth — *Down with the Bastile!*
Can ye tame a people now?
Try them — flatter, promise, vow,
Swear their wrongs shall be redressed—
30 But patience — time will do the rest;
Swear they shall one day be fed —
Hark! the People — *Dead for Dead!*

Calculating statesmen quail —
Proud aristocrat grows pale;

225

35 Savage sounds that deathly song:
Hark! — *A bas les Tyrans!*
Blindly now they wreak revenge —
How rudely do a mob avenge!
What coronetted Prince or Peer
40 Will not the base born slavelings fear?
Sooth, their cry is somewhat stern:
Aristocrats, à la Lanterne!
Ghastly fruits their lances bear —
Noble heads, with streaming hair;
45 No reverence for rank and law:
A wilder shout — *A bas le Roi!*

Now, the bloody work is done—
On they stride o'er prostrate throne;
Royal blood of King and Queen
50 Streameth from the guillotine;
Wildly on the people goeth,
Reaping what the noble soweth —
Little dreamed he, prince or peer,
Of *who* should be his heritor.
55 Hunger, now, at last is sated
In halls where once it wailed and waited —
Wild Justice fiercely rules the laws
Which failed to right a people's cause.
On that Human Ocean floweth,
60 Whither stops it no one knoweth —
Surge the wild waves in their strength
Against all chartered rights at length —
Throne, and King, and Noble fall;
But the People — they hold Carnival.

A Lament for the Potato
A.D. 1739
(From the Irish)
LADY WILDE

There is woe, there is clamour, in our desolated land,
And wailing lamentation from a famine-stricken band;
And weeping are the multitudes in sorrow and despair,
For the green fields of Munster lying desolate and bare.

5 Woe for Lorc's ancient kingdom, sunk in slavery and grief;
Plundered, ruined, are our gentry, our people, and their Chief;
For the harvest lieth scattered, more worth to us than gold,
All the kindly food that nourished both the young and the old.
Well I mind me of the cosherings, where princes might dine,

10 And we drank until nightfall the best seven sorts of wine;
Yet was ever the Potato our old, familiar dish,
And the best of all sauces with the beeves and the fish.
But the harp now is silent, no one careth for the sound;
No flowers, no sweet honey, and no beauty can be found;

15 Not a bird its music thrilling through the leaves of the wood,
Nought but weeping and hands wringing in despair for our food.
And the Heavens, all in darkness, seem lamenting our doom,
No brightness in the sunlight, not a ray to pierce the gloom;
The cataract comes rushing with a fearful deepened roar,

20 And ocean bursts its boundaries, dashing wildly on the shore.
Yet, in misery and want, we have one protecting man,
Kindly Barry, of Fitzstephen's old hospitable clan;
By mount and river working deeds of charity and grace:
Blessings ever on our champion, best hero of his race!

25 Save us, God! In Thy mercy bend to hear the people's cry,
From the famine-stricken fields, rising bitterly on high;
Let the mourning and the clamour cease in Lorc's ancient land,
And shield us in the death-hour by thy strong, protecting hand!

A Supplication

LADY WILDE

'De profundis clamavi ad te domine'.

By our looks of mute despair,
By the sighs that rend the air,
From lips too faint to utter prayer,
    Kyrie Eleison.

By the last groans of our dying,
Echoed by the cold wind's sighing
On the wayside as they're lying,
    Kyrie Eleison.

By our fever-stricken bands
Lifting up their wasted hands
For bread throughout the far-off lands,
    Kyrie Eleison.

Miserable outcasts we,
Pariahs of humanity,
Shunned by all where'er we flee,
    Kyrie Eleison.

For our dead no bell is ringing,
Round their forms no shroud is clinging,
Save the rank grass newly springing,
    Kyrie Eleison.

Golden harvests were are reaping,
With golden grain our barns heaping,
But for us our bread is weeping,
    Kyrie Eleison.

Death-devoted in our home,
Sad we cross the salt sea's foam,
But death we bring where'er we roam,
    Kyrie Eleison.

Whereso'er our steps are led,
They can track us by our dead,
Lying on their cold earth bed,
    Kyrie Eleison.

25 We have sinned — in vain each warning —
Brother lived his brother scorning,
Now in ashes see us mourning,
                    Kyrie Eleison.

Heeding not our country's state,
Trodden down and desolate,
30 While we strove in senseless hate,
                    Kyrie Eleison.

We have sinned, but holier zeal
May we Christian patriots feel,
Oh! for our dear country's weal,
                    Kyrie Eleison.

Let us lift our streaming eyes
35 To God's throne above the skies,
      He will hear our anguished cries,
                    Kyrie Eleison.

Kneel beside me, oh! my brother,
Let us pray each with the other,
For Ireland, our mourning mother,
                    Kyrie Eleison.

The Voice of the Poor
LADY WILDE

Was sorrow ever like to our sorrow?
            Oh, God above!
Will our night never change into a morrow
            Of joy and love?
5 A deadly gloom is on us waking, sleeping,
            Like the darkness at noontide,
That fell upon the pallid mother, weeping
            By the Crucified.

Before us die our brothers of starvation:
10   Around us are cries of famine and despair

Where is hope for us, or comfort, or salvation —
    Where — oh! where?
If the angels ever hearken, downward bending,
    They are weeping, we are sure,
15   At the litanies of human groans ascending
    From the crushed hearts of the poor.

When the human rests in love upon the human,
    All grief is light;
But who bends one kind glance to illumine
20   Our life-long night?
The air around is ringing with their laughter —
    God has only made the rich to smile;
But we — in our rags, and want, and woe — we follow after,
    Weeping the while.

25   And the laughter seems but uttered to deride us.
    When — oh! when
Will fall the frozen barriers that divide us
    From other men?
Will ignorance for ever thus enslave us?
30   Will misery for ever lay us low?
All are eager with their insults, but to save us,
    None, none, we know.

We never knew a childhood's mirth and gladness,
    Nor the proud heart of youth, free and brave;
35   Oh! a death-like dream of wretchedness and sadness,
    Is life's weary journey to the grave.
Day by day we lower sink and lower,
    Till the God-like soul within,
Falls crushed, beneath the fearful demon power
40   Of poverty and sin.

So we toil on, on with fever burning
    In heart and brain;
So we toil on, on through bitter scorning,
    Want, woe, and pain:
45   We dare not raise our eyes to the blue heaven,
    Or the toil must cease —
We dare not breathe the fresh air God has given
    One hour in peace.

We must toil, though the light of life is burning,
50   Oh, how dim!
We must toil on our sick bed, feebly turning
            Our eyes to Him,
Who alone can hear the pale lip faintly saying,
            With scarce moved breath
55 While the paler hands, uplifted, aid the praying —
            'Lord, grant us *Death!*'

Work While It is Called Day

LADY WILDE

'No man hath hired us' — strong hands drooping
    Listless falling in idleness down;
Men in the silent market place grouping
    Round Christ's cross of silent stone.
5 'No man hath hired us' — pale hands pining,
    Stalwart forms bowed down to sue —
'The red dawn is passed, noon is shining,
    But no man hath given us work to do.'

Then a Voice seemed to peal from the heights of heaven: —
10   'Men', it said, 'of the Irish soil!
'I gave ye a land as a Garden of Eden,
    'Where you and your sons should till and toil;
'I set your throne by the glorious waters,
    'Where ocean flung round you her mighty bands,
15 'That your sails, like those of your Tyrian fathers,
    'Might sweep the shore of a hundred lands.

'Power I gave to the hands of your leaders
    'Wisdom I gave to the lips of the wise,
'And your children grew as the stately cedars
20   'That shadow the streams of Paradise.
'What have ye done with my land of beauty?
    'Has the spoiler bereft her of robe and crown?
'Have my people failed in a people's duty?
    'Has the wild boar trampled my vineyard down?'

231

25 'True', they answered, faint in replying,
   'Our vines are rent by the wild boar's tusks;
 'The corn on our golden slopes is lying,
   'But our children feed on the remnant husks.
 'Our strong men lavish their blood for others;
30   'Our prophets and wise men are heard no more;
 'Our young men give a kiss to their mothers,
   'Then sail away for a foreign shore.'

 Then the Lord came down from the height of heaven,
   Came down to that garden fair to view,
35 Where the weary men waited, from morn 'till even,
   For some one to give them work to do.
 'Ye have sinned', He said, and the angel lustre
   Darkened slowly as bright clouds may;
 Weeds are growing where fruit should cluster —
40   'Yet ye stand idle all the day.'

 'Have ye trod in the furrows, and worked as truly
   'As men who knew they reap as they sow?
 'Have ye flung in the seed and watched it duly,
   'Day and night, lest the tares should grow?
45 'Have ye tended the vine my hand hath planted?
   'Pruned and guided its tendrils fair,
 'Ready with all things that might be wanted
   'To strengthen the fruit its branches bear?

 'Who knoweth the time of the new dispensations;
50   'Go on in my faith, and the light will come;
 'The last may yet be first amongst nations;
   'Wait till the end for the final doom.'
 The last may be first! Shall our country's glory
   Ever flash light on the path we have trod?
55 Who knows? Who knows? for our future story
   Lies hid in the great sealed Book of God.

The Extermination

RICHARD D'ALTON WILLIAMS

'Dominus pupillum et viduam suscipet.' — Ps. 145.

When tyranny pampered and purple-clad minions
    Drive forth the lone widow and orphan to die,
Shall no angel of vengeance unfurl his red pinions,
    And, grasping sharp thunderbolts, rush from on high.?

5   'Pity! oh, pity! — a little while spare me:
    My baby is sick — I am feeble and poor;
In the cold Winter blast, from the hut if you tear me,
    My lord, we must die on the desolate moor!'

    'Tis vain — for the despot replies but with laughter,
10   While rudely his serfs thrust her forth on the wold:
Her cabin is blazing from the threshold to rafter,
    And she crawls o'er the mountain, sick, weeping, and cold.

Her thinly-clad child on the stormy hill shivers —
    The thunders are pealing dread anthems around —
15 Loud roar in their anger the tempest-lashed rivers —
    And the loosened rocks down with the wild torrents bound.

Vainly she tries in her bosom to cherish
    Her sick infant boy, 'mid the horrors around,
Till, faint and despairing, she sees her babe perish —
20   Then lifeless she sinks on the snow-covered ground.

Though the children of Ammon, with trumpets and psalters,
    To devils poured torrents of innocents' gore,
Let them blush from deep hell at the far redder altars,
    Where the death-dealing tyrants of Ireland adore!

25 But, for Erin's life-current, thro' long ages flowing,
    Dark demons that pierce her, you yet shall atone;
Even *now* the volcano beneath you is glowing,
    And the Moloch of tyranny reels on the throne.

Hand in Hand

RICHARD D'ALTON WILLIAMS

Our bounteous God gave the fertile sod
    To sustain his people well,
And not that you of a vampire few
    Should make this earth a hell.
5   We are not brutes whom your pleasure suits
    To harness, to lash, and spurn,
But love for love, all tribes above,
    And hate for hate, return.

Come! hand in hand, at Heaven's command,
10   Whose voice through the people rolls,
Let us bravely stand for our lives and land,
    And prove that men have souls!

Must we live and die in the pauper's stye,
    The sweltering poorhouse den,
15   Where your pride and lust and rapine thrust
    The souls of immortal men?
And then you prate of their brutal state,
    Who've made them the things they are —
By the Hosts on High, it were better to die
20   A thousand times in war!

Then hand in hand, at Heaven's command,
    Whose voice through the people rolls,
Let us bravely stand for our lives and land,
    And prove that men have souls!

25   O sons of men, called of prophet pen —
    Than angels scarcely less —
Who can trace one sign of a birth divine
    In your woeful wretchedness?
Man, maid, and boy know not hope nor joy;
30   The light from your eyes has flown —
All peace and love have soared above,
    And your hearts are turned to stone.

Yet hand in hand, at Heaven's command,
    Whose voice through the millions rolls,

35   Let us bravely stand for our lives and lands,
               And prove that men *have* souls!

         We have many a bed of Wicklow lead,
               And stronger Leitrim veins,
         Whence the iron ore may make something more,
               Perchance, than bolts and chains.
40   If the scythe and spade, like an iron blade,
               Should rust 'neath the landlord's heel,
         There are gows enow in the land, I know,
               To turn them both to steel!

45   Then hand in hand, at Heaven's command,
               Whose voice through the millions rolls,
         Let us bravely stand for our lives and land,
               And prove that men have souls!

         The young ash trees shall dance on the breeze,
50   In the strife for the soil to join,
         And the forests of larch take life, and march
              From the Suir and the storied Boyne.
         At length we stand, an united band,
               Prepared to die or do —
55   If no gentler hand can save the land,
               We'll have O'Neil's *lamh ruadh.*

         And hand in hand, at Heaven's command,
               Whose voice through the people rolls,
         We'll bravely stand for our lives and land,
60   And prove that men have souls.

         From Tyrawley, too, 'Lamh lauder aboo!'
               Shall be heard like a larum-drum,
         And a burning sleet and a winding sheet
               Portend your hour is come —
65   Your hour of doom; from their shroudless tomb
               Shall rise your victims slain,
         Whose guiltless blood, an awful flood,
               Shall fall in a fiery rain —

         When hand in hand, at Heaven's command,
70   Whose voice even death controls,

We bravely stand for our lives and land,
    And prove that men have souls.

The dark winds blow, and the grave lights glow,
    And the sky hath a feverish glare,
75 As to and fro in woe they go,
    On the labouring midnight air;
Then the troubled hosts of our brethren's ghosts,
    With a sound like unsheathing swords,
On the blast aghast have passed up fast
80   To the throne of the Lord of Lords!

Swear hand in hand, at Heaven's command,
    Whose voice through the storm-wind rolls,
To bravely stand for your lives and land,
    And prove that men have souls.

Kyrie Eleison

RICHARD D'ALTON WILLIAMS

Life and death are in thy hand,
    Lord, have mercy!
The blight came down at Thy command,
    Christ, have mercy!
The famine pang and fever pain
Tear the nation's heart in twain —
5 Human aid is sought in vain —
    Parce nobis, Domine!

Loud, more loud, their footsteps fall,
    Lord, have mercy!
Heaven is one vast funeral pall,
    Christ, have mercy!
Twin destroyers, hand in hand,
They stalk along the blasted land —
10 Who before their frown shall stand?
    Parce nobis, Domine!

Without a grave, like weeds to lie,
    Lord, have mercy!

Despairing thousands wait to die,
$$\text{Christ, have mercy!}$$
The famished infant vainly cries —
Its mother dead beside it lies —
15 Let our anguish pierce the skies —
$$\text{Parce nobis, Domine!}$$

Outcast of the nations, long,
$$\text{Lord, have mercy!}$$
We bear a foreign tyrant's wrong,
$$\text{Christ, have mercy!}$$
Black our fearful crime must be,
With triple scourges lashed by Thee —
20 Famine, Plague, and Slavery —
$$\text{Parce nobis, Domine!}$$

Oh! if torture might atone,
$$\text{Lord, have mercy!}$$
With tears of blood before Thy throne,
$$\text{Christ, have mercy!}$$
Six hundred years we toil in chains;
We sow, but aliens reap our plains:
25 The life is frozen in our veins—
$$\text{Parce nobis, Domine!}$$

Disarmed and bleeding, here apart,
$$\text{Lord, have mercy!}$$
A vulture preys upon our heart,
$$\text{Christ, have mercy!}$$
Oh! bitter is our Helot doom —
In life no joy, in death no tomb —
30 Despair and vengeance rule the gloom —
$$\text{Parce nobis, Domine!}$$

Without a prayer or passing bell,
$$\text{Lord, have mercy!}$$
The shroudless armies hourly swell,
$$\text{Christ, have mercy!}$$
The dying, ghastlier than the dead,
With blanched lips have vainly said,
35 'Give us this day our daily bread' —
$$\text{Parce nobis, Domine!}$$

237

Woe! woe! to feel the life-blood freeze,
                    Lord, have mercy!
Fruitlessly, by slow degrees,
                    Christ, have mercy!
Oh! had we fallen on the plain
In rapid battle swiftly slain,
40   We had not perished thus in vain—
                    Parce nobis, Domine!

The grave shall wider, deeper grow,
                    Lord, have mercy!
My soul forebodes a darker woe,
                    Christ, have mercy!
No food on earth — no health in air —
The sword were mercy to despair.
45   Avenger! when thine arm is bare,
                    Parce nobis, Domine!

Their God is wroth, our foemen say:
                    Lord, have mercy!
Our Father! turn Thine ire away.
                    Christ, have mercy!
Bid Thine angel cease to slay —
Have mercy, Heaven, on feeble clay —
50   Hear Thy stricken people pray
                    Parce nobis, Domine!

Before the isle is all a grave,
                    Lord, have mercy!
Arise! mysterious God, and save;
                    Christ, have mercy!
But if the pestilential sun
Must see us wither, one by one,
55   Thy hand hath made — Thy will be done —
                    Parce nobis, Domine!

Lord of Hosts

RICHARD D'ALTON WILLIAMS

Lord of Hosts! in vain for pity
    Tyrants long we prayed, but now
To Thee we cry from plain and city —
    Rise, and judge between us, Thou!
To glut the rage of English Mammon
    We mourn a yearly million slain;
And reap from graves the plague and famine,
    Pouring forth our blood like rain.

Every heart is bare before Thee —
    If with sacrilegious lips
And lying tongue we dare adore Thee,
    Strike us down in foul eclipse!
If we seek revenge or plunder,
    Or to crush a brother's creed,
Blast us with Thy fiercest thunder —
    Leave us in our hour of need.

If we seek but justice purely,
    Earth and Hell our foes may be;
Thou wilt bless our banner surely,
    And Thy smile is victory!
Ere we burst the chains that gore us,
    Ere the tide of battle rolls,
May thine angels camp around us,
    Nerve our hearts and cleanse our souls!

Lord of Hosts! in tears before Thee
    See the prostrate people kneel —
Hear the starving poor implore Thee —
    Smile on Freedom's sacred steel!
By His blood who lived to love us,
    Toiled to teach, and died to save —
By Thyself, just God! above us,
    Grant us Freedom, or the grave!

Vesper Hymn
to the Guardian Angels of Ireland
RICHARD D'ALTON WILLIAMS

Sinking afar o'er the deep's mighty fountains,
 While the sun's rayless brow upon night's bosom faints;
Descend, Guardian Spirits! encamp on our mountains,
 And lovingly watch o'er the Island of Saints.

5 And while to His ear rise your 'thrice holy' numbers,
 May an aura divine through night's solitudes blow,
Which shall fill with strange music our many-dreamed slumbers,
 And wrap the full heart in oblivion of woe.

When sleep, sorrow's tomb with her flowery wand sealing,
10 The soft pall of silence o'er Life's battle flings,
Then glimpses of Eden in visions revealing,
 O'ershadow our rest with your sheltering wings.

And let us, in dreams of the soul's native regions,
 Behold — what saint only or poet may say —
15 Spear, banner, and falchion of cherubim legions
 Proudly waved in the blaze of angelic array!

From the rill-gushing mountains, the thrones of your glory,
 The towers of your watching, the homes of your love,
Look down on our slavery's tear blotted story,
20 And rush to our rescue with strength from above.

Ere the black steed of Famine, in tempest descending,
 The young harvest tramples still greenly that springs,
Oh! yet, o'er the vales' precious fruitfulness bending,
 Expand the vast shields of your emerald wings.

25 And ere shroud mantled Pestilence' noisome breath wither
 The flow'rs through which lately young Health,
  smiling, trod,
Whence the tree of Life blossoms, Raphaël! oh! hither,
 On balm-dropping pinion, come, 'Healing of God!'

Till, from Famine and Plague and worse Thraldom emerging,
30 More purified, chainless, and chastened we stand:
All hearts to one centre, united, converging,
 And Love, Peace, and Plenty, replenish the land.

240

Come! come to us, Angels of Hope and of Healing,
    With chaplet of snowdrop and plumes of the dove —
35 And, like rainbow-clad show'rs to the fainting earth stealing,
    Come, green-winged Mercy and fire-arrowed Love!

PART VI

'Best Pillar of Thy Throne'

THE UNIONIST REACTION

Lines Written the Day before
the Queen's Arrival in Dublin
ANONYMOUS

As some fair vision, radiant o'er with light,
Breaks with bright glories on the gloom of night,
Distant tho' yet, but still whose coming ray,
Sends forth the twilight, heralding the day —
5 She comes, to cheer with hope that 'nighted shore
Where plague and famine heaped their spectre store,
Where infant suffering, and maturer life,
Fell faint and dying, 'midst destruction's strife,
×And the whole land, like some colossal deck,
10 Struggled and sunk — a mighty social wreck:
Queen of Imperial greatness, o'er whose power
No clouds are spread, no adverse fortunes lower —
Thy people free; best pillar of thy throne,
Which, 'midst the shock of states stands firm alone;
15 Be thine the hand to cheer the fainting heart,
To act the mother's, as the Monarch's part,
O'er the sad scene to shed thy cheering light,
And from thy well loved isle to chase the night;
To bid the din of civil discord cease,
20 And hush each cry of party into peace,
To drive contending factions from the land,
And join the people in one heart and hand.
What though some vows of fealty have been broken?
Some words of passion have been rashly spoken —
25 Still are they surface-specks; no deeper sore
Cankers the general heart, sound to the core.
Let no disturber from a foreign land
On words of passing anger take his stand,
Nor vainly hope to raise Rebellion's flame.
30 A tower of strength it stands — the Royal Name.
Come when she may, the echoing shout will prove
The deep devotion of her people's love.
Hibernia well may mark the happy hour,
Which brings Victoria to her emerald bower,
35 And fills up hope, long shadowed forth in thee,
Illustrious Queen — most gentle Majesty.

Bright Were the Days

LIEUT. THOMAS ACRES OGLE

Oh! bright were the days when our country was feeding
On praties and butter-milk, three times a day,
And Paddy first learned the old Irish breeding,
To wield his shillelah, and have his own way;
But now the big lumpers won't grow in old Erin,
And the gorsoons are lean, as the pigs in the sty,
And there's not a soul from granny to the bairn,
But this blessed minute could sit down and cry.

Oh! the old times are gone, when in Erin so glorious,
We drank our own potheen, and heeded not care —
And the brave hearts that loved her, were ever victorious,
With their pretty skullcrackers, at pattern and fair;
And the boys danced all day with the light-hearted colleens,
To the bagpipes' sweet music, in the shebeen and tent;
'Mid the braying of asses, and squeaking of bonneens,
And we drank, swore, and courted, wherever we went.

Oh! land of the shamrock, though poor and forlorn,
And the lumpers no longer will grow in thy soil, —
And thy famous knee-breeches are faded and torn,
With the sweat of thy brow, and the brunt of thy toil;
I love thy big bogs and thy bare bawns as dearly,
As when youthful vigour warmed every joint,
And though fortune has dealt her hard strokes so severely,
Thou'll be happy again on *potatoes* and *point!*

On the Death of the Rev. Robert Traill, D.D.

A SOUTHERN

In the forefront of the deadly fight 'gainst fearful odds he stood,
A minister of Him whose life was pass'd in doing good;
Myriads had fallen by his side, exhausted, famish'd, spent,
Yet still the warrior held his ground, on deeds of mercy bent.

A deadly foe assail'd them there — a monarch dread was he;
All times, all places, and all men have own'd his sovereignty;

This cruel tyrant was king death, who laid his dart aside,
And with a sword in either hand, smote thousands and they died.

10 In his right hand the famine blade was grasp'd with surest hold,
And this resistless weapon slew the people, young and old;
Nor yet less deadly was the wound caused by the fever blade,
Which, in its burning sweep, men's homes their piles funereal
      made.

But who was he, this hero brave, that stood against the foe,
Who met and warded from the poor so many a well-aimed blow?
15 Who did resist the dread approach of death, in fierce array,
And keep the iron-hearted king from his dire work away?

It was the noble high-soul'd TRAILL, the poor man's trusty
      friend
Who long time from starvation's pangs did helpless crowds
      defend;
Day after day, week after week, this patriot toiled and strove,
20 Contended with and baffled death, by faith and zeal and love.

There have been warriors who fought on glory's battle plain,
And mariners who braved the storms and dangers of the main,
There have been patriots who have toil'd, and martyrs who have
      bled,
But Traill, no nobler heart than thine, e'er went down to the
      dead!

25 In every good and noble work his talents were employed.
The efforts of all Christian men his Christian aid enjoy'd;
But judge the pastor's weight of care, his load of bitter grief,
When hundreds fell on every side, for whom he'd no relief.

He saw his flock o'erwhelmed and crush'd — his heart bled at
      the sight,
30 He saw a dark and angry cloud, foreshowing stormy night;
He saw the wasted forms of those who sighed and pined for
      food,
Yet in his post of gloom and death the reverend warrior stood!

His own resources had been drained — still did the victims fall;
Then in impassioned strains, at last, did he for succour call;
35 And succour came — and so the lives of multitudes were sav'd,
But still the broad black flag of death above them darkly wav'd.

246

Upon the right hand famine smote; but while the victims pined
Before the naked withering blade, in Traill a shield they find;
For to the rescue quick he rush'd, and robbed death of his prey,
40   And many a drooping household cheer'd, for many a weary day.

Upon the left hand fever raged, and groups lay here and there,
Some in their huts with broken roofs, some in the open air;
To bring this suffering crowd relief, and soothe their pain and
      woe,
Seemed a high duty to his soul, which he could not forego.

45   Like as, when winds and waves combine their fury to molest
Some little bark, which peacefully rode on the ocean's breast,
And the tir'd helmsman doth behold, yet will not quit his post,
The billows, which with maddening surge, sweep on, a fearful
      host;

So he, the pilot of a bark toss'd by life's wildest storm,
50   As one by one the billows swept above each sinking form,
But held the rudder with a grasp more desperate and strong,
And brav'd, with a heroic breast, the waves which roll'd along.

'Twas dreadful agony to him those awful sights to see,
Which, like a wild and feverish dream, haunted his memory;
55   He saw the people pine for food, and saved all he could save;
He saw the region all around one black and hideous grave!

Closer upon the weary man sick, starving creatures press,
Who with their parch'd and burning tongues the generous giver
      bless!
Does he not shun infection's touch, and shrink from scenes so
      dread? —
60   No! tho' 'tis death their forms to see, those spectres must be fed.

Woe to that starving multitude! alas, their well-tried friend
Is absent! Where, oh! where is he, his mighty aid to lend?
Alas, for them upon the bed of sickness now he lies,
To the discharge of duties dread a living sacrifice!

65   Weeks have roll'd by. Many poor forms uncoffin'd graves have
      found,
Or are — oh, awful sight and sad! — decaying overground!

And there are moving skeletons, of every size and form,
Breathing and living, who'll find rest soon from this blighting
    storm.

And he who, with devotedness worthy of his holy faith,
70   Had fought for others, is, at last, in conflict fierce with death.
But does death conquer? — Does he lay this noble spirit low?
He does not — for his Saviour Christ had vanquish'd this last
    foe.

'Tis true the saint's heart ceased to beat; cold have his hands
    become,
And lips that eloquently told the whole truth now are dumb;
75   'Tis true that all on earth of him is cold and lifeless dust,
But his spirit walks enthron'd and free, among the pure and just.

And the heartless tyrant, death, has fail'd to win him for his
    prey;
Christ won a triumph o'er the grave, and bore the palm away;
And so the martyr's end was 'peace' — his life has just begun,
80   And on his brow now beams the crown by Jesu's pure blood won.

No more those scenes of ghastly awe, those spectral sights he'll
    see,
No tear-drop falls, no want is known, where he will ever be;
No toil is needful or requir'd — no cares can there molest;
All, all is joy and peace and love; sunshine and light and rest!

85   The heat and burden of the day long had his spirit borne;
That toil is past, and his is free, no more he'll grieve or mourn,
He was a burning, shining light; that light is now remov'd,
But it is blazing round the throne of Him, whom he had lov'd.

His name and memory a place will still find on the earth,
90   A grateful nation in their hearts will prize his matchless worth.
Bless'd with the highest, noblest gifts, he gave them to the Lord
Whom he had serv'd; and now he has his heavenly reward.

Upon this earth the warrior's form will ne'er again be seen;
His battle-plume will wave no more where the dread fight had
    been;
95   Years will roll on and many come to muse upon his grave,
And say, 'There Ireland's martyr lies; the gifted, good, and
    brave!'

The Irish Emigrant's Farewell
in the Famine Year
A SOUTHERN

From a land of want and weeping,
    Sorrow, grief, despair, and woe,
Where grim death vast spoils is reaping,
    We, the broken-hearted go,
To provide a happier dwelling
    Far across the moaning sea,
Whose white billows now are swelling
    Whilst we bid farewell to thee.

What tho' tempest, hail, and thunder,
    Whirlwind and hurricane,
Rend lov'd Erin's form asunder
    And convulse her heart with pain;
What altho' her lot be anguish,
    We still love her not the less,
But shall, wheresoe'er we languish,
    Her and hers for ever bless!

Happier days may yet await us,
    Scenes more pleasant glad the eye,
But even these shall not elate us
    While o'er Ireland's fate we sigh:
What that fate may be hereafter
    Is to us a thing unknown,
But the voice of joy or laughter,
    From her stricken soil has flown.

Yet her hills may sound with gladness,
    Her green vales with deep shouts ring
While we may, oppress'd with sadness,
    Feel the exile's bitter sting.
Be it so — farewell, dear Erin,
    Land of mightiest grief, farewell!
We our weary course are steering
    Far from where thy children dwell.

The Summer of 1847 in Ireland:
The Second Famine Year
A SOUTHERN

The winter and stormy spring have past,
The joyous summer has come at last,
And the glorious sun, as in days of old,
Spreads over the country his beams of gold,
5   And nature bursts into life and glee,
But our isle has lost all its gaiety.

Can our hearts rejoice while Erin lies
O'erwhelmed by dread calamities,
Which, with the might of a thunder storm,
10   Have blighted her lov'd and lovely form,
Have crush'd her spirit, and bow'd her head,
And made her the isle and home of the dead?

First, famine came and assail'd the poor:
What madd'ning pangs did they then endure!
15   They fell! and how dreadful was their fall,
And how vain for succour their anguish'd call!
They fell! and as living they got no bread,
Even biers and graves were denied the dead!

The fever, with burning breath then came,
20   With eyes of fire and touch of flame,
And wither'd up the forms of those
Who had been sure pierc'd by famine's throes,
Till the ablest man and his lusty sons
Were nothing but creeping skeletons!

25   The daughters, too, of the Emerald Isle,
The last to murmur, and first to smile —
Yes, they, the flowers of Erin's soil,
Nourish'd with anxious care and toil,
Have calmly droop'd their heads in the grave,
30   And died with those whom they could not save.

Thus famine and fever, distress and pain,
The broken heart and the scorchèd brain,

And death, to whose sceptre e'en kings must bow,
Are all familiar to Erin now;
35 And can we, who're spared, in this hour rejoice,
With spirits gay, and with merry voice?

Oh, no! the summer will smile in vain,
It will not bring us the lost again;
The sun on his bright career may go,
40 But the lights of many hearts are low;
Nature may shout with her million tongues,
We cannot chorus her sweet, glad songs.

The hearts of those who have seen this woe
Can never more on this earth o'erflow;
45 The buoyant step and the cheerful air
Will be reckon'd amongst the things that were;
The joyous shout and the thrilling strain
Will only meet a response of pain!

Still bow we obedient to God's behest,
50 Who ordereth all things for the best,
And who from evil can bring forth good
And change despair into gratitude —
Tho' the heart be heavy, and dim the eye,
On Him, on Him we will still rely.

Stanzas on the Death
of Daniel O'Connell, Esq., M.P.

ROBERT YOUNG

The Man of the People, whose dignified name,
Through most of the universe soared high in fame,
Has pass'd as a wave that recedes from the shore,
And Erin again shall behold him no more:
5 From time to eternity hurried away;
Call'd hence by a mandate which all must obey.

No more shall his eloquence, burning and strong,
Which roll'd like a torrent, impetuous along,

251

The torpid arouse, or the timid affright,
10   And turbulent feelings, or tranquil, excite,
Lead captive minds of his audience at will,
And make them at pleasure his wishes fulfil.

Behold him at Tara and old Mullaghmast,
Commander-in-chief over multitudes vast,
15   The ruler to whom they in homage bow'd down,
A monarch in all but the sceptre and crown;
Whilst his ample coffers with cash always teem'd,
And he, in his greatness, omnipotent seem'd.

Oh! had he green Erin lov'd better than Rome,
20   He morally great could have made her become;
Industry, contentment, and peace widely spread,
And to independence his countrymen led;
But all his exertions were put forth to raise
Rome's priests, the Church of Old England abase.

25   Deep hatred to Britain, her throne, and her laws,
He loudly proclaim'd, amidst shouts of applause,
From *rebels in heart*, who attended his call,
And echoed his treason throughout Burgh-quay Hall;
Declaring that nought but the Union's repeal
30   The dangerous wounds of the nation could heal.

Thus seeds of sedition and strife widely sown,
Sprung rapidly up, bearing fruits too well known —
Of bloodshed and hate, mid-day murder and crime,
More horrid than ever stain'd country or clime:
35   Men of the same soil placed in hostile array,
Prepared to encounter in deadly affray.

Such doings the vengeance of Heaven call 'd forth,
To visit the Island, East, West, South and North,
With *Famine* and *Pestilence*, sweeping away
40   Some thousands, and spreading surprise and dismay;
And but for the *SAXON* — held up as their foe —
The poor of the land would have all been laid low.

And now, in the midst of the crisis severe,
The man, of all others, whom millions held dear,

45   Has breathed out his last, in a land far remote —
        By Death's mighty hand unexpectedly smote —
        Cut off and deprived of his long-cherished hope,
        Of being absolved from his sins by the Pope.

        But why, when preparing this life to depart,
50   Bequeath the Italians his large *Irish heart*?
        The people, from whom all his opulence came,
        Had surely upon it by far the best claim.
        He boasted how dearly his country he loved,
        But to it, when ending his course, *heartless* proved!

PART VII

'Erin, I Fear 'Tis Very Like You'

THE BRITISH CONTRIBUTION

From:

The Farmer of Inniscreen:
A Tale of the Irish Famine in Verse
ANONYMOUS

Across the sea in Ireland,
    Just eighteen years ago,
A dreadful famine came from God,
    And filled the land with woe.

5   There was no food, there was no work,
    There was no hope of food,
And over every country place
    The fearful famine spread.

And when the old potatoes failed,
10   The people's hope failed too;
They had no heart to work for bread,
    They knew not what to do.

The turf lay useless in the fields,
    They had no mind to toil;
15   The wild weeds grew upon the fields,
    For no one tilled the soil.

Some seed was sown, but never grew —
    There came a curse from heaven;
And wise men said the land had sinned,
20   And had not been forgiven.

The poor-houses were full of men,
    And women sick and thin;
And daily more came to the door,
    When they were full within.

25   The little children — helpless things! —
    Grew sick and weak, and cried;
And many babes, for want of milk,
    Sank helplessly and died.

Good gentlemen in every town
30   Did what they could to save
The starving people from their fate,
    And from the pauper's grave.

The Potato Crop, 1846

ANONYMOUS

Alas! the foul and fatal blight
Infecting Raleigh's grateful root,
Blasting the fields of verdue bright,
That waves o'er Erin's favourite fruit.
5   The peasant's cherished hope is gone,
His little garden pride is o'er,
Famine and plague now scowl upon
Hibernia's fair and fertile shore.

Yet, well the statesman's eye foresaw
10   The monster evil; well his heart
Felt how unjust must be the law,
That starves the cot and chains the mart.
Boldly the patriot-path he trod
Through obloquy, reproach and scorn —
15   His sole reward the smile of God,
And the blessings of the yet unborn.

And what can equal that reward?
Not all the gold-mines of Peru:
When black and blighted lies the sward,
20   Aid hastens o'er the billows blue;
Employment gives the peasant bread,
Gives hope and virtue. Therefore Bless'd
And honoured by the heart and head
Which cheer the humble and oppressed.

25   Th' example fructifies, and men
Devote them to their country's good
Improvement bids the hill and glen
Contribute to the nation's food.
The swamp is drained — the dismal fen
30   Shall smile to heaven with golden grain
Outrage is fetter'd in his den,
And Justice indicates her reign.

Hence out of evil good may spring,
Social and physical. The land
35   Lacks but the care of men to bring

Forth happiness, the helping hand
Alone is needed. Property
Has duties which will be fulfill'd:
And the fair Island yet shall be
40 Such as the voice of nature will'd.

And oh! not only there, but here,
Even in a land with riches rife,
Want shivers o'er the hearthstone drear,
And chills the blood of human life,
45 This too shall end; the struggling poor
Possess an humbler brother's claim;
Eliza's law may yet restore
Old England's charitable fame.

Erin go Bragh!

BRITANNICUS

Erin go bragh! — if bragh may mean bragging,
  Faith, it were folly to beg you do that, —
Sweet Irish modesty rather wants gagging,
  Divil a patting needs delicate Pat:
5 Oh! and the blarney he tells of his country,
  Isle of Calypson, and 'jim o' the say,' —
While the stern truth, to shame his effront'ry,
  Shows a grim desert in rotting decay.

Dreary and desolate, ugly, and endless
10   Stretches your mountains, your bog, or your moor,
Dotted with hovels, where famish'd and friendless
  Are on their dunghills your barbarous poor;
Erin, — don't brag; from ocean to ocean
Never was seen such a terrible place,
15 Dante himself might have caught a new notion
  In an Inferno of you and your race.

Erin go bragh! — if bragh may mean braying —
  Faith, and your ears are as long as your tail,
Silly and sad is the game that you're playing,
20   Erin go bragh! and Hurrah for Repale!

258

Why, you're the fool of the universe, surely,
  Thus to destroy all your help and your hope;
Or do you think that it's limitless purely
  Because you cut off the far end of the rope?

25 Erin, on your side is virtue intirely,
  And on the Saxon's perdition and guilt;
Och, and O hone! but we've governed you direly,
  Beautiful innocent, smother'd and kilt!
You are *not* murderous, reckless, and shameless—
30 You are *not* indolent, subtle, and wile;
Honours unnumbered, unequalled, and nameless,
  Never were known in the Emerald Isle!

Oh! but 'that country doth alter men's natures',
  O History writes, and, by Patrick, it's true —
35 Brutalised feelings and monkeyfied features,
  Erin — I fear it is very like you!
Aye, and to 'cram, blaspheming your feeder;'
  This is your motto (I quote by the book):
Moloch and Bel! — if you follow your leader,
40 Much like a devil, fair Erin, you look!

Erin go bragh! go softly, go humbly,
  Down in the ashes, confessing your crimes;
Guilt-laden people! in penitence, dumbly,
  Take for the better a Briton's bold rhymes:
45 Mercy is swift to forgive and forget;
  Only repay not blessings with curses,
Britain to thee shall be generous yet!

Enigmatica: A Riddle
CHLOE

My first is rage, and fury dire,
And oft occasions warlike fire:
My second farmers have, I trow,
To drain, to till, to sow, to plough.
5 My whole was fruitful, green and fair;

259

No reptile breath'd in its pure air;
The poorest ne'er refused to share
With poorer still their humble fare,
And cordial greetings loved to give,
10   With hearty prayers that you may live
A thousand years, and ne'er grow old.
Those voices now are sad and cold;
Thousands are numbered 'midst the dead
Who once poured blessings on your head,
15   Whilst famine and disease replace
The hearty meal and joyous face.
The plant they fondly used to prize
Lies blasted now before their eyes:
No marriage chimes salute the ear,
20   The dismal toll alone you hear.
May Heaven again its blessings pour
Upon this suffering Nation's shore!
And health and plenty soon abound
Where pestilence and want are found,
25   And every one their trifle give,
To aid these suffering men to live.

The Spectre

H.D.

Far west a grim shadow was seen, as 'tis said,
Like a spectre from Famine and Pestilence bred:
His gaunt giant-form, with pale Poverty wed,
    Meteor-like, fraught with awe, flashed in view:
5   Some exclaim'd it was naught but a shadow of night, —
Some derided the Seer who proclaim'd its dread might, —
But at length all confess'd his forebodings were right;
    The event quickly prov'd them too true.

261

The fell Spectre advanc'd, — who the horrors shall tell

10   Of his galloping stride, as he sounded the knell

Of thousands on thousands who 'neath his eye fell?

        Death cast the sure dart at his nod:

Now to low feeble moan sinks the sufferer's last cry,

As the pestilent fiend to each victim draws nigh,

15   Swift the death-smitten body is laid out hard by, —

        'Tis a dread visitation of God.

Ah! Erin, late isle of the smile and the tear,
Erst blent like the rainbow, to hope ever dear,
Light again the soft smile to thy sorrow once near,
     So radiant will bright joyous beam:
Shall thy woe, sprung from famine's assault, never cease?
Ne'er more let thy feuds thy dark sufferings increase;
Then naught shall arrest the gay sunshine of peace,
     Blotting out the dark storm's lurid gleam.

20

Ne'er dream that thy sister fails fondly to love thee,
Ne'er think that in pride she would fain rise above thee,
Ne'er imagine, if Fate with its sorrows yet prove thee,
    There fails in her eye the soft tear:
Thine uplifting pride of her statesmen would be,
30   With delight would her sons thy prosperity see,
And if sorrow yet hang o'er thy blighted roof-tree
    They pray renew'd joy may be near.

Mortality in Skibbereen.

L.

The 'Keen' comes wailing on the wind,
    That sweeps o'er Erin's mountains blue;
It chills the heart of Earl and hind —
    It lends the land a ghastly hue!
5   The song of death by Death is chanted!
    The dying bear the shroudless dead;
Th' uncoffin'd clay a grave is granted —
    The very worm averts his head.

Darkly proceed the famish'd cotters;
10   To-morrow may behold their grave:
The young man towards the churchyard totters —
    The bravest heart no more is brave.
Those grey hairs may have known the wave
    Where Nelson's signal boldly flew:
15   Perchance they dared the Gallic glaive,
    And bear the scars of Waterloo.

Slowly the gaunt procession wends —
    The blessed voice of hope is faint;
The spotless stole Religion rends
20   In misery o'er the dying pliant:
While Pestilence on sable wings
    Aids vulture Famine in the feast,
Which view well with the offerings
    Paid to the Plague-Scourge of the East.

25 And yet — oh! paradox — oh! shame! —
   Oh! blind improvidence! The land
 Is of the best that ever came
   Forth from its mighty Maker's hands.
 Fertile and fair, it should have been
30   The glory of the British crown:
 And *now*, behold the shudd'ring scene! —
   The seedless fields — the spectral town.

 But Nature vindicates her God;
   Teaches a lesson from the soil:
35 A voice springs from the blighted sod
   In mercy for the sons of toil,
 Fair Nature's energies expire
   When rack'd for one poor parcel root;
 And Labour merits better hire
40   Than the sad fare of Raleigh's fruit.

 'The 'Keen' comes wailing on the blast,
   The voice of Winter joins the dirge;
 The shadows of Despair are cast
   Around the new grave's narrow verge.
45 Oh! let us hope that day will rise
   To dissipate this fearful gloom;
 And bring the blessings of the skies
   To raise a nation from her tomb.'

Sketches in the West of Ireland
C.C.T.

Uncoffin'd, unshrouded, his bleak corpse they bore,
From the spot where he died on the cabin's wet floor.
To a hole which they dug in the garden close by;
Thus a brother hath died — thus a Christian must lie!

5 'Twas a horrible end and a harrowing tale,
To chill the strong heart — to strike revelry pale.
No disease o'er this Victim could mastery claim,
'Twas Famine alone mark'd his skeleton frame!

265

The bones of his Grandsire and Father too, rest
10   In the old Abbey-yard, by the holy rites blest;
Their last hours were sooth'd by affection's fond cares,
Their last sighs were breath'd midst their friends tearful prayers!

Unshriven, untended, this man pass'd away,
Ere time streak'd one hair of his dark locks with gray;
15   His requiem the wild wind, and Ilen's hoarse roar,
As its swollen waves dash on the rock-girded shore.

PART VIII

'We'll Soon Have Cheap Flour and Plenty of Meal'

STREET BALLADS

Another Version of Soyer's Soup
ANONYMOUS

Air — 'Widow Machree'

Arrah Judy acra, did you hear any news?
          Oh hone a vourneen machree!
With their infernal talk my head is confused,
          Oh hone a vourneen machree!
They invented a plan to entrap our poor men,
To bring a tin can off for pottage, you see;
5   The news was so brief of this parish relief,
          Oh hone a vourneen machree!

If you seen my poor man with his old black tin can
          Oh hone a vourneen machree!
You'd think that the world was near at an end,
          Oh hone a vourneen machree!
At this time the French cook served us all up with soup;
I ne'er seen such a group in his kitchen, you see,
10   While our bones was near smashed waiting for the trash,
          Oh hone a vourneen machree!

Then Soyer the boy kept up the royal square,
          Oh hone a vourneen machree!
If you chance to get in you are sure of your share,
          Oh hone a vourneen machree!
For he gave it quick and could make it thick,
And by steam he fed thousands, I'm sure, every day,
15   But they couldn't be sure while they stood on his floor,
          Oh hone a vourneen machree!

While the broth it was thickening with onions and meal,
          Oh hone a vourneen machree!
The impatient mob, sure they shoved in the rails,
          Oh hone a vourneen machree!
Then a poor Connaught man they threw into the soup,
And the steam was so strong, by the powders you see,
20   That those infernal rogues boiled the poor man and his brogues,
          Oh hone a vourneen machree!

A New Song Called
The Emigrant's Farewell to Donegal
ANONYMOUS

Good people on you I call, give ear to those lines you soon shall
    hear;
I'm caused to weep deprived of sleep for parting from my
    relations dear;
My hardships here I can't endure, there's nothing here but
    slavery,
I will take my lot and leave this spot and try the land of liberty.

5   Farewell dear Erin, fare thee well, that once was call'd the Isle
    of Saints,
For here no longer I can dwell, I'm going to cross the stormy
    sea,
For to live here I can't endure, there's nothing here but slavery,
My heart's oppress'd, I can find no rest, I will try the land of
    liberty.

My father holds five acres of land, it was not enough to support
    us all,
10   Which banishes me from my native land, to old Ireland dear I bid
    farewell.
My hardships here I can't endure, since here no longer I can stay
I take my lot and leave this spot and try the land of liberty.

My love, you know that trade is low, provisions they're
    exceeding high,
We see the poor from door to door craving their wants we can't
    supply,
15   To hear their moans, their sighs and groans, with children naked,
    cold, and bare,
Craving relief, it renews my grief as we have nothing for to
    spare.

So now my dear you need not fear the dangers of the raging sea,
If your mind is bent I am content, so now prepare and come
    away.
My dear, if you'll agree to marry me, I'll quickly prepare,
20   We'll join our hands in wedlock's bands and we will stay no
    longer here.

It was in the year of '46 I was forced to leave my native land,
To old Ireland I bid adieu and to my fond relations all,
But now I 'm in America, no rents or taxes we pay at all,
So now I bid a long farewell to my native and old Donegal.

A New Song on the Rotten Potatoes
ANONYMOUS

You landlords of Ireland I'd have you beware,
And of your poor tenants I 'd wish you'd take care,
For want of potatoes in this present year
From the crutch to the cradle are trembling with fear.

5   See how starvation meets us in the face;
But relief is expected from each foreign place,
Come sell all your cattle and don't keep a tail
Before that you part with your corn or meal.

Through Ireland the potatoes do rot in the field,
10   If you were to see them it would make your heart bleed;
If they don't get relief then the poor must prevail
And fight till they die for their corn and meal.

Then next try the landlord and see what he'll do,
For they know the potatoes are rotten all through;
15   Tell them for your rent that you'll give them good bail
Before that you'll part with your corn or meal.

If then to your wishes they will not comply,
Then tell them at once that you'd rather to die
For your family is starving for want of the grain,
20   Then why should you part with your corn or meal.

There are some of those landlords playing their pranks,
And sending the tenants to draw in their ranks
They'll have them like foxes all caught by the tail,
And then you must part with your corn and meal.

25   Let the Whigs and Repealers all join heart and hand,
And likewise the Tories to come on one plan,

To boldly come forward and never to fail,
And then we will have both our corn and meal.

Come cheer up good people, you need never fear,
30 For the rents they must fall upon this present year;
Sure they can't tyrannize or attempt to prevail,
To make you to part either corn or meal.

Do not be down-hearted but cheer up once more,
The provision is coming from each foreign shore,
35 Good beer, flour, and butter, rich sugar and tea,
From Russia and Prussia and America.

The potatoes have failed since the year Forty-Five;
The labourers will flourish and trade will revive;
Public works & railroads will commence without fail,
40 And then we can purchase both corn and meal.

So now my good people you need never fear;
Old Ireland will prosper on this present year;
But instead of potatoes, believe what I say:
We'll have cheap loaf with a good cup of tea.

We'll Soon Have Cheap Flour and Plenty of Meal
ANONYMOUS

You boys of Tipperary attend to my ditty,
A few simple verses I wish to lay down,
Concerning those ruffians — I mean the managers
That plunder the people in country and town.
5 For this present season our pockets are draining,
Which leaves the poor people alas to bewail;
But don't be complaining — I'll tell you the reason
We'll soon have cheap flour and plenty of meal.

There's a big-gutted miser — his name I'll not mention —
10 You all know him well, he lives in the main street.
Not long ago this fellow was begging,
He don't know his friends when he does them meet;

By selling bad bread he raised up his head —
He'll get a downfall for that, I go bail —
15   In spite of such fellows that plunder the people,
We'll soon have cheap flour and plenty of meal.

We are backed by the Queen, it is plain to be seen:
Our ports she has opened to prosper our trade,
She is a true friend to all our brave sons,
20   That earn their bread by plough and the spade.
Sure, this very spring many ships they will bring
From Quebec, Philadelphia, and likewise Orleans,
Tho' much were distressed in parts of the west,
We'll soon have cheap flour and plenty of meal.

25   In Dublin, fair city, there was a great meeting,
Where thousands assembled, it's plain you may see:
There was Protestants, Catholics, Dissenters, & Quakers
That laid down their money both gallant and free;
Free seed to provide for the good of our nation,
30   Employment to bring unto old Grannuaile;
The truth I am telling without any lying,
We'll soon have cheap flour and plenty of meal.

There is a few more that now I will mention:
There is Father John, a pious divine,
35   He is generous and kind and liberal of mind;
He is good to the poor, as all creatures do find:
Mr. O'Brien, he is right good also,
No matter what creed, for that I'll go bail;
He will relieve them, without hesitation,
40   May he never want flour and plenty of meal.

So now to conclude and to finish these verses:
May trade and commerce soon bless our isle,
Unite all together like brother and brother,
And then all our foes they can't us beguile;
45   If we had fair play on this present day,
The foes of old Ireland we would revile,
In spite of John Bull and the bugs of this nation,
We'll soon have cheap flour and plenty of meal.

Notes on the Poems

'A Lay of the Famine'. *A Treasury of Irish Poetry in the English Tongue* ed. S.A. Brooke and T.W. Rolleston (London: Smith, Elder & Co., 1900), p. 179.
> Line 21:   'ululu': Onomatopoeic rendering of the keen, or lament for the dead.

'The Song of the Famine'. *Dublin University Magazine* Vol. 30, No. 175 (July, 1847).

'The Wanderer'. *The Nation* Vol. 7, No. 24 (Feb. 9, 1850).

'The Poor Little Maiden'. William Allingham (b. Ballyshannon, Co. Donegal, March 19, 1824; d. Hampstead, England, Nov. 18, 1899); although his verse suggests the influence of his friends from the literary world of Victorian England, notably Tennyson, many of Allingham's poems show a keen sympathy with the plight of the Irish peasantry in the years following the Famine; this is particularly true of his best work, the long poem *Lawrence Bloomfield in Ireland* (1864). 'The Poor Little Maiden' appeared in his first collection, dedicated to Leigh Hunt: *Poems* (London: Chapman & hall, 1850), p. 98.

'The Young Street Singer'. *Poems* (London: Chapman & Hall, 1850), p. 244.

'Lay of the Famine: The Irish Husband to his Wife'. *Dublin University Magazine* Vol. 35, No. 205 (March, 1850). 'W.C.B'. was possibly William Carr Boyd, who completed a B.A. at Trinity College in 1851.

'The Last Appeal'. *The Irishman* Vol. 1, No. 34 (Aug. 15, 1849).

'And the Famine Was Sore in the Land: 1847'. John Swanwick Drennan (1809-1893) was a medical doctor and son of the author the United Irishman manifesto, William Drennan, *Glendalloch and Other Poems by the Late Dr. Drennan, With Additional Verse by His Sons* (Dublin: William Robertson, 1859), p. 110.

'A Wail: 1847'. *Glendalloch* (Dublin: William Robertson, 1859), p. 82.
> Line 21:   'Cairns of Meath': The neolithic burial mounds of Newgrange, Knowth, and Dowth.

Line 21:   'Cashel's station': The Rock of Cashel, Co. Tipperary; site of a number of churches, dating back to the 5th cent.

Line 24:   'Glendalloch': Monastic settlement in Co. Wicklow.

'1848'. William Drennan, Jr. (1802-1895). Lawyer, and son of the author of the United Irishman manifesto, William Drennan, *Glendalloch* (Dublin: William Robertson, 1859), p. 151.

Line 4, etc: 'Thrasea': Publius Clodius Thrasea Paetus (d. A.D. 60) Roman senator famous for his opposition to Nero.

Line 5:   'Helvidius': Helvidius Priscus (fl. ca. A.D. 60) Roman stoic who opposed Nero on the principle that an emperor should be bound by the decisions of the Senate.

Line 9:   'Tantalus': In Greek mythology, a man punished by the gods by being placed within sight of fruit which he could never reach.

'Lament of the Irish Emigrant': Lady Dufferin (b. 1807; d. London, June 13, 1867). Born Helen Selina Sheridan, this grand-daughter of the playwright Richard Brinsley Sheridan married the Marquess of Dufferin in 1825. Her sentimental Irish poems were much anthologized. Her 'Lament' can be found in *Songs, Poems and Verses* (London: John Murray, 1894).

'A Christmas Chime for 1849'. *Dublin University Magazine* Vol. 35, No. 205 (Jan, 1850).

'To the Cholera'. John Keegan (b. Queen's Co. [Co. Laois], 1809; d. Dublin, 1849) was educated at a hedge school, and wrote much fugitive verse in the journals of the period. He was a victim of the cholera epidemic of 1849, and was buried in a pauper's grave in Glasnevin. *Cork Magazine* Vol. 2, No. 13 (Nov., 1848).

Line 16:   'Tamerlaine': Notoriously cruel Scythian conqueror, made famous in plays by Marlowe and Rowe.

Line 28:   'Romaunt of Sue': *The Wandering Jew* (trans. 1844), an enormously popular novel by Eugene Sue (1804-1857), which ends with the deaths from cholera of its two heroines.

Line 34:   'Leo': Pope Leo X, Giovanni de Medici (1475-1521) patron of the arts and excommunicator of Luther.

Line 34:   'Wellesley': Arthur Wellesley (1769-1852), first Duke of Wellington, hero of Waterloo.

'The Dying Mother's Lament'. *Legends and Poems* (Dublin: Sealy, Byrne & Walker, 1907), p. 509.

'Home Again'. Mary Kelly (b. ca. 1825, Headford, Co. Galway; d. Brisbane, Australia, May, 1910) wrote as 'Eva' for *The Nation, The United Irishman*, and *The Irish Felon*; her involvement with nationalist politics brought her into contact with Dr. Kevin Izod O'Doherty, to whom she became engaged. O'Doherty was transported in 1848, and Kelly followed him to Australia, where they were married. 'Home Again' can be found in *Poems By 'Eva' of The Nation* (Dublin: M.H. Gill & Son, 1909), p. 65.

'A Scene for Ireland'. *Poems By 'Eva' of the Nation* (Dublin: M.H. Gill & Son, 1909), p. 57.

'One of Many'. *The Irishman* Vol. 1, No. 25 (June 23, 1849).

'A Lament'. William Pembroke Mulchinock (b. Tralee, Co. Kerry, March, 1820; d. Sept., 1864) was one of the mainstays of the short-lived *Cork Magazine*; wrote for *The Nation* as 'W.P.M., and 'Heremon'; emigrated to New York in 1849, but returned to Ireland in 1850. The list of 'patrons' for his *Ballads and Songs of W.P.M.* includes Emerson, Irving, and Longfellow. 'A Lament' first appeared in the *Cork Magazine* Vol. 2, No. 14 (Dec., 1848).
Lines 57-8:   'Sodom, Gomorrah': In subsequent reprintings of the poem, the lines were dropped comparing the desolation of Sodom and Gomorrah with that of Ireland.

'The Old Story'. *Cork Magazine* Vol. 2, No. 13 (Nov. 1848).

'Song of the Ejected Tenant'. *Ballads and Songs of W.P.M.* (New York: T.W. Strong, 1851), p. 200.
Line 21:   'ululu': Onomatopoeic rendering of the keen, or lament for the dead.

'Ireland's Lament'. Jeremiah O'Ryan (b. Bansha, Co. Tipp., ca. 1770; d. Bansha, March, 1855) wrote in local journals as 'Darby Ryan'. His lengthy 'Lament' appears in his only volume, *The Tipperary Minstrel* (Dublin: Marcus Maddigan, 1861), p. 15
Line 14:   'Moloch': False idol; see Amos 5:26.

'The Eviction'. Michael Segrave (b. Drogheda, Co. Louth, 1823; d. Wigan, May 3, 1875) emigrated to Lancashire in 1840 to work as a weaver; joined the Chartist movement, and wrote for *The Irishman*. 'The Eviction' can be found in Ralph Varian's *Ballads, Popular Poetry and Household Songs of Ireland* (Dublin: M.H. Gill & Sons, 1877), p. 109.

'The Boreen Side'. James Tighe (b. Carrickmacross, Co. Monaghan, 1795; d. Dublin, Nov. 17, 1869) ran a bookshop in Great Britain St., Dublin; wrote temperance tracts; a friend of Mangan, he contributed to the *Irish Penny Journal* and *The Irishman* , in which 'The Boreen Side' appeared: Vol. 1, No. 39 (Sept. 29, 1849).

'The Irish Mother's Lament'. Elizabeth Willoughby Varian (b. Ballymena, Co. Antrim, ca. 1830; d. ca. 1903) wrote for *The Nation* as 'Finola'; in 1871 married poet and editor Ralph Varian. Her 'Lament' can be found in *Poems by 'Finola'* (Belfast: John Henderson: 1851), p. 117.
Line 29:   'Mavoureen': Ir. 'My darling'.

'The Tabinet Weaver'. *Poems* (Belfast: Henderson, 1851), p. 114.
Title: 'tabinet': A costly watered fabric of silk and wool.

'Drimin Donn Dilis'. John Walsh (b. Cappoquin, Co. Waterford, April 1, 1835; d. Cashel, Co. Tipp., Feb. 1881) worked as a teacher; a frequent contributor to the journals of the time, including *The Nation*, for whom he wrote as 'J.W'. and 'Boz'; *The Irishman* as 'Shamrock' and 'Lismore'; the *Waterford Citizen* as 'A Capppoquin Girl'. 'Drimin Donn Dilis' can be found in Stopford Brooke and T.W. Rolleston, eds. *A Treasury of Irish Poetry* (London: Smith, Elder, 1900), p. 185.

Title: 'Drimin Donn Dilis': Ir. 'Dear brown cow'.

'Lament of the Ejected Irish Peasant'. *Dublin University Magazine* Vol. 35, No. 205 (Jan. 1850). It was republished as a broadside, available in the White Collection, Trinity College, Dublin.

Line 6: 'A gradh geal . . .' Ir. 'O bright love of my heart'.

'The Itinerant Singing Girl'. Lady Wilde (b. Wexford, ca. 1824; d. London, Feb. 3, 1896), born Jane Francesca Elgee, is perhaps better remembered as 'Speranza', the name under which she wrote for *The Nation*. In 1851 she married William Wilde (knighted 1864), and became the mother of Oscar Wilde. 'The Itinerant Singing Girl' was first published in *The Nation* Vol. 7, No. 19 (Dec. 29, 1849).

PART II

'A Land Become a Monument'

AUBREY DE VERE & THE RELIGIOUS RESPONSE

'The Desolation of the West'. Aubrey Thomas de Vere (b. Curragh Chase, Co. Limerick, Jan. 10, 1814; d. Curragh Chase, Jan. 21, 1902), as a landlord and man of letters took an active part in the cultural life of both England and Ireland. He was a friend of Ruskin, Tennyson, and Newman, in whose footsteps De Vere followed when he became a Roman Catholic in 1851. In 1882 he published a verse translation of the Irish epic, the *Táin Bó Cuailnge*, entitled *The Foray of Queen Maeve*. He spent much of the Famine on his estate, and in 1848 wrote about the state of Ireland in *English Misrule and Irish Misdeeds*. 'The Desolation of the West', can be found in his *Irish Odes and Other Poems* (New York: The Catholic Publications Society, 1869), p. 40.

Epigraph: 'Misgravit Judah . . .' 'Judah has gone into exile because of affliction'. Lam. 1:3.

Lines 19-21: 'race of old Ulster driven': The Cromwellian Act of Settlement (1652) drove much of the Catholic population of Ulster into Connaught.

Line 53: 'her Faith': The Roman Catholic church, which De Vere joined in 1851; the poem is dated Dec. 12, 1860.

Line 62: 'New Heaven': 'And I saw a new Heaven and a new earth'. Rev. 21:1.

Line 69: 'that City': The New Jerusalem of Rev. 21.

'Ireland: 1851'. *Irish Odes* (New York: Catholic Publications Society, 1869), p. 159.

'Irish Colonization: 1848': First appeared in the *Dublin Univerity Magazine* Vol.

34, No. 199 (1849), p. 110.
Line 24:   'Hesperean': Hesperius, land of the west.
Line 26:   'Iris': In Greek mythology, goddess of the rainbow, and mes-
              senger of the gods.
Line 65:   'old torn Poland . . .' Poland was partitioned as a spoil of war
              three times, in 1772, 1793 and 1795.

'Ode: After One of the Famine Years'. *Irish Odes* (New York: Catholic Publications
      Society, 1869), p. 40.
Line 22-3:   'Tuileries . . . Invalides': Parisian public buildings attacked by
              the mob in 1792.
Line 93:   'Blessed the mourners': The Sermon on the Mount: i.e. 'Blessed
              are they that mourn; for they shall be comforted'. Mt. 5:4.

'The Sisters: Or, Weal in Woe'. *Irish Odes* (New York: Catholic Publications
      Society, 1869), p. 174.

'Widowhood: 1848'. *Irish Odes* (New York: Catholic Publications Society, 1869),
      p. 149.

'The Year of Sorrow: Ireland — 1849'. *Irish Odes* (New York: Catholic
      Publications Society, 1869), p. 141.

'Sonnet: 1849': Ellen Fitzsimon (b. Westland Row, Dublin, Nov. 12, 1805; d.
      London, Jan. 27, 1883). The eldest daughter of Daniel O'Connell, Fitzsimon
      wrote for *The Nation* .as 'L.M.F'. Her 'Sonnet' is from *Darrynane in Eighteen
      Hundred and Thirty-Two and Other Poems* (Dublin: W.B. Kelly, 1863), p. 99.
Line 14:   Whom the Lord loveth . . .' 'For whom the Lord loveth he
              chasteneth, and scourgeth every son he receiveth'. Heb. 12:6.

PART III

'To Help Old Ireland in Another Rhyme'.

SATIRES AND DIALOGUES

'Dublin: A Poem'. Sir Samuel Ferguson (b. Belfast, March 10, 1810; d. Howth, Aug.
      9, 1886) was a successful lawyer, an antiquarian, and one of the leading Irish
      poets of his age, whose reputation today rests on his verse translations of Irish
      epics, such as his *Congol* (1872). During the Famine, his political sympathies
      began to move away from the unionism he had espoused as a younger man.
      'Dublin' first appeared in the *Dublin University Magazine*, Vol. 34, No. 199
      (July, 1849). Two sections of the poem have been omitted; one of 204 lines,
      beginning at line 106; and another of 24 lines, beginning at line 126.
Line 6:   'Californian gold': The California gold rush of 1849 widened
              the gulf between the poverty of Ireland, and the potential of the
              New World.

Line 19: 'Champion's van': Ralph W. Champion, coal merchant and furniture van-proprietor, of 50 Denzille St., Dublin.

Line 20: 'King William': Statue of William III which stood on College Green, facing the gates of Trinity College.

Line 22: 'the Bank': The Bank of Ireland building on College Green; formerly the Irish House of Parliament (1782-1800).

Line 24: 'Grattan': Henry Grattan (1746-1820) Irish statesman; the key figure in the establishment of the Irish Parliament of 1782.

Line 27: 'Bushe': Charles Kendal Bushe (1767-1843); one of the members of the Parliament of 1782 who opposed the Act of Union.

Line 27: 'Plunket': William Conyngham Plunket (1764-1854); one of the members of the Parliament of 1782 who opposed the Act of Union.

Line 36: 'Beresford': John Beresford (1738-1805); as Commissioner of Revenue for Ireland was responsible for the construction of the Custom House in 1780.

Line 52: 'D —': Probably either John Blake Dillon (1816-1866), or Michael Doheny (1805-1863), both of whom were Young Irelanders who went to New York after the failure of the 1848 rising.

Line 54: 'Lachesis': In Greek mythology, one of the Three Moirae, or Fates; the 'caster of lots'.

Line 57: 'Menenius': The pen-name of Digby Pilot Starkey, a unionist pamphleteer of the period; i.e. *Luck and Loyalty*, 1848.

Line 58: 'Sartorius': Ernest Sartorius, German religious pamphleteer; a translation of his *Doctrine of the Person and the Work of Christ* was distributed by the Religious Tract Society in 1838.

Line 70: 'Sub prohibitione superûm': Under the prohibition of a superior.

Line 71: 'sorites': A logical sophism formed by an accumulation of arguments.

Line 78: 'a million too few': The Poor Inquiry Commission of 1836 estimated that over 2 million persons were living in poverty in Ireland. This was interpreted by some economists as a 'surplus population', of whom Ireland had to dispose.

Line 104: 'Hoyle': Edmund Hoyle (1672-1769) Author of rule books for whist, backgammon, and numerous other games.

Line 104: 'Priscian': Priscianus Caesariensis (fl. ca. 500 A.D.) Latin grammarian.

Line 147: 'Codrus': A legendary king of Athens.

Line 158: 'half-acre': The Gregory Clause stated that anyone holding more than a quarter acre of land was not eligible for public relief.

Line 162: 'Arturius': Arthur; e.g. a king or ruler.

Line 194: 'road': see note to 'Inheritor and Economist' line 445, on p. 280.

Line 204: 'Ribbon Lodge': See note to 'Inheritor and Economist', line 198, on p. 279.

Line 204:   'Orange Lodge': Society founded in 1795 to defend protestant-
              ism, and later unionism.
Line 205:   'Bann': River in Co. Antrim and Co. Derry.
Line 206:   'Lagan': River running through Belfast.
Line 218:   'dare not hang': See note to 'The Famished Land', line 14 on p.
              289.
Line 220:   ''Tis conscience . . .': *Hamlet*, Act III, Scene i.
Line 225:   'one short bill': The Constitution of 1782.

'Inheritor and Economist: A Poem'. *Dublin University Magazine* Vol. 33, No. 197
(May, 1849). A section of the poem 120 lines long has been deleted, beginning
at line 500.
Line 4:   'catallacticals': A proposed name for the study of political econ-
              omy; 'the science of exchanges'.
Line 13:   'Liebig': Justus Von Liebig (1803-1873), German chemist;
              *Organic Chemistry In Its Applications to Agriculture and
              Physiology* (1840).
Line 38:   'Free Trade': The great debate over the repeal of the tariffs on
              imported grain reached a crisis in the winter of 1845 with the
              first reports of famine in Ireland.
Line 82:   'Bonnycastle': John Bonnycastle (ca. 1750-1821), author of
              many standard textbooks on elementary mathematics; *The
              Scholar's Guide to Arithmetic* (1780).
Line 94:   'Parkes': Isaiah Parkes; *Essays on the Philosophy and Art of
              Land Drainage* (1848).
Line 139:   'Napier': Probably Sir Charles James Napier (1782-1853), mili-
              tary hero of the Sikh Wars of the 1840s.
Line 146:   'Lucretius': Roman poet (ca. 99 B.C. - ca. 55 B.C.), author of
              On The Nature of Things.
Line 154:   'Calliope': Muse of epic poetry.
Line 155:   'Clio': Muse of history.
Line 198:   'Ribbon-lodge': A secret, loosely organized agrarian paramil-
              itary organization.
Line 214:   'anti-phlogistics': Flame retardants.
Line 214:   'phlebotomy': Theraputic blood-letting.
Line 247:   'who's to pay?': The conviction of government policy-makers
              that 'Irish property should pay for Irish poverty' meant that the
              landlords in the most destitute Poor Law Unions — those least
              able to pay — had the highest poor rates.
Line 309:   'Heraclitus': Ephesian philosopher (fl. ca. 500 B.C.) whose best
              known utterance, 'It is not possible to step twice into the same
              river', encapsulates his concept of eternal mutability.
Line 320:   'Shere Sing': Shir Singh, Sikh commander in the second British-
              Sikh War (1848-9).
Lines 369-71: 'Indian Corn': Known popularly as 'Peel's Brimstone', it caused
              severe digestive problems for those unused to preparing and

eating corn meal.

Line 375:   'Scire facias': A judicial writ requiring the party concerned to 'show cause' why execution should not be taken.

Line 400:   'four hundred millions debt': The Irish national debt on the eve of the Act of Union was £21 million; the English, £461 million.

Line 405:   'If Dorsetshire and York . . .': cf. 'If Cornwall had been visited with the scenes that have desolated Cork, would similar arguments [concerning the cost of relief efforts] have been used?' Isaac Butt, *A Voice For Ireland*, 1847.

Line 409:   'slave-owners': cf. 'To replace the lost food by foreign corn would have required an appropriation of twenty million sterling — the same amount which has been devoted, without scruple, to turning West Indian negroes wild'. John Mitchel, *The Last Conquest of Ireland (Perhaps)*, 1861. The money was given as compensation to slave-owners after the abolition of slavery in 1833.

Line 445:   'roads': Relief work was only allowed to be 'non-productive', so as not to interfere with the free market; hence, there was much unnecessary building and rebuilding of roads, many of which were left torn up when the public works ended in the Spring of 1849.

Line 507:   'Castle-Rack-Rent': Maria Edgeworth's novel, *Castle Rackrent* (1800) dealt with the decline of an estate.

Line 524:   'Todd and Burns': Dublin drapers, located at 47 Mary St., and 24 Jervis St.

Line 545-6: 'Diocletian . . . Constantine': Diocletian, Roman emperor (r. 284-305 A.D.) inaugurated the last and most severe persecution of Christians. Coins of his reign depicted emperors and were thus objected to by Christians. Constantine (r. 306-337 A.D.) succeeded Diocletian and became a Christian in A.D. 312.

Line 547:   'the sign': Before the battle of Milvian Bridge (A.D. 312), Constantine was reputed to have been told in a dream by Christ to paint crosses on all his soldier's shields; 'By this sign shall you conquer' — which Constantine did.

'The Potato Commission'. Edward Forbes, head of the Geological Museum, Jermyn Street, Dublin. Forbes originally wrote the song for the amusement of his colleagues; it was subsequently reprinted in *The Bentley Ballads; Comprising the Tipperary Hall Ballads* (London: R. Bentley, 1876).

Line 2:   'Potato Commission': In Oct. of 1846, Sir Robert Peel appointed Dr. Lyon Playfair (1818-1898), a chemist who had studied under Liebig [see note on p. 279 to 'Inheritor and Economist', line 13], and the botanist Dr. John Lindley (1799-1865) to determine the cause of the potato blight.

Line 7:   'Sir Robert': Sir Robert Peel (1788-1850), prime minister at the onset of the Famine.

Line 11: 'King Dan': Daniel O'Connell (1755-1847) 'The Liberator', head of the Repeal Association.

Line 13: 'Prince John': John O'Connell (1811-1858), son of Daniel O'Connell and heir apparent to the leadership of the Repeal Association.

Line 13: 'Smith O'Brien': William Smith O'Brien (1803-1864), one of the most popular of the Young Ireland leaders.

Line 45: 'Decaine': Joseph Decaisne (1807-1882), French botanist.

Line 45: 'Kutzing': Friedrich Kützing (1807-1893), German botanist.

'A Dialogue between an Irish Agent and a Tenant'. James Martin (b. Oldcastle, Co. Meath, 1782; d. Oldcastle, 1860), beginning in 1811, published nearly twenty small books of satiric verse, primarily in rhymed couplets, extolling a pre-Connellite nationalism. His 'Dialogue' was privately printed in volume of that name (Dublin, 1848). Martin supplies numerous scriptural notes for the poem, the most pertinent of which have been retained.

Line 90: 'field to field': 'Woe unto them who join house to house, that lay field to field till there be no place, that they may be placed alone in the midst of the earth!' Isa. 5:8; also Hab. 2:9-10; Prov. 30:4.

Line 94: 'oppress the poor': 'Deliver the spoiled out of the hand of the oppressor; and do no violence to the stranger, the fatherless, or the widow. . . . But if ye will not hear these words, I swear by myself, saith the Lord, that this house will become a desolation. Jer. 22:3-5; also Ps. 14:4; Ezek. 22:7.

Line 101: 'The land': 'The land shall not be sold forever; for the land is mine'. Lev 25:23.

Line 183-4: 'faith not works': 'By works a man is justified, and not by faith only'. Jas 2:24.

'The Mirror of Satire: A Rhapsody'. *John and Mary: A Modern Irish Tale, etc.* (Trim: Henderson Bros., 1855), p. 89.

PART IV

'One Whom Some Have Called A Seer'

JAMES CLARENCE MANGAN

A Vision of Connaught in the Nineteenth Century'. *The Nation* Vol. 5, No. 250 (July 17, 1847). Internal evidence suggests that Mangan is again playing with the conventions of authorship, as he did in his pseudo-translations, and wrote this parody of himself. It was published with the following notice: 'Mangan, exactly a year ago, wrote "A Vision of Connaught in the Thirteenth Century", which, as it may have escaped the memory of some of our readers, we republish. Now, we ask our readers to compare it, line by line, with this graphic composition by a younger Mangan, and pronounce with us in favour of the new comer'.

Epigraph: 'Et moi . . .': Mangan's epigraph for the original reads: "Et moi, j'ai éte aussi en Arcadi — And I , I too have been a dreamer". Inscription on a painting by Poussin'.

Line 6:   'highways': See note on p. 280 to 'Inheritor and Economist', line 445.

Line 12:   Randolph Routh': Sir Randolph Routh (1785-1858); from Nov. 1845 until Oct. 1848 superintended the distribution of famine relief, for which he was knighted in April of 1848.

Line 33:   'Soyer': Alexis Benôit Soyer (1809-1858) French chef of London's Reform Club, who devised a soup for the Irish poor costing only £1 per 100 gallons. Fashionable Dublin flocked to view his soup kitchen in Phoenix Park. The *Freeman's Journal* exclaimed on April 6, 1847:

'Dublin society pays 5 shillings each to see paupers feed on Soyer's soup. Five shillings each to watch the burning blush of shame chasing pallidness from poverty's wan cheek! When the animals in the Zoological Gardens can be inspected at feeding time for sixpence!'

See also 'Another Version of Soyer's Soup' on p. 268.

Line 37:   'the Hall': Conciliation Hall, Burgh Quay, Dublin; headquarters of O'Connell 's Repeal Association.

Line 38:   'the change': The 'repeal rent', weekly donations which financed the Repeal Association. Contributions dropped to a mere £12 from the entire country on the week of June 6, 1848.

Line 55:   'Freeman': *Freeman's Journal*, pro-O'Connell Dublin newspaper.

'The Famine'. James Clarence Mangan (b. Dublin, May 1, 1803; d. Dublin, June 20, 1849) the poète maudit of 19th cent. Dublin, was both the most experimental and the most tormented Irish poet of the period. In spite of a life of grinding poverty, and addictions to alcohol and opium, he nonetheless managed to produce a large body of poetry that is receiving ever-increasing critical attention. He died during the cholera epidemic of 1848, his body emaciated by malnutrition. 'The Famine', his last published poem, appeared in *The Irishman* Vol. 1, No. 23 (June 9, 1849), eleven days before his death.

Lines 5-7:   'Tishbite seer': The prophet Elijah, who from the top of Mount Carmel saw 'a little cloud ariseth out of the sea'. 1 Kings 18:44.

Line 15:   'Simoom': A desert wind.

Line 35:   'Pharos': The great lighthouse at Alexandria.

'The Funerals'. *The Irishman* Vol. 1, No. 13 (Mar. 31, 1849).

'Lamentation of Jeremias over Jerusalem'. Duffy's *Irish Catholic Magazine*, April, 1847. A paraphrase of the first chapter of the Book of Lamentations; each stanza corresponds, more or less, to a verse of the original. The epigraph is not from the Bible.

'The Peal of Another Trumpet'. *The Nation* Vol. 4, No. 186 (May 2, 1846) .

Title: 'Trumpet': Trumpets figure prominently in Biblical prophecy; cf. Ezek. 7:14, 33:3; Rev. 8, 9, and 11.

Epigraph: 'Mdlle Lenormand': Marie Anne Adelaide Lenormand (1772-1843), rose to prominence during the French Revolution by providing prognostications for Danton, Marat, and Robespierre: later a confidante of Napoleon.

Line 82:   'St. Leon': Eponymous hero of a novel (1799) by William Godwin.

'Pompeii'. *Duffy's Irish Catholic Magazine* (April, 1847).

Title: 'Pompeii': City destroyed by the eruption of Mount Vesuvius on Aug. 24, A.D. 79.

'Siberia'. *The Nation* Vol. 4, No. 184 (April 18, 1846).

'Song of the Albanian'. *The Nation* Vol. 5, No. 254 (Aug. 14, 1847).

Title: '1826': The siege of Mesolonghi; despite being reduced to a diet of seaweed, the inhabitants of the town made a final effort to attack the besieging Turks in April, 1826. They were defeated and massacred.

Line 8:   'dominant Moslem': Albania did not finally achieve independence from Turkey until 1913.

Line 10:   'Góvria': Mountain to the west of Mesolonghi.

Line 43:   'glorious Greece': Greece achieved independence from Turkey in 1830: the death of Byron in 1824 during the Greek War of Independence popularized philhellenism among admirers of romanticism.

Line 50:   'khandjer': A curved Eastern dagger.

'A Vision: A.D. 1848'. *The United Irishman* Vol. 1, No. 3 (Feb. 26, 1848).

Line 27:   'a Man': Daniel O'Connell (1775-1847), who between 1839 and 1842 established the Repeal Association.

Line 49:   'people by millions': O'Connell's famous 'monster meetings', at Tara and Mullaghmast, drew vast crowds.

Line 101:   'trumpet... in John': Trumpets figure prominently as harbingers in Rev. 8, 9 and 11.

'A Voice of Encouragement — A New Year's Lay': *The Nation* Vol. 6, No. 274 (Jan. 1, 1848).

Line 25:   'Milton': 'Which way shall I fly,
Infinite wrath, and infinite despair?
Which way I fly is hell, my self am hell;
And in the lowest deep, a lower deep
Still threatening to devour me opens wide,
To which the hell I suffer seems a heaven'.
Paradise Lost *Book IV, Lines 73-8*.

Line 48:   'Son of Man cometh': A misquotation of Matt. 24:44; 'Therefore be ye also ready, for in such an hour as ye think not the Son of Man cometh'.

Line 67: 'comet-sword': 'A blazing star or comet appeared for several months before the plague'. Daniel Defoe, *Journal of the Plague Year*. Ironically, the passage is from Defoe's denunciation of 'fortune-tellers, cunning-men, and astrologers'.

'The Warning Voice'. *The Nation* Vol. 4, No. 176 (Feb. 21, 1846).

Line 74: 'Sea of clear glass': 'And I saw, as it were, a sea of glass mingled with fire, and them that had gotten the victory over the beast'. Rev. 15:2.

'When Hearts Were Trumps'. *The Irishman* Vol. 2, No. 4 (Jan. 26, 1850).

Line 3: 'slight leaven and largest lumps': 'Know ye not that a little leaven leaveneth the whole whole lump'. Cor. 5:6 Leaven, a piece of fermented bread added to new bread is used throughout the Bible to represent impurity.

Line 11: 'Gall's and Spurzheim's bumps': Franz Joseph Gall (1785-1828) and Johann C. Spurzheim (1776-1832), neuroanatomists whose theories of the physiological structure of the brain gave credence to the practice of phrenology.

Line 17: 'Ninety-Three': See also Lady Wilde's 'France in 'Ninety-Three' on p. 225.

Line 21: 'Clubs': The radical arm of the repeal movement was divided into a number of semi-autonomous Confederate Clubs.

Line 23: 'Castle-Hercules': Dublin castle, seat of the British administration of Ireland.

Line 35: 'Brummell ... D'Orsay': George 'Beau' Brummell (1778-1840) and Alfred G.G. D'Orsay (1801-1852), Regency leaders of fashion.

'Lament for Clarence Mangan'. Richard D'Alton Williams (b. Dublin, Oct. 8, 1822; d. Thibodeaux, Louisiana, July 5, 1862) was a medical student when he began writing for *The Nation* as 'Shamrock' and 'D.N.S'. In 1848 he co-founded the *Irish Tribune* with Kevin Izod O'Doherty; the two were later tried for treason felony, but Williams was acquitted: he emigrated in 1851. His 'Lament' was originally published as 'Implore Pace For Clarence Mangan' in *The Irishman* Vol. 1, No. 27 (July 7, 1849). Mangan died on June 20, 1849.

Epigraph: 'Oft with tears . . .': From Mangan's 'To Joseph Brenan: A Reply', first published in *The Irishman* Vol. 1, No. 22 (June 2, 1849).

Line 19: 'Tyrconnell and Tyrone': Mangan's 'Lament For The Princes of Tyrone and Tyrconnell' (1840).

Line 21: 'Bosphorus': A phrase from Mangan's 'The Wail and Warning of the Three Khalendeers' (1844).

Line 22: 'elfin mariners': Mangan's 'The Fairies' Passage' (1848).

Line 23: 'Lady Agnes': perhaps Williams is thinking of 'Lady Eleanora' in Mangan's translation of Rükert's 'Ride Around the Parapet' (1842).

Line 24:   'Cáhal Mór': The central figure in Mangan's 'Vision of Connaught in The Thirteenth Century' (1846).

Line 24:   'Roisin Dubh': Mangan translated this Irish poem twice, as 'Dark Rosaleen' (1846) and 'Roisin Dubh' (1849).

Line 27:   'the warnings': cf. Mangan's 'A Warning Voice' (1846) on p. 152.

Line 29:   'tranced vision': cf. Mangan's 'A Vision' (1848) on p. 146.

Line 58:   'Trisagion': An angelic hymn to God.

PART V

'The Bright-Eyed and the Bold'

THE NATIONALIST CHALLENGE

'Be Free'. *The Irishman* Vol. 1, No. 31 (Aug. 4, 1849).

Line 9:   'sun to rule. . .': 'And God made two great lights: the greater light to rule the day, and the lesser light to rule the night'. Gen. 1:16.

Line 27:   'Felony': see note to 'The Famished Land', line 14 on p. 289.

Line 41:   'I gave a king . . .': I gave thee a king in mine anger, and took him away in my wrath'. Hos 13:11.

'How Shall We Hail the Spring?' *The United Irishman* Vol. 1, No. 7 (March 25, 1848).

Line 16:   'Golconda': Former name of Hyderbad, celebrated for its diamonds.

'The Plucking of the Shamrock'. *The Nation* Vol. 6, No. 286 (March 25, 1848).

'Thanatos, 1849'. *The Irishman* Vol. 1, No. 18 (May 5, 1849).

Title: 'Thanatos': Gk. 'Death'.

Epigraph: 'Him that dieth . . .' 1 Kings 16:4.

Line 10:   'Apollyon': 'And there came out of the smoke locusts upon the earth. . . . And they had a king over them, who is the Angel of the bottomless pit, whose name is Apollyon'. Rev. 9:3,11.

Line 34:   'Sennacherib': King of Assyria (r. 704-681 B.C.), invaded Judah in 701 B.C.; mentioned in 2 Kings.

'Present and Future'. *Echoes From Parnassus: Selected from the Original Poetry of the Cork Southern Reporter* (Cork: Southern Reporter, 1849), p. 12.

'A Song of Ulster'. Francis Davis (b. Hillsborough, Co. Down, March 7, 1810; d. Belfast, Oct. 7, 1885). A weaver by trade, Davis wrote for *The Nation* as 'The Belfast Man': in 1850 he established his own newspaper, the *Belfast Man's Journal*, which ran for three months. 'A Song of Ulster' can be found in his collected poems, *Earlier and Later Leaves* (Belfast: Patrick Mallon, 1878), p, 267.

Line 17:   'Dutchman': William of Orange.

Line 77:   'upas': A mythical tree which cast a poisonous shadow.

'The Artisan's Apology for Emigrating'. John De Jean Frazer (b. Birr, Kings Co. [Co. Offaly], 1809; d. Dublin, March, 1852)A carpenter by trade, Frazer wrote for *The Nation* and *The Irishman* under the names of 'John De Jean', 'J. De J'. and 'J'. A prolific poet during the Famine years, he wrote much less after the death of his son in 1849. A collected edition of his *Poems* (Dublin: McGlashan) was brought out by a group of his admirers in 1851 to assist him financially. Nonetheless, he died in poverty the following year. 'The Artisan's Apology' first appeared in *The Irishman*, Vol. 1. No. 38 (Sept. 22, 1849).

'Extermination'. *The Irishman* Vol. 1, No. 40 (Oct. 6, 1849).

Title: 'Extermination': The word 'extermination' was used in the nationalist press of the period as a synonym for 'eviction'. See also R.D. Williams, 'The Extermination' on p. 233.

'The Harvest Pledge': *The Nation* Vol . 6, No. 301 (July 8, 1848).

Title: 'Harvest Pledge': It was an open secret in the Summer of 1848 that the leaders of the insurrectionary Confederate Clubs had decided to defer the rebellion until after the harvest had been gathered. Hence, the extra connotation of the word 'harvest' in 1848. See also Thomas D'Arcy McGee, 'A Harvest Hymn' on p. 196.

'The Lost Labour'. *The Irishman* Vol. 1, No. 24 (June 16, 1849).

'The Spring Flowers'. *The Nation* Vol. 5, No. 234 (April 3, 1847). Stanzas IV and V were added to the version of the poem published in Frazer's *Poems* (Dublin: McGlashan, 1851), p. 237.

'The Three Angels'. *Cork Magazine* Vol. 1, No. 10 (Aug., 1848).

'The Queen's Visit'. *The Irishman* Vol. 1, No. 31 (Aug. 4, 1849) . 'J'. is possibly John De Jean Frazer.

Title: 'Queen's Visit': Queen Victoria visited Ireland in August of 1849; see E.W. Varian's 'Our Welcome' on p. 214. See also 'Lines Written the Day before the Queen's Arrival in Dublin' on p. 244.

'Rhymes for the Landlorded'. William James Linton (b. London, Dec. 7, 1812; d. New Haven, Conn., Dec. 29, 1897) was a dedicated Chartist who wrote for *The Nation* as 'Spartacus' in hopes of uniting his cause with that of Young Ireland. In 1866 he emigrated to America, where he became the leading engraver of his age, and author of numerous books on the subject; he received an honorary doctorate from Yale in 1891. His 'Rhymes' were reprinted in Martin MacDermott's *New Spirit of the Nation* (London: T. Fisher Unwin, 1894), p. 85.

'A Mystery'. Denis Florence MacCarthy (b. Dublin, May 26, 1817; d. Blackrock, Co. Dublin, April 7, 1882) was respected during his lifetime for his translations of Calderon: however, his most popular works were the poems he published in *The Nation* as 'Desmond' or 'D.F.M.C'. 'A Mystery' has been much anthologized, and can be found in MacCarthy's collected *Poems* (Dublin: M.H. Gill & Sons, 1882); it first appeared in *The Nation* Vol. 5, No. 245 (June 19, 1847).

Line 6: 'Istambol': The famine aid sent to Ireland from Turkey was used by Irish nationalists as an indictment of the English reluctance to provide relief funds, as 'Turk' had long been a synonym for 'tyrant'. cf. 'They [the peasantry] were driven out of house and home in the black '47 . . . . Even the Grand Turk sent us his piastres'. 'The Citizen' in James Joyce's *Ulysses*.

'A Very Old, Old Man'. Martin MacDermott (b. Dublin, April 8, 1823: d. Dublin, April 25, 1905) was a Young Irelander who wrote for *The Nation* and the *Irish Felon* under his initials. He later became an architect, and worked for a time in Egypt; edited *The New Spirit of the Nation* (1894) and *Songs and Ballads of Young Ireland* (1896). 'A Very Old, Old Man' first appeared in *The Nation* Vol. 5, No. 272 (Dec. 18, 1847).

'The Famine in the Land'. Thomas D'Arcy McGee (b. Carlingford, Co. Louth, April 13, 1825; d. Ottawa, Ontario, April 7, 1868) emigrated to Boston in 1842; returned to Dublin in 1845 to work as a journalist, eventually becoming co-editor of *The Nation*, for which he wrote as 'Amergin'. He emigrated again in 1849, and went on to play a key role in the Confederation of Canada in 1867. He was assassinated by a disgruntled Fenian. 'The Famine in the Land' can be found in *The Poems of Thomas D'Arcy McGee* (London: D & J Sadlier, 1869). It originally appeared in *The Nation* Vol. 5, No. 236 (April 17, 1847) as 'Life and Land'.

Line 17: 'Gonsalvo . . . the Cid': Spanish warrior heroes; the first Gaelic invasion of Ireland was supposed to have been made by the Milesians, an Iberian tribe, ca. 1300 B.c.

Line 20: 'Roncevalles': Site of battle in Penninsular War, July 25, 1813; Marshall Stoult was repulsed by the British forces with heavy losses on both sides. A large number of Irishmen fought in the Penninsular army.

Line 21: 'Mariner': Christopher Columbus.

Line 51: 'Cleena': One of the legendary names for Ireland.

Line 55: 'Mononia': An ancient name for Munster.

'A Harvest Hymn'. *The Nation* Vol. 6, No. 298 (June 17, 1848).

Title: 'Harvest': See note to 'The Harvest Pledge' on p. 286.

'The Living and the Dead'. *The Nation* Vol. 5, No. 243 (June 5, 1847).

'The Three Dreams'. *Poems* (London: D & J Sadlier, 1869) p. 104.

Line 39: 'Tanist': The heir of a Celtic chieftain.

Line 39:   'Kerne': Irish foot-soldier.
Line 45:   'Milesius': Head of the Celtic tribe believed to have moved to
              Ireland from Spain. See note to 'The Famine in the Land', line
              17 on p. 287.

'The Woeful Winter'. *Poems* (London: D & J Sadlier, 1869), p. 343.
Line 13:   'Brian': Brian Boru (940-1014) one of the earliest Irish leaders
              to attempt to forge a national army from feuding tribes.
Line 13:   'Owen': Owen Roe O'Neill (ca.1590-1649) like Brian Boru,
              sought to create an Irish nation in the face of tribal loyalties.
Line 21:   'Romans': The Roman Empire was never to include Ireland;
              indeed, in the 4th cent. Roman Britain was frequently harassed
              by Irish raiders.
Line 23:   'Harold': Harold (ca. 1022-1066) King of England prior to the
              Norman conquest; sheltered with Dermot, King of Dublin, in the
              winter of 1051 during political troubles in England.
Line 23:   'Bruce': Edward Bruce (d. 1318), King of Ireland, and younger
              brother of Robert Bruce, King of Scotland.

'Patrick's Day, 1847'. *The Nation* Vol. 5, No. 234 (April 3, 1847).

'Pro and Con'. *The Irishman* Vol. 1, No. 32 (Aug. 11, 1849).
Line 9:   'eastern woe': Plagues were popularly believed to originate in
              the Middle East at the time of the Famine. See also 'Mortality in
              Skibbereen' on p. 264, and T.D. McGee's 'The Woeful Winter'
              on p. 199.

'Famine and Exportation'. John O'Hagan (b. Newry, March 19, 1822; d. Dublin,
     Nov. 12, 1890) Studied at Trinity College, Dublin; wrote for *The Nation* as
     'Siabh Cuilinn' and 'Carolina Wihelmina;' became a barrister, and was
     appointed chairman of the Irish Land Commission in 1881; wrote a study of
     Ferguson's poetry. His 'Famine and Exportation' can be found in *Songs and
     Ballads of Young Ireland* (London: Downey, 1896), p. 177.

'The Battle of Antioch'. John Thomas Rowland (b. Collon, Co. Louth, ca. 1825; d.
     Drogheda, Co. Louth, 1875) wrote for *The Nation* and *The Irishman* as
     'J.T.R.'; later became a solicitor; translated 'The Prophecy of MacAuliffe'
     from the Irish for Nicholas O'Kearney's *The Prophecies of St. Columbkille*,
     etc., (1856). 'The Battle of Antioch' is from *The Irishman* Vol. 2, No. 2 (Jan.
     12, 1849).
Line 2:   'Antioch': During the 1st Crusade, the city of Antioch (today
              Antakya, Turkey) was entered by the crusaders on June 8, 1098.
              Four days later they in turn were besieged by Kerbogha of
              Mosul, until a crusading sortie crushed Kerbogha on June 28.
              Antioch was the base for the successful march on Jerusalem the
              following year.

Line 7:   'Orontes': River Orontes, which runs into Antioch.
Line 76:   'Raymond of Toulouse': Raymond IV (1043(?)-1105), a leader
            of the lst Crusade.

'The Leaves Are Blighted'. *The Irishman* Vol. 1, No. 38 (Oct. 2;, 1849).
Line 16:   'Ard Righ': Ir. High King.

''Tis Evening Now'. *The Irishman* Vol. 1, No. 46 (Nov. 17, 1849).
Line 21:   'Greedan': Mythological drink said to have provided inspiration.

'The Famished Land'. *The Nation* Vol. 5, No. 224 (Jan. 23, 1847).
Line 14:   'felons': 'Felon' was made a key word of the period by the
            creation of the special offence of 'treason felony', which allowed
            the authorities to convict a person of treason without being
            obliged to create a martyr by executing him. One of the nation-
            alist newspapers of 1848 was *The Irish Felon*.

'Advice'. *The Irishman* Vol. 1, No. 29 (July 21, 1849).
Lines 21-2: 'Mitchel, Davis, Meagher, Duffy': The leaders of Young
            Ireland, John Mitchel (1815-1875); Thomas Davis (1814-1845);
            Thomas Francis Meagher (1793-1867); Charles Gavan Duffy
            (1816-1903).
Line 32:   'Felon': see note to 'The Famished Land', line 14 above.

'Our Welcome'. Elizabeth Willoughby Varian (b. Ballymena, Co. Antrim, ca. 1830;
d. ca. 1903) wrote for *The Nation* as 'Finola;' in 1871 married Cork poet and
editor Ralph Varian. 'Our Welcome' is from her *Poems by 'Finola'* (Belfast:
John Henderson, 1851), p. 112.
Line 1:   'thee': Queen Victoria, who visited Ireland in August, 1849: she
            first landed at Cobh (renamed 'Queenstown' for the occasion),
            only 50 miles along the coast from the much publicized devas-
            tation at Skibbereen. See also 'The Queen's Visit' on p. 188 and
            'Lines Written the Day before the Queen's Arrival in Dublin' on
            p. 244.

'Proselytizing'. *Poems* (Belfast: Henderson, 1851), p. 41.
Title: 'Proselytizing': The attempts by some Protestant relief workers
            to include religious instruction with famine aid infuriated many
            Catholics.

'The Enigma'. Lady Wilde (b. Wexford, ca. 1824; d. London, Feb. 3, 1896), born
Jane Francesca Elgee, is perhaps better remembered as 'Speranza', the name
under which she wrote for *The Nation*; her article 'Jacta alea est' was responsible for the paper's prosecution in 1848. In 1851 she married William
Wilde (knighted 1864), and became the mother of Oscar Wilde. Her *Poems*
were published in 1864 (Dublin: James Duffy). 'The Enigma' is from *The
Nation* Vol. 6, No. 293 (May 6, 1848).

'The Exodus'. *Poems* (Dublin: Duffy, 1864) p. 43.

Line 1:   'A million...': Ironically, the Census of 1851 was compiled by the man Speranza was to marry that same year, William Wilde.

'The Famine Year'. Originally titled 'The Stricken Land' in *The Nation* Vol. 5, No. 224 (Jan. 23, 1847).

Line 46:   'Angel of the Trumpet': 'And the seventh angel sounded... and the nations were angry, and Thy wrath is come, and the time of the dead, that they should be judged'. Rev. 11:15-6.

'Foreshadowings'. *The Nation* Vol. 7, No. 3 (Sept. 9, 1849).

Line 1:   'Oremus': L. 'Let us pray'.

Line 2:   'Patmos': 'I, John ... was in the isle that is called Patmos, for the word of God'. Rev. 1:9.

Line 6:   'mystical seals': 'And I saw when the Lamb opened one of the seals ... and, behold, a white horse; and he that sat on him had a bow: and a crown was given unto him, and he went forth conquering, and to conquer'. Rev 6:1-2.

Line 16:   'pale steed': 'And I looked, and, behold, a pale horse, and his name that sat on him was Death' Rev 6:8. The pale horse is the fourth in the sequence.

Line 20:   'war-steed': 'And there went out another horse that was red; and power was given to him that sat on it to take peace from from the earth'. Rev. 6:4 The second horse of the sequence.

Line 30:   'black steed': 'And I beheld, and lo, a black horse; and he that sat on him had a pair a pair of balances in his hand'. Rev. 6:5 The third horse of the sequence.

Line 50:   'Rama': 'A voice was heard in Ramah, lamentation and bitter weeping'. Jer. 31:15.

Line 54:   'Hypage, Satana': Gk. 'Begone Satan!' Mat. 4:10. The words uttered by Christ during his forty days in the wilderness.

Line 60:   'Trisagion': An angelic hymn of praise.

Line 61:   'Palm-branches': 'And, lo, a great multitude stood before the throne, and before the Lamb, clothed with white robes, and palms in their hands'. Rev. 7:9.

Line 63:   'jewelled-walled city': The New Jerusalem. 'And the foundations of the wall of the city were garnished with all manner of precious stones'. Rev. 21:19.

Line 68:   'mystical vial': The seven vials, or bowls, of wrath 'containing the seven last plagues; for in them is filled up the wrath of God'. Rev. 15:1.

Line 70:   'rainbow-crowned angel': 'And I saw another mighty angel come down from heaven, and a rainbow was on his head ... when he shall begin to sound, the mystery of God should be finished, as he hath declared to his servants, the prophets'. Rev. 10:1,7.

'France in '93: A Lesson from Foreign History'. *The Nation* Vol. 5, No. 233 (March 27, 1847).

Line 3:   'famished cry for Bread': In April of 1793, the poor of Paris took to the streets to protest against the high cost of food.

Line 26:   'Bastile': The Bastile was actually stormed by the mob in 1789.

Line 49:   'à la Lanterne': The street lamps, 'lanterne de rue', provided a convenient scaffold for hanging aristocrats during the era of mob rule.

Line 49:   'King and Queen': Louis XVI was guillotined on Jan. 21, 1793; Marie Antoinette was guillotined Oct. 14 the same year.

'A Lament for the Potato: A.D. 1739'. *Poems* (Dublin: Duffy, 1864), p. 63.

Title: '1739': There was a famine due to widespread crop failure in Ireland during the years 1739-41; it was particularly severe in Munster.

Line 5:   'Lorc': A legendary king of Munster, reputedly grandfather of Brian Boru.

Line 29:   'Fitzstephen's clan': The Fitzstephens had been major land-holders in Munster since the 12th century.

'A Supplication'. *The Nation* Vol. 5, No. 272 (Dec. 18, 1847).

Epigraph: 'De profundis ...': 'Out of the depths have I cried unto thee, O Lord'. Ps. 130:1.

Line 3:   'Kyrie Eleison': Gk. 'Lord have mercy'. See also R.D. Williams' 'Kyrie Eleison' on p. 236.

Lines 16-18:   'Golden harvests, etc.': Stanza 6 did not appear in the original version of the poem from *The Nation*, but is found in all subsequent reprintings.

'The Voice of the Poor'. *The Nation* Vol. 6, No. 294 (May 13, 1848).

Line 6:   'darkness at noontide': 'And when the sixth hour was come, there was darkness over the whole land until the ninth hour'. Mk. 15:33; also Mt. 27:45; Lk. 23:44.

'Work While It Is Called Day'. *The New Spirit of the Nation* ed. Martin MacDermott. (London: T. Fisher Unwin, 1894), p. 119.

Title: 'Work While ...': 'Work while it is called Today, for the Night cometh, wherein no man can work'. Thomas Carlyle, *Sartor Resartus.*

Line 15:   'Tyrian fathers': One of the more dubious myths of the origins of the Irish people maintained that Ireland was originally settled by Phoenician sailors. Tyre was one of the chief seaports of Phoenicia on the Syrian coast.

Line 51:   'The last may yet be first': 'The last shall be first, and the first last'. Mt. 20:16; also Mk. 10:31: Lk. 13:30.

'The Extermination'. Richard D'Alton Williams (b. Dublin, Oct. 8, 1822; d. Thibo-deaux, Louisiana, July 5, 1862) was a medical student when he began writing for *The Nation* as 'Shamrock' and 'D.N.S'. In 1848 he co-founded the *Irish Tribune* with Kevin Izod O'Doherty; the two were later tried for treason felony, but Williams was acquitted; he emigrated in 1851. 'The Extermination' can be found in *The Poems of R.D. Williams* (Dublin: Duffy, 1901), p. 25.

Title: 'Extermination': The word 'extermination' was used in the nationalist press of the period as a synonym for 'eviction'. See also J. D. Frazer, 'Extermination' on p. 172.

Epigraph: 'Dominus . . .': Not from the remarkable Ps. 145 at all, but a misquotation of Ps. 146:9: 'Dominus custodit advenas, pupillum et viduam suscipet; et vias peccatorum disperdet'. 'The Lord preserveth the strangers; He relieveth the fatherless and widow; but the way of the wicked he turneth upside down'. Since the British were often referred to as 'strangers' one suspects Williams' omission is intentional.

Line 21: 'Ammon': 'The children of Ammon have ripped up women with child in Gilead, that they might enlarge their border'. Amos 1:13.

'Hand in Hand'. *The Nation* Vol. 8, No. 9 (Oct. 26, 1850).

Line 10: 'the people': 'vox populi, vox dei'. [Williams' note].
Line 42: 'gows': Blacksmiths.
Line 56: 'lamh ruadh': Ir. 'red hand', symbol of Ulster.
Line 61: 'lamh lauder aboo': Ir. 'The strong arm forever'.
Line 62: 'larum-drum': Battle drum.

'Kyrie Eleison'. *Poems* (Dublin: Duffy, 1901), p. 150.

Title: 'Kyrie Eleison': Gk. 'Lord, have mercy'. The words are used as a response in both the Catholic and Anglican liturgies.
Line 6: 'Parce nobis, Domine': L. 'Spare us, Lord'.
Line 28: 'Helot': A class of serfs in Sparta.

'Lord of Hosts'. *The United Irishman* Vol . 1, No. 15 (May 20, 1848).

'Vesper Hymn to the Guardian Angels of Ireland'. *Poems* (Dublin: Duffy, 1901), p. 149.

Line 27: 'Raphaël': One of the three angels mentioned in the Bible (1 Chr. 26:7); the name means 'God has healed'.

PART VI

'Best Pillar of Thy Throne'

THE UNIONIST REACTION

'Lines Written the Day before the Queen's Arrival in Dublin'. *Dublin University Magazine* Vol. 34, No. 201 (Sept. 1849).

Title: 'Queen's Arrival': Queen Victoria arrived in Dublin on Aug. 6, 1849. See notes to E.W. Varian's 'Our Welcome' on p. 289. See also 'The Queen's Visit' on p. 188.

'Bright Were the Days'. Lieut. Thomas Acres Ogle lived at Carnsore Pt, Co. Wexford. His *Wild Flowers of Poetry* was published in Dublin, 1865. 'Bright Were The Days', can be found in *An Anthology of the Potato* ed. Robert McKay, (Dublin: Allen Figgis & Co. , 1961), p. 64.

Line 5: 'lumpers': A large, watery variety of potato extremely popular at the time of the Famine.

Line 24: 'potatoes and point': A traditional expression; before taking a bite of potato, one would 'point' the potato at a piece of bacon.

'On the Death of the Rev. Robert Traill, D.D'. *Lays for Patriots* (Dublin: Samuel B. Oldham, 1848), p. 131.

Title: 'Traill': Church of Ireland vicar of Schull during the Famine, who made super-human efforts on behalf of the poor of all creeds. He died of typhus late in 1847.

'The Irish Emigrant's Farewell in the Famine Year'. *Lays For Patriots* (Dublin: Samuel B. Oldham, 1848),p. 108.

'The Summer of 1847 in Ireland: The Second Famine Year'. *Lays for Patriots* (Dublin: Samuel B. Oldham, 1848), p. 114.

'Stanzas on the Death of Daniel O'Connell, Esq., M.P'. Robert Young (b. 1800, Fintona, Co. Tyrone; d. ca. 1870) was a nailor who wrote as 'The Fermanagh True Blue'. D.J. O'Donoghue remarks archly of Young: 'In the 1860s he was awarded £50 a year by the Government, ostensibly for literary ability, but as he had none, it must have been for political services'. His *Poetical Works* were published in Derry: Derry Standard Office, 1863.

Title: 'O'Connell': Daniel O'Connell (b. 1775; d. May 15, 1847) died in Genoa while on a pilgrimage to Rome.

Line 13: 'Tara . . . Mullaghmast': Sites of two of the most successful 'monster meetings' of the Repeal Association.

Line 28: 'Burgh-quay Hall': Conciliation Hall, Burgh Quay, Dublin, headquarters of O'Connell's Repeal Association.

Line 50: 'heart': Although O'Connell's body was returned to Dublin for burial, his heart was buried in Rome.

PART VII

'Erin, I Fear 'Tis Very Like You'

THE BRITISH CONTRIBUTION

'The Farmer of Inniscreen: A Tale of the Irish Famine in Verse'. (London: Jarrold and Sons, 1863). One of 'Jarrold's Household Tracts For The People'. 'These tracts are worthy of the attention of all who seek to promote the moral and religious improvement of their families and of the people at large. Price —twopence'.

'The Potato Crop, 1846'. *Illustrated London News* Vol. 9, No. 244 (Aug. 29, 1846).
Line 9:   'the statesman': Sir Robert Peel (1788-1850) realized in the autumn of 1845, ahead of most of the rest of his government, that Ireland was on the verge of a major famine, and ordered £100,000 worth of Indian meal to be purchased as emergency supplies.
Line 11:   'the law': The Corn Laws. See note to 'Inheritor and Economist', line 38 on p. 279.

'Erin go Bragh!' *The Nation* Vol. 6, No. 297 (June 10, 1848). 'A writer in the last number of the University Magazine says: "The whole English Press, without distinction of party, seems animated by the one common object of vilifying and holding up to odium everything in our country". And here is a commentary on the text, which some English writer has flung in our face'.

'Enigmatica: A Riddle'. *Enigmatica: Or Original Rhymes and Riddles* (Bideford: W. Cole, 1847), p. 3. 'The profits arising from this little work are intended for the poor Irish sufferers'.
Lines 1-2:   'My first . . .' Ire.
Lines 3-4:   'My second . . .' Land.

'The Spectre'. *The Spectre: Stanzas with Illustrations* (London: Thomas M'Lean, 1851). 'In Ireland's late calamity, the earnest endeavour of Englishmen of all ranks to alleviate, by vast pecuniary contributions, the suffering of her starving sons, spoke, so as not to be mistaken, the sympathy of brothers'. 'Prefactory Remarks'.

'Mortality in Skibbereen'. *Illustrated London News* Vol. 10. No. 5 (Jan. 30, 1848). The poem was originally untitled: the title is from the article in which it originally appeared.
Line 24:   'the East': Plagues were popularly believed to originate in the Middle East at the time of the Famine. See also T.D. McGee's 'The Woeful Winter' on p. 199, and Miro's 'Pro and Con' on p. 202.

'Sketches in the West of Ireland'. *Illlustrated London News* Vol . 10, No.250 (Feb. 13, 1847). The title of the poem is drawn from the article in which it originally appeared; the poem was untitled. This article, with illustrations by James Mahony, was the first to make the British public aware of the scale of the destitution in Ireland. Its focus on West Cork made 'Skibbereen' a by-word for the devastation of the Famine.

PART VIII

'We'll Soon Have Cheap Flour and Plenty of Meal'
STREET BALLADS

'Another Version of Soyer's Soup'. Broadside: White collection, No. 250; Trinity College, Dublin.

Title:	'Soyer's Soup': Alexis Benôit Soyer (1809-1858), French chef of London's Reform Club, set up a soup kitchen in Dublin's Phoenix Park, where he dispensed a soup of his own devising that cost a mere £1 per 100 gallons. See note to 'A Vision of Connaught in the Nineteenth Century', line 33 on p. 282.
Line 1:	'Oh hone . . .' Ir. 'Alas for the darling of my heart'.

'A New Song Called The Emigrant's Farewell to Donegal'. Broadside: National Library of Ireland, ca. 1847.

'A New Song on the Rotten Potatoes'. Broadside; White Collection, No. 140; Trinity College, Dublin.

'We'll Soon Have Cheap Flour and Plenty of Meal': Broadside: White Collection, No. 168, Trinity College, Dublin.

Line 18:	'our ports': The repeal of the Corn Laws. See note to 'Inheritor and Economist', line 38 on p. 279.
Line 25:	'great meeting': The Mansion House meeting of Oct. 28, 1845, called to deal with the the impending Famine, brought together a heterogeneous group, including Daniel O'Connell and the Duke of Leinster.
Line 27:	'Quakers': The Society of Friends did more than any other single organization to provide effective relief.
Line 34:	'Father John': Probably John McHale (1791-1881), Archbishop of Tuam; influential church leader and man of letters.
Line 37:	'Mr. O'Brien': William Smith O'Brien (1803-1864), Protestant land-owner and Young Irelander; as an M.P. he brought in several bills for poor relief in the 1830s; led the ill-fated rising of 1848.

Author Index